Three Steps to He…

Three Steps to Heaven

Untimely Deaths in the Music World

Roma Wheaton

WARNER BOOKS

A *Warner* Book

First published in Great Britain in 1993 by Warner Books
Reprinted 1994

A CIP catalogue record for this book
is available from the British Library.

ISBN 0 7515 0401 7

Typeset by
Hewer Text Composition Services, Edinburgh
Printed in England by Clays Ltd, St Ives plc

Warner Books
A Division of
Little, Brown and Company (UK)
Brettenham House
Lancaster Place
London WC2E 7EN

Dedicated to the memory of
my friend Mary Downing
who died too young

And my father
a 'hillbilly music' man
who loved rock 'n' roll

With special thanks
to my family
for all their support and encouragement

NAME	REASON FOR DEATH	AGE	DIED
1950s			
Hank Williams	Alcohol/Morphine	29	1953
Johnny Ace	Accidentally Shot Himself	25	1954
Charlie Parker	Drugs/Alcohol	34	1955
Buddy Holly	Plane Crash	22	1959
Ritchie Valens	Plane Crash	17	1959
The Big Bopper	Plane Crash	28	1959
Billie Holiday	Drugs/Alcohol	44	1959
Mario Lanza	Heart Attack	38	1959
1960s			
Eddie Cochran	Car Crash	21	1960
Johnny Horton	Car Crash	33	1960
Patsy Cline	Plane Crash	30	1963
Hawkshaw Hawkins	Plane Crash	41	1963
Johnny Burnette	Drowned	30	1964
Sam Cooke	Shot	29	1964
Jim Reeves	Plane Crash	40	1964
Alma Cogan	Cancer	34	1966
Otis Redding	Plane Crash	26	1967
Brian Jones	Drowned under influence of Drugs/Alcohol	27	1969
1970s			
Jimi Hendrix	Drugs	27	1970
Janis Joplin	Heroin	27	1970
'King' Curtis	Stabbed	37	1971
Duane Allman	Bike Crash	24	1971
Jim Morrison	Cardiac Arrest	27	1971
Gene Vincent	Perforated Ulcer	36	1971
Clyde McPhatter	Alcohol	38	1972
Ron 'Pigpen' McKernan	Drugs/Alcohol	27	1973
Bobby Darin	Following Heart Surgery	37	1973
Gram Parsons	Drugs/Alcohol	26	1973
Jim Croce	Plane Crash	30	1973
'Mama' Cass Elliott	Heart Attack	32	1974
Paul Kossoff	Drugs	25	1976
Florence Ballard	Heart Attack	32	1976
Phil Ochs	Suicide	35	1976

Tommy Bolin	Drugs/Alcohol	25	1976
Elvis Presley	Drugs	42	1977
Marc Bolan	Car Crash	29	1977
Ronnie Van Zant	Plane Crash	28	1977
Sandy Denny	Brain Haemorrhage	31	1978
Keith Moon	Drugs/Alcohol	31	1978
Donny Hathaway	Suicide	33	1979
Sid Vicious	Heroin	21	1979
1980s			
Ian Curtis	Suicide by Hanging	23	1980
John Lennon	Shot	40	1980
John Bonham	Alcohol	32	1980
Tim Hardin	Drugs	39	1980
Bob Marley	Cancer	36	1981
Mike Bloomfield	Heroin	36	1981
Harry Chapin	Car Fire	38	1981
Karen Carpenter	Cardiac Arrest due to Anorexia Nervosa	32	1983
Dennis Wilson	Drowned under influence of Drugs/Alcohol	39	1983
Billy Fury	Heart Attack	41	1983
Marvin Gaye	Shot by his Father	44	1984
Rick Nelson	Plane Crash	45	1985
Phil Lynott	Drugs	34	1986
Peter Tosh	Stabbed/Shot	42	1987
Andy Gibb	Cardiac Arrest caused by Drugs	30	1988
1990s			
Stevie Ray Vaughan	Plane Crash	35	1990
Steve Clark	Alcohol	30	1991
Steve Marriott	Died in Fire	44	1991
Freddie Mercury	AIDS	45	1991

Contents

Acknowledgements

A book covering such a diverse number of personalities requires extensive research. During the preparation of this manuscript I gathered information from a wide range of books, periodicals and documentaries and I am very grateful for the valuable information they provided. Whilst it would be impossible to list them in their entirety I have found the following books indispensable: Jim Goldbolt's *The World of Jazz*; Martin Williams' *The Jazz Tradition*; *The Faber Companion to 20th-Century Music*; *The Guiness Book of Rock Stars*; *The Guiness Who's Who of Country Music*; *Hard Rock and Heavy Metal Encyclopedia*; Greil Marcus' *Mystery Train*; John Savage's *England's Dreaming*; *Encyclopedia Metallica*; *N.M.E. Who's Who in Rock and Roll.*

I also dipped into several periodicals – *Guitar World*; *Guitar School*; *Vox*; *Rolling Stone*; *Q*; *RCD*; *Jazz* – which afforded me valuable insight into the music world.

One of the difficulties in researching a book of this nature is to vivify the artists. For this I turned to the excellent selection of video and films available, in particular I recommend Channel 4's 'Sound Stuff'.

I am very grateful to Rob Wheaton, Sheila Thompson and David Ostrer for their help in gathering material. Also the Countess Diana de Rosso, the Music Department at the Berkshire Library, and Miss Skinner, Head of Music at Licensed Victuallers Schools.

Preface

Three Steps To Heaven is a tribute to a select group of musicians bound together by the untimeliness of their deaths. It was Eddie Cochran's biggest hit, but, ironically, when it topped the music charts, he had already climbed that short staircase.

Fate seems to have a way of striking down young and gifted personalities. And although untimely death is not a phenomenon restricted to those in the entertainment world, their very celebrity makes them the object of our voyeuristic interest.

At what age do we judge a death to be a premature? The Bible sets man's lifespan at seventy, three score years and ten. And despite enjoying better health and living longer nowadays, we live in a youth orientated society and are considered over the hill at fifty. Thus, forty-five seemed to be a reasonable demarcation point for the purposes of this book.

I have attempted to be comprehensive and include all those who have written their way into the twentieth-century musical Hall of Fame by an early death. And I apologise beforehand for any omissions which may come to light; they are not deliberate.

To a certain extent all the personalities defined herein have become cult figures. Some, like Buddy Holly, Jimi Hendirx and Elvis Presley have moved into the realms of legend.

Would they have retained this superstar status had they lived into old age? Or would they have worn out their creativity and disappeared into obscurity? On this we can only speculate, for death has frozen them forever-young in our minds.

For the best part of a year I immersed myself, through the written word and film footage, in the lives of these personalities. Some I liked, some I didn't. But it was a voyage of discovery and always fascinating as such. When the manuscript was finally completed I felt I was saying farewell to old friends.

The music of these tragic victims of fate has been kept alive by the wonders of modern technology. I hope their stories will live on through these pages.

Jimi Hendrix said it all with his words: 'It's funny the way most people love the dead. Once you're dead, you've got it made for life.'

Roma Wheaton 1993

Introduction

The Greek dramatist Menander (340–291 BC), said, 'Whom the gods love, die young'. This has certainly been the case in the music world this century. Under the glaring spotlight of the world's press, one young rock star after another has hurtled to an early death. Like shooting stars, they blaze flamboyant paths across our skies. Then, on reaching their zenith, they flare brightly but briefly, before plunging to earth, leaving only a sad trail in the heavens to mark their passing.

From the jazz age of Billie Holiday to the punk era of Sid Vicious, each generation has created its own heroes, remaining faithful to them even when a new wave of music arrives on the scene and signals the end of their reign.

In the 1950s, teenagers came of age and were recognised as a potent market force. And because of this increased consumer demand, and the power of the press to maximise the 'man of the hour', many a monster was created.

Rock stars began to make enormous amounts of money and lives of excess became almost commonplace. But the price of fame and glory is high. Drugs, always part of the musician's culture, became more freely available. Many stars, unable to cope with their celebrity and the loneliness and isolation of life on the road, turned to them, and alcohol, for solace.

Live fast and die young seemed to be the motto of the sixties and seventies. Drug abuse accounted for many of the early deaths. But speed, in its mechanical form, also took a toll: motorcycle, car and plane crashes claimed victims, too.

These, then, are the stories of those sacrifices to the gods.

Billie Holiday

Real Name:	Eleanora Fagan
Born:	7 April, 1915, Baltimore, Maryland, USA
Died:	17 July, 1959
Age:	44

The legendary jazz singer Billie Holiday began life as Eleanora Holiday. She later changed her name to Halliday, then to her father's name, Holiday, before eventually becoming known as Lady Day.

The illegitimate daughter of a banjo-playing guitarist, Eleanora inherited her love of music from her father, Clarence. Her parents married after her birth but later divorced when Clarence Holiday abandoned Eleanora and her mother, Sadie Fagan, to play guitar with a band. Eleanora was only a baby at that time and her early years were very hard. It is thought that she was involved in childhood prostitution and she herself mentioned a Baltimore brothel in her autobiography, *Lady Sings The Blues*. However, this claim has been refuted by people who knew Eleanora in those early years.

One of Eleanora's favourite occupations was going to the movies, and her ambition was to be a film star. When, in her teens, she started singing in Harlem nightclubs, Eleanora adopted the Christian name of her favourite actress, Miss Billie Dove.

Billie was an incredibly beautiful girl; large (she weighed nearly fifteen stone) but with a good figure. She was tall with a golden brown skin and a style very much her own. By the time she was eighteen, Billie was attracting the attention of audiences and critics alike with her unique voice and natural sense of rhythm and harmony. It was at this early stage of her career that she gained the nickname of Lady because of her ladylike attitude.

Billie had begun smoking marijuana when she was very young, sometimes leaving the club where she was performing to smoke a joint in Central Park between sets. She loved good living and all the trimmings of success. She had a lusty appetite for sex and enjoyed a succession of lovers. Unfortunately, her taste in men wasn't very good, and it was because of one that Billie later became a heroin addict. She also enjoyed a drink with her fellow musicians but she showed no signs of alcoholism in those early days.

In 1935, Billie began the recording career that was to bring her worldwide fame. She also made her début at the famous Apollo Theatre in Harlem. On the advice of her personal manager, Joseph Glaser, Billie began to diet and managed to slim down. A contract to tour with the Count Basie Band, singing jazz and blues, was the next step in Billie's career and her time with them proved very successful.

Her career was now well established, and in 1936, Billie felt financially able to set up her beloved mother Sadie in a small New York restaurant. However, Billie had become disenchanted with life on the road. The relationship between her and the management of the Count Basie Band became strained and Billie was asked to leave.

Within a month she had joined Artie Shaw's band, billed as Lady Day. A close friend had shortened her surname in jest and it stuck. At the beginning of the tour all seemed to be going well but, with the introduction of another singer to the band, resentment grew and Billie left.

A town girl at heart, Billie returned to New York where, in 1939, she was on the opening bill at a fashionable new club, the Café Society. Billie used this period of her career to polish her act, introducing a song about oppression that was to bring her greater fame. 'Strange Fruit' was a deeply moving song about lynching in the South, and Billie's rendition mesmerised her audiences. She also added torch songs of despair and hopelessness to her repertoire, pouring a wealth of expression into them and attracting large audiences.

A short-lived engagement to her piano accompanist, Sonny White, was followed by a string of casual relationships. In 1941, while she was performing at the Famous Door, Billie started dating a man she had known for many years, Jimmy Monroe. Billie's mother and her manager disapproved, considering Monroe a bad influence on Billie, but, following a whirlwind romance, the two were married. The couple left New York immediately after the wedding as Billie had some professional engagements to fulfil.

She had always spent her money as quickly as she made it and, when her marriage ran into difficulties, Billie returned to the New York clubs to work in an effort to stabilise her affairs. She had undergone some personality changes, too. Generally well known to be of a cheerful, if unpredictable, disposition, Billie was now polished and sophisticated on stage, but erratic and given to wild rages off it. She suffered from melancholia and resorted to opium for solace. When the opium made her feel sick and seemed to affect her singing voice, she turned to heroin.

During the early 1940s, Billie continued to play the clubs, spending all the money she earned on drugs. As she was afraid of endangering her voice and losing her hard-won popularity, she was able to control her heroin intake.

In 1945, divorced from Monroe, Billie married trumpeter Joe Guy. With his help she formed her own band and they toured the country billed as Billie's Big Band. But bookings were scarce and, desperate for some money, Billie returned to her solo career.

The following year, Billie travelled to Hollywood to make the film, *New Orleans*. It received good reviews but didn't make Billie the star she wanted to be. The nightclub business was also facing a recession and there was very little work forthcoming. Billie used this lull in her career to try and kick her heroin habit. She entered a clinic and came out clean, but once back on the club circuit, she found she could not do without the consolation of drugs.

Meanwhile, Billie's career was rocketing. She had signed a recording contract with Decca, and the records she made with them had a more universal pop appeal. Among these, Billie's emotive rendering of 'Loverman' and 'Porgy' are classics of American popular song.

But her personal life was again in disarray. In 1947, she was arrested for drug possession and, after a month of anxiety while she waited for the case to come to trial, she was sentenced to a year and a day in jail. Following her release she sought to re-establish her career, but the police refused to issue her with a cabaret card, which precluded her working in any New York nightclubs, and she was forced to undertake out-of-town tours.

Billie's stay in prison had also sapped her confidence. Physically, she was well, and looking as beautiful as ever, but sometimes her depressions overwhelmed her. She continued to tour but her appearances were often erratic; she would arrive late for shows or, if she felt the audience was not appreciative enough, she would curtail her numbers.

Joe Guy and Billie had long since gone their separate ways and now Billie was involved with John Levy, the manager of the Club Ebony where Billie performed in June, 1948. He took over the management of her affairs and arranged another tour for her. In 1949, she and Levy were in Hollywood where Billie was playing Billy Berg's club. On New Year's Eve, Billie complained that a customer had accosted her and a fracas broke out. One of the guests was stabbed by Levy, and he and Billie were charged with assault with a deadly weapon.

A couple of weeks later, they were both arrested again and charged with possession of opium. Billie, who had been determined to stay off drugs following her prison sentence, maintained her innocence and was later acquitted. Levy, taking all Billie's money with him, fled the state. The publicity had not harmed Billie's popularity, however, and her career enjoyed a resurgence.

In 1951, Billie got married again, this time to her new manager, Louis McKay. The next few years were good ones for Billie: Although she was still prohibited from working in New York clubs, television had opened up new horizons for her and she had many jazz club and tour bookings.

Billie's craving for drugs resurfaced in 1956 and she was again arrested. She entered a clinic and broke her habit, but back on the road, she began to drink heavily. Although her final years were plagued by alcohol consumption, Billie reached new heights with her singing, pouring all the grief and tragedy of her personal life into her recordings.

Her drinking began to adversely affect her health. By this time she was very thin (weighing only about eight stone), and her marriage had fallen apart. Because of her erratic bursts of temper many of her friends had fallen by the wayside, too.

By 1959, she was still working steadily but her heart wasn't in it. Her health had deteriorated alarmingly and she was short of money. She accepted an offer to sing at a concert in May, 1959 for the paltry sum of $300, but during the concert she collapsed and had to be admitted to hospital.

Billie was diagnosed as suffering from cirrhosis of the liver and seemed to be responding to treatment when, in her hospital bed, she was arrested on a narcotics charge. She was subjected to two weeks of police harassment but nonetheless seemed to be improving when suddenly, on 17 July, she died of heart failure. Such was Billie's insecurity that she had taped $750 to her leg, as the nurses discovered after her death.

Dozens of musicians attended the memorial service held for this great artiste, the most memorable jazz singer of her age.

In 1972, a film was made of Billie's life, based on her autobiography *Lady Sings The Blues*. Diana Ross portrayed this sad 'Lady'.

Ironically, although Billie died almost destitute, her husband, their divorce not having been finalised, benefited from the thousands of dollars that accrued posthumously from Billie's recordings.

Charlie Parker

Full Name: Charles Christopher Parker Jr
Born: 29 August, 1920, Kansas City, Kansas, USA
Died: 12 March, 1955
Age: 34

There were three main interests in Charlie Parker's life: music was the earliest and principal one, closely followed by drugs and sex. Nicknamed 'Yardbird' or 'Bird' because of his love for fried chicken, Charlie was a natural musician. He began playing the saxophone in a high school band, but school was not for him, and he quit when he was fifteen. Within the year he had begun his professional career playing with Jay McShann's bluesy Kansas City Band.

Charlie was a master of improvisation and he played his saxophone at a dizzying speed. Unfortunately, he tried to live his life at the same reckless pace. Drugs were part of the jazzman's culture and Charlie had been introduced to both drugs and alcohol at a very young age. His addiction was to last throughout his tumultuous life.

Charlie's love of women was almost as strong as his addiction to drugs and alcohol and, at the age of sixteen, he married for the first time. In his short life he married four times and had two children, although only two of his marriages were legally recognised. These factors, plus the energy he expended in his playing, would contribute to the severe mental disorders that beset him in his early twenties.

By the age of twenty, Charlie had made his way to New York where he made his début at one of Dizzy Gillespie's jazz sessions at the 18 Club. He and Gillespie began an association that was to continue for many years. Together with Thelonius Monk, Kenny Clarke and a few others, they were the pioneers of the revolutionary jazz movement called bebop. Bebop, later shortened to bop, was a form of jazz characterised by rhythmic and harmonic complexity usually played off the beat. Swing was hot but bebop was cool. Charlie, adding his own blues-orientated sound and the originality of his improvisation, became a master. Success came too slowly, though, for Charlie, who lived life in the fast lane and always knew what he wanted. However, until 1945, when he formed his own group, he had to be content with working with other bands.

With the formation of his own group, which included the young Miles Davis, his extraordinary virtuosity became apparent. He had always commanded the respect and admiration of his fellow musicians for his work, even though they abhorred his drug addiction and the abuse he inflicted on his body. But nobody could help Charlie as he plunged heedlessly towards self-destruction.

In 1946, he was arrested and committed to Camarillo State Hospital for six months. His ability to produce wonderful music was in no way impaired, and he later composed 'Relaxing at Camarillo' in memory of his stay there. Revitalised by his treatment, Charlie picked up the pieces of his life and, continuing his collaboration with Gillespie, returned to produce more soaring, innovative music.

The first recordings Charlie made under his own name were 'Koko' and 'Billie's Bounce' (1947), two strikingly original pieces. But Charlie was already beginning to burn out and it is generally thought that by 1950 he was past his best.

During the early 1950s, whether performing in concert or playing at Birdland, the famous jazz club named in his honour, Charlie's appearances became increasingly erratic. He had a peptic ulcer and legend has it that he invented the 'Nightcap' cocktail of milk and whisky because he couldn't give up alcohol. His general state of health had been affected by his voracious appetite for drugs and alcohol, and he had severe mental problems. In 1954 he tried to commit suicide and was admitted to a psychiatric hospital for detoxification. Nonetheless Charlie still reigned supreme as the major alto saxophone player of his time.

Sadly, at the age of thirty-four, his body burnt out and abused by years of addiction, Charlie died of a heart attack. The doctor who later examined his body estimated his age as over fifty, demonstrating the toll that a lifetime of excess had taken on his body.

The 1988 film *Bird* directed by Clint Eastwood, relates the sorry story of Charlie's life. The haunting soundtrack is composed of original Charlie Parker recordings.

Charlie Parker's inner spirit found freedom in his music, which soared and dived in the effortless manner of a bird in flight. His influence lingers on in many of the musicians of today. Sadly, one of those disciples, Brian Jones, also chose to echo the pattern of Charlie's personal life.

Mario Lanza

Real Name:	Alfredo Arnold Cocozza
Born:	31 January, 1921, Philadelphia, Pennsylvania, USA
Died:	7 October, 1959
Age:	38

Mario Lanza's parents, like many other Italians, left Italy for America in search of a better life. Mario's father was a great music-lover and Mario was raised to the sound of Enrico Caruso's singing. Mario was himself possessed of a powerful, although untrained, voice and he loved to imitate Caruso.

Always rebellious, and never academic, Mario was expelled from high school and began a series of odd jobs. Appropriately enough, he was working as a piano mover when Sergei Koussevitsky, the celebrated conductor of the Boston Symphony Orchestra, heard him sing and arranged for him to appear at the Berkshire Music Festival in 1942.

A contract to sing on a Columbia tour followed but the entry of the United States into the Second World War interrupted Mario's career. After completing a stint in the Air Force he returned to the concert circuit where, in

1948, MGM heard him perform at the Hollywood Bowl and offered him a contract. Rumour circulated that for the Hollywood Bowl audition, Mario and his manager, Sammy Weiler, had somehow faked a recording of Mario's to sound like Enrico Caruso. Whatever the truth, it was on the strength of this that Mario was offered a contract.

Musicals were in vogue at that time and MGM thought that Mario, with his handsome, Latin features and glorious voice, would be a perfect leading man. His first musical film was *The Midnight Kiss* (1949). He starred opposite Kathryn Grayson, playing a truck driver with a natural singing voice who becomes an opera star. *The Toast of New Orleans* (1950) followed. Mario again co-starred with Kathryn Grayson, this time playing a singing fisherman (with a powerful voice) who becomes an opera singer . . . Unfortunately, *The Toast of New Orleans* wasn't the toast of anywhere else, and Mario's Hollywood career might have come to an abrupt end but for one thing: one of the songs from the film, 'Be My Love', became a hit and made Mario Lanza a household name.

MGM were delighted, and immediately assigned Mario to play his hero, the legendary singer Enrico Caruso, in a new film. *The Great Caruso* (1951) was a tremendous hit at the box office, the public loved the pop opera they were being offered and Mario loved the fame.

The studio, however, was less exuberant. Although the film was bringing in a lot of money their star had turned into a monster. Mario was wild and unpredictable. He had always had a heavy build and loved to consume prodigious amounts of food. He frequently had to diet for a film role and, consequently, his weight fluctuated madly. He also had an insatiable appetite for alcohol, and later, drugs. There were stories of his womanising but these were not substantiated by the rumours that his personal hygiene was less than impeccable.

Mario, upset by these tales, blamed MGM for the adverse publicity and delayed the start of his next film. Kathryn Grayson, for undivulged reasons, refused to co-star with him and the studio was forced to find a new female lead. Eventually *Because You're Mine* (1952) went into production. This time Mario played an opera singer who joins the Air Force and, once again, the film was a success.

But Mario's personal life was in disarray. He was in dispute with the studio and, because of his temperamental reputation, it was proving very difficult to cast his leading lady in *The Student Prince*. Ann Blyth eventually accepted the part and production began. Mario recorded the songs but he was engaged in a legal battle with MGM and filming was delayed. When these difficulties were resolved another attempt was made to go into production but, once again, temperament reared its head, and MGM were without a star. In desperation they cast a young unknown actor, Edmund Purdom, in the lead, miming to Mario's voice. The film had been two years in the making and MGM, feeling they had suffered enough, terminated Mario's contract.

A rapid decline now occurred in Mario's career. He was obese, the constant bingeing and dieting had taken a toll on his his voice and his health was suffering. His behaviour became erratic, he missed night-club bookings and had to suffer the indignity of miming to his own records on television.

However, Warner Brothers decided to take a chance on him and they signed him to a 'two-film contract'. The first, *Serenade* (1956), about a peasant boy who becomes (what else?) an opera singer, did remarkably well at the box office.

Nevertheless, Warner Brothers mysteriously decided to buy out the second half of Mario's contract.

Now Hollywood turned its back on Mario and he decided to return to his singing. He had an unfulfilled ambition to prove that he could be a great tenor and conquer the operatic world. He rejoined the concert circuit and continued to record popular songs. But he had either misjudged his own abilities or had left it too late.

In 1958 he decided to accept a couple of European film offers, *The Seven Hills of Rome* and *For the First Time*, tempted by the opportunity to work in Italy, the home of opera. Unfortunately, both sank without trace although his version of the song 'Arriverderci Roma' (1958) was a hit.

The following year, while still filming in Rome, Mario, aged thirty-eight, collapsed and died of a massive heart attack. But his popularity lives on, there are still good sales of his records and he has posthumous fan clubs. In his home town of Philadelphia there is also a Mario Lanza Park.

Hedda Hopper, the famous Hollywood columnist, wrote of him, 'He recognised no authority, no discipline, no frontiers except his own gigantic appetite for food, drink and women'. These words echo those Charlie Parker's doctor used of him: 'A man who lives for the pleasure principle: drugs, sex, food, music . . .'

Hawkshaw Hawkins

Real Name: Harold F. Hawkins
Born: 22 December, 1921, Huntingdon, West Virginia, USA
Died: 5 March, 1963
Age: 41

Like any good hillbilly singer, Hawkshaw Hawkins began singing on the radio in his teens. In his early twenties he had a recording contract with King Records, appearing on all the important country radio programmmes. By 1947 he had his first country hit, 'Sunny Side Of The Mountain'.

Hawkshaw Hawkins had all the personality and good looks usually associated with country singers but he had something extra, musical foresight. He added amplified guitars, more piano and updated the tempo. Even so, he was just on the threshold of his success at the time of his death.

In 1954, he accepted the supreme accolade for any western singer and joined The Grand Ole Opry. His wife, Jean Shepard, was also a country star with the Opry. On the night of 5 March, 1963, Hawkins called his wife to tell her he was flying back from a charity concert although weather conditions were not good.

Hawkins never made it back. He was another victim of the fatal flight that killed Patsy Cline and Cowboy Copas. His widow was left to bring up their two children, and in the wake of her husband's death she had a string of hits.

On the day of the memorial service, in fitting tribute to the Nashville stars local radio devoted the airwaves to the recordings of Patsy Cline, Hawkshaw Hawkins and Cowboy Copas. Hawkins' recording of 'Lonesome 7–7203', released shortly before his death, climbed quickly to the Number One position in the charts.

Jim Reeves

Full Name:	James Travis Reeves
Born:	20 August, 1923, Galloway, Texas, USA
Died:	31 July, 1964
Age:	40

In 1964, the world of country and western music lost another of its brightest stars in a plane crash when velvet-voice 'Gentleman' Jim Reeves followed Hank Williams, Patsy Cline, Hawkshaw Hawkins and Cowboy Copas to an untimely death.

Jim Reeves was a farm boy, one of the requirements for a true country and western singer. But as a boy Jim didn't want to be a singer. His was the all-American dream, to be a professional baseball player. For a short time he was the pitcher for the St Louis Cardinals but an injury put paid to this career.

Undaunted by this turn of events, Jim returned to Texas and his second love, music. Fame and fortune in the country music world is hard to come by and Jim supplemented his singing income by working as DJ for the local radio station.

In 1953, on the night Hank Williams died, Jim was asked to replace him on *Louisiana Hayride*, a popular country music radio programme. Although Jim was older than Hank, he came to success much later, and only after Hank had vacated the position of king of country and western music. As luck would have it a representative of a record company was in the audience and Jim was offered a contract.

He had two hits in the country chart that year, 'Mexican Joe' and 'Bimbo', before he was invited to join Nashville's Grand Ole Opry, the home of country and western music, in 1955.

But Jim, with his smooth, deep voice, was better suited to the new trend of music that was in vogue in the south, violins and vocal backing replacing the twang of hillbilly instruments. Jim made the final transition from country to pop music with his song 'He'll Have To Go' (1959), for which he is best remembered. In 1960, when Johnny Horton was killed in a car accident, Jim replaced him as the most popular country singer. Yet again, Jim Reeves was in the right place at the right time. His next album, 'Touch Of Velvet,' was composed entirely of popular music and made Jim the first country star to produce a pop album.

It wasn't only in his native state of Texas that Jim's popularity reigned. He was well known throughout North America, and in 1962 he took his music to Africa, returning there in 1963 to make a film, *Kimberley Jim*.

In May 1964, Jim said prophetically: 'What I dislike most is the travelling. The main trouble and danger, maybe, with tours, is getting there and back'. Two months later Jim was piloting his single-engine plane home to Nashville through driving rain. With him was his fellow musician, Dean Manuel. Their plane crashed in dense foliage and, because of the extreme weather conditions, and despite the huge search party sent out, it took two days to recover the bodies.

Mary Reeves, Jim's widow, kept his music alive throughout the sixties and seventies. During Jim's career he had forty-six Top Ten hits and six posthumous Number Ones which made him the best selling country singer ever.

In 1981, through the wonders of modern science, 'Have You Ever Been Lonely', an electronically-created duet between Jim Reeves and Patsy Cline, made a ghostly appearance in the charts.

Hank Williams

Full Name:	Hiram Hank Williams
Born:	17 September, 1923, Mount Olive, Alabama, USA
Died:	31 December, 1953
Age:	29

Gospel, soul, blues and country and western music have all contributed to the overall sound that synthesised from rhythm and blues into rockabilly, rock 'n' roll and, later, rock. Country music, the folk music of the southern United States, originated among the poor hard-working people who toiled long hours for little reward. It brought colour to their lives and gave them an outlet for their emotions. Songs that dealt with the vices of men – adultery and drinking – were sung, usually accompanied by a piano, in seedy bars. These bars were known as honky-tonks, hence honky-tonk music.

Hank Willams was brought up in poverty in Alabama. He was born in Mount Olive but the family later moved to Montgomery, the town which Hank always considered his home. His mother was an organist and singer for the Baptist Church and she took her son along to accompany her. The rest of Hank's musical training came from a black street singer named Tee-Tot, who also taught him the guitar.

Hank's singing career got off to a good start when he won first prize at an amateur night performance, singing his own composition 'The WPA Blues'. The WPA – Works Progress Administration – was a government organisation which sought to find work for the many who were unemployed in those years.

By the age of fourteen Hank had formed his own band called Hank Williams and The Drifting Cowboys. Hank always considered himself a cowboy and dressed the part, although of course, he had probably never even seen a horse. As well as music, alcohol featured very strongly in Hank's life. He had begun to drink when he was very young and was an alcoholic by the time he was fifteen. He drifted from place to place, playing and singing in the honky-tonks of the south.

Tall, dark and handsome (albeit balding), Hank was very attractive to women. At the age of nineteen he met and fell in love with Audrey Mae Sheppard Guy, a girl who, like Hank, had aspirations to be a country singer. Their decision to marry seems to have been a sudden one because the ceremony took place in a gas station. This isn't quite as odd as it may seem, since the owner of the gas station was the town Justice of the Peace.

Audrey was an ambitious girl and she was to have a major influence on Hank's career. She was able to provide what he needed most, direction and impetus. She encouraged his songwriting and, shortly after their marriage, Hank secured a recording contract with Sterling Records, later moving to MGM.

His star in the ascendant, Hank became a regular on *Louisiana Hayride*. However, a country singer cannot consider himself a real star until he has received the great accolade of being invited to become a member of Nashville's Grand Ole Opry.

The Grand Ole Opry is the home of the country and western music industry; more than a theatre, it is an institution. In June, 1949, Hank was invited to audition at an evening performance. He walked on to the stage an unknown country singer, sang 'Lovesick Blues', a number inspired by Audrey, received a standing ovation, was recalled for *six* encores and walked off a star. 'Lovesick Blues' immediately zoomed to Number One in the country music charts.

Hank was a big star now and making a lot of money, but he was also consuming a great quantity of alcohol. He began to miss performances and, when he did appear, he was liable to forget the words of his songs. On one occasion he set a hotel room on fire and on another he fell off the stage. To make matters worse, he and Audrey were having marital difficulties. While Hank was out on the road, Audrey was out enjoying herself. Decked out in fur and jewels she went out on the town, reputedly inspiring Hank to write another of his very successful numbers, 'Your Cheatin' Heart'.

Hank began supplementing his alcohol intake with drugs. An old back injury, exacerbated by his fall from the stage, was giving him trouble and he was taking chloral hydrate for the pain. In 1952, The Grand Ole Opry, disapproving strongly of his behaviour, fired him. Audrey, too, had had enough, and she divorced him.

Taking a beautiful nineteen-year-old girl, Billie Jean Jones Eshlimar, with him, Hank ran home to his mother. Hank and Billie Jean were married on the stage of the municipal auditorium in New Orleans. The ceremony, which was well attended, was a case of 'come one, come all', if you could afford to buy a ticket, you were welcome. In fact, the event proved so popular that Hank and Billie Jean gave an evening show as well as a matinee.

Not long after their wedding Hank was admitted to hospital suffering from acute alcohol intoxification. As soon as possible he discharged himself and was promptly arrested for drunkenness. Meanwhile, though, his songs were flourishing. Many of them are still familiar to us today, recorded by other artists: 'Long Gone Lonesome Blues', 'Your Cheatin' Heart' and 'Jambalaya'. But despite its auspicious beginning his marriage wasn't thriving and there were rumours that the couple were to part.

On the night of 31 December, 1952, on route to a concert in Canton, Ohio, Hank climbed into the back of his baby blue Cadillac. With him, for company, he had some painkillers and a bottle of beer. At his first stopover in Knoxville, Tennessee, Hank appeared ill. Nevertheless, the trip was resumed that same evening. When the chauffeur drew up at a gas station in Oak Hill, Virginia some hours later, he found Hank dead. It was later suggested that Hank had already been dead at the earlier stopover but the chauffeur denied this vehemently.

The verdict of the inquest was that Hank had died of a heart attack caused by excessive drinking and this has been the accepted cause despite the rumours to the contrary.

Hank Williams was indisputedly the king of country and western music and his funeral was suitably impressive. Twenty thousand mourners, including two black-swathed widows, attended his funeral in Montgomery, Alabama. The service was broadcast by two radio stations for all those unable to attend. Death at twenty-nine brought immortality to Hank Williams and his music.

The two widows continued to fight for many years after his death over which one was rightfully entitled to call herself Mrs Hank Williams, and who was entitled to the greater share of his fortune. Audrey's claim was that, as she had been married to Hank for ten years, and was the mother of his son, Hank Williams Jnr, and that because most of his songs had been written for her, she should retain the right. Billie Jean, despite the fact that her first marriage had not been dissolved at the time of her marriage to Hank, claimed that she had been his wife at the time of his death, and therefore *she* was entitled to his name and royalties.

It was not until 1975 that the court case between the two widows was finally resolved, and Billie Jean, as Hank's common-law wife, was granted the widow's rights. Audrey, however, died that year and it is she who lies buried beside Hank in Oakwood Cemetery, Montgomery, Alabama.

In 1961, Hank was elected by his fellow musicians to the Country Music Hall of Fame, for not only was he the king of country and western music, he was also a pioneer of rhythm and blues and rock. A film biography of Hank's life, entitled *Your Cheatin' Heart* and starring George Hamilton, was made in 1964. Audrey served as adviser so naturally Billie Jean hardly featured.

Another court battle took place in the 1980s. A young girl called Cathy Stone claimed that she was Hank William' illegitimate daughter and therefore entitled to a share of his estate. Needless to say, Hank's son, Hank Williams Jnr, and Billie Jean Williams Horton were not at all pleased by this development. Cathy Stone had been adopted by Hank's mother, Lilly Stone, and the court ruled that she was indeed Hank's daughter but that, because of her adoption, she had no legal right to a part of the estate. An appeal is still being considered. Miss Stone, in the meantime, changed her name to Jett Williams and is herself an aspiring country singer.

In 1991, a life-size bronze statue of Hank Williams was erected in the Montgomery city car park in his memory although, with all the legal wrangling that has occurred, it seems unlikely that he would have been forgotten in any case.

Johnny Horton

Full Name: John Horton
Born: 3 April 1927, Tyler, Texas, USA
Died: 5 November 1960
Age: 33

Johnny Horton, otherwise known as The Singing Fisherman, began a career in the fishing industry, but soon moved on to become a professional musician. Very handsome, with a rich deep voice that was equally suited to the raucous tones of honky-tonk or the softer sound of country music, he was an up-and-coming star at the age of twenty-six when he married Hank Williams's widow, Billie Jean.

In 1959, he had a huge hit with 'The Battle Of New Orleans', which transcended the country-pop music barrier and was a Number One hit in both charts. In 1960 he had another major hit with 'North To Alaska'. In November of that year, Johnny was performing in Austin, Texas. After the show he and two others climbed into Johnny's white cadillac to make the journey home. There was a head-on collision and, at the age of thirty-three, Johnny Horton was dead and poor Billie Jean was a widow once again.

Johnny Ace

Real Name:	John Marshall Alexander Jr
Born:	9 June, 1929, Memphis, Tennessee, USA
Died:	24 December, 1954
Age:	25

Johnny Ace, the son of a preacher, was reared on the gospel and church music of the southern United States. Rhythm and blues, the dominant music of the black culture at that time, was his great love. Following his demobilisation from the United States Navy at the end of the Second World War, Johnny decided to follow a career as a musician.

He joined The Beale Streeters, a rhythm and blues band, originally as a pianist, becoming their vocalist in 1949. His first single, recorded with The Beale Streeters, was 'My Song', which immediately reached to the Number One position in the R&B chart. Johnny's next five singles were also hits and he toured the southern states exhaustively to promote them.

Life on the road was hard and tiring and the musicians were obliged to find various ways to entertain themselves and relieve the tedium. On Christmas Eve, 1954, Johnny was appearing in a concert in Houston, Texas. To while away the time during the intermission, he indulged in a game of Russian roulette and shot himself, one instance in which most definitely 'the show couldn't go on'. Theories that he was murdered by a hired killer were quickly discounted.

The release of Johnny's 'Pledging My Love' was the first posthumous rock 'n' roll hit and it is now regarded as a standard rock ballad. Both Elvis Presley and Roy Orbison later covered it. Poor Johnny, on the brink of the big time, foolishly gambled with his life and, at the age of twenty-five, the promising talent of his music was lost.

Alma Cogan

Full Name:	Alma Angela Cogan
Born:	19 May, 1932, London, England
Died:	26 October, 1966
Age:	34

Alma Cogan's parents were of Russian descent. Their families had emigrated to Britain in order to avoid the pogroms that were prevalent in Russia at the time. They settled happily into life in Britain, Alma's father anglicising his name by changing it from Kogin to Cogan.

The Cogans' ran a tailoring business and were constantly on the move, from Golders Green to Reading, then to Worthing, finally returning to London. Despite this, Alma's family life was very happy. The whole family loved music and entertainment and the children – Alma had one brother and one sister – were expected to entertain at family gatherings.

Alma's mother, Fay, was very musical herself: as a young girl she had played the piano at the local cinema to accompany silent films. She recognised Alma's musical ability, and enrolled her in dancing, singing and piano lessons, taking her to sing at tea dances as soon as she was old enough.

Following the war, the American influence was very strong in the entertainment world and Alma was a great devotée of the cinema. She entered as many talent competitions as her mother could find and, at the age of fourteen, while the family was living in Worthing, Alma was proclaimed Sussex Queen of Song.

Alma was a tall, striking brunette, full-busted with a tiny waist. By the age of fifteen she had secured her first professional engagement at the Grand Theatre, Brighton. In 1949, she made her London début in the chorus of *High Button Shoes*. Another star in the making – Audrey Hepburn – was also in the chorus line, and she and Alma struck up a friendship.

When High Button Shoes closed, Alma relied on cabaret work. In 1950, she signed a contract with HMV, but Walter Ridley, a producer with the company, advised her to carry on with singing lessons and personal appearances to gain experience.

Both Alma's parents had been endlessly encouraging and supportive, and when her father died unexpectedly in 1952, Alma was very distressed. She had always had a close relationship with him and she regretted that he had not lived to see her become a star.

Alma was beginning to achieve a measure of fame on the radio. In the early fifties television was still in its infancy and radio was the major medium of entertainment. Alma was well-suited to radio: she didn't have a truly great voice but she compensated with her musical ability, ebullient personality and unique style. She had also developed her own vocal idiosyncrasy and became known as 'the girl with the giggle in her voice'.

Later in 1952 Alma was forced to take a six-month break from singing. She had lost her voice, possibly as a result of the distress of her father's death, and needed to rest. She returned to the stage, touring with *Mr Pastry Comes to Town*, before being offered a regular spot on the popular radio show, *Take It From Here*. Her first recording for the show, 'To Be Worthy Of You', was not a hit. However, she remained with this show for three years, sharing the spotlight with actress and comedienne June Whitfield.

Alma made her first television appearance in 1953, singing a song that was ideally suited to her voice and personality, 'Bell Bottom Blues'. This song was a runaway hit and was the first of twenty that Alma recorded in her career. She released eight more singles in 1954, scoring a great success with 'I Can't Tell A Waltz From A Tango'. Alma rapidly became one of the most popular faces on television. After the austerity of the war years, the public loved the catchy songs she sang, as well as her happy personality and extravagant costumes. Alma laughed and the audience laughed with her.

Alma had originally harboured an ambition to be a dress designer and now she brought this talent to bear in creating the most wondrously flamboyant dresses. She wore huge bouffant skirts decorated with flounces, frills, sequins, beads and feathers, and these became her trademark. She was, at twenty-one, a fine figure of a woman, and she emphasised her height with very high heels and her tiny waist with flouncy skirts.

One of the few stars that did not have a personal manager, Alma liked to be in full control of her life. Her career was everything to her, and she managed her affairs with the shrewdness of a hard-headed businesswoman, reinventing herself as styles and trends changed. She had enormous confidence, which enabled her to promote herself to the press, who loved her. She gave endless interviews and attended every event that might gain her useful publicity. Blessed with a very generous nature, Alma shared everything she had, devoting as much time and talent as she could spare to charity.

In 1955 Alma had her first Number One hit with 'Dreamboat'. Now a well-established television star, she also loved to perform in pantomime. She had always encouraged and enjoyed audience participation, knowing that it kept her in touch with her fans.

Alma was fiercely loyal to her friends. She included many men among them – Danny Kaye, Cary Grant, Tommy Steele, Sammy Davis Jnr, Jerry Lewis, Lionel Bart, John Lennon, the list is endless – but she never married. When questioned by the press she replied that the right man had never come along. Alma was so ambitious and single-minded about her career that it is doubtful whether she ever had any time left over for romance.

As amenable as she was to the press, Alma considered that her private life was her own. She loved to entertain and was renowned for her inventive parties. Invitations were much sought-after and any occasion proved a good excuse for a gathering. All of Alma's parties were elaborate and many had a theme. One in particular attracted the attention of the press when they saw the guest list: it included Chuck Berry, Gene Pitney, The Beatles, The Rolling Stones, Cliff Richard and many other notable celebrities.

In 1957, Alma made her American debut on the *Ed Sullivan Show*, a hugely popular television programme in the United States which showcased new talent. Alma was well received and invited to return later in the year for an engagement in the Persian Room at New York's Plaza Hotel. In order to appeal to a more international audience, Alma added jazz songs to her repertoire, and even went as far as recording one on her return to the United Kingdom, to the surprise of her British fans.

Between 1958 and 1962 Alma undertook a series of tours. Her first trip was to Iceland, and her travels were to include Ireland, South Africa, most of Europe, Israel and Kenya. In each place she tried to learn a little of the language. This must have presented a challenge to her when, in 1962, she went to Japan. Her hit single 'He Just Couldn't Resist Her With Her Pocket Transistor' was a great success with the Japanese, and so was Alma. On this visit she made her first colour television appearance and was delighted to see how effective her dresses looked on the screen.

The early sixties saw the arrival of a new era in pop music. The Beatles were all the rage and Alma decided that she needed to update her image. She adopted a more svelte way of dressing, leaving the old bouffant look of the fifties behind. The 'beehive' was the popular hairstyle of the day and this suited Alma well, allowing her to show off her large collection of earrings.

Although the transition in her style worked well, Alma was disappointed with the direction her career was taking. Her next single, 'Just Once More', didn't sell well in Britain and Alma saw her fame slipping away. Never dispirited for long, and still very popular on the international cabaret circuit, Alma undertook tours of Britain, Europe, Australia and the Far East.

In 1965, it seemed that she had finally met Mr Right. Brian Morris was the owner of a very popular London club, the Ad Lib. He and Alma shared many interests, and, most importantly, a sense of humour. It seemed Alma had finally found happiness. But fate was against her. She had to go into hospital for an operation, ostensibly for appendicitis, but, unbeknown to her, she had cancer.

After recovering from the surgery, and still unaware of the seriousness of her illness, Alma tried to put her career back on course. She embarked on a tour of Sweden, where she was still very popular, but collapsed at the end of the tour and had to be flown home. She died later that year, aged only thirty-four, a victim of stomach cancer.

Alma Cogan, with her catchy sentimental songs, warm sense of humour and glamorous style, brought a great deal of pleasure to many people. She was much loved and her memory lingers on.

Patsy Cline

Real Name:	Virginia Patterson Hensley
Born:	8 September, 1932, Winchester, Virginia, USA
Died:	5 March, 1963
Age:	30

Patsy Cline, undisputably one of the most gifted of country and western vocalists, poured all the emotions and experiences of her life into the ballads for which she became famous.

Patsy's mother, Hilda Hensley, had been abandoned by her husband when her children were young and was forced to raise the family on her own. Patsy, who had always been musical, made her debut singing country songs on the local radio station when she was only fourteen. As soon as she was old enough, she began to sing in the local taverns to augment the family income, and at the age of fifteen Patsy made her début on the Grand Ole Opry.

In 1956 Owen Bradley, a Nashville record producer, signed her to record 'Walking After Midnight'. To gain additional publicity for the single, Hilda Hensley was persuaded to present Patsy on the amateur television talent programme *Arthur Godfrey's Talent Scouts*. This was the only push the song needed: it went straight into the country and pop charts and Patsy's career was launched.

Despite the fact that this record was such a hit, it made little money for Patsy. She claimed that most of the income went direct to the record companies. Her subsequent singles failed to make much of an impression on the pop market and Patsy returned to Nashville, where she was regarded as a superstar.

Patsy married young, and with her career just beginning, she began to feel the restrictions of married life. Gerald Cline, her first husband, was very kind and gentle, but Patsy wanted more excitement in her life. When she was cited as co-respondent in her manager's divorce, she and Gerald decided to go their separate ways.

Physically, Patsy was very attractive. A brunette, she had a good figure and a very suggestive way of walking which she emphasized by wearing fringed cowgirl outfits. She had gained a reputation for sexual promiscuity and rumours abounded that she had slept her way to fame. Whether this was true or not, it appears that when she was on tour, she did like to have someone around to keep her bed warm.

While performing at the Rainbow Room, a local tavern, Patsy met her second husband, Charlie Dick. Theirs was a very turbulent relationship, often punctuated by bouts of violence from Dick, who was extremely jealous. Patsy retired briefly to have a child but, when Dick was drafted, Patsy was left alone to care for the family and she went back to work.

A big spender, she needed to supplement the income from her records with tours of the taverns and honky-tonks of the southern states. Being on the road, singing in sleazy clubs and staying in motels was not a glamorous way of life. The one part of it that Patsy liked was the driving. She had a white Cadillac and she drove it recklessly. One night, in 1961, she drove into another car and was thrown through the windscreen. She suffered a fractured hip and multiple face lacerations and it was some months before she could work again.

Determination drove Patsy on and, with the help of her manager, Randy Hughes, and record producer Owen Bradley, she rebounded to produce 'I Fall To Pieces', which she recorded while still on crutches. Now Patsy was back in the big time with a hit that once again transcended the country chart to reach the pop charts.

Patsy's unique vocal talents and ability to communicate her emotions enabled her to reach beyond the world of country music. Her next single, 'Crazy', was also a success and both 'Crazy' and its 'B' side, 'Who Can I Count On?', did well in the pop charts.

The pressures of supporting a family and coping with her turbulent marriage kept Patsy working hard throughout 1962. She was a regular star of The Grand Ole Opry and was voted the Country Music Association Entertainer of the Year. Despite the volume of work she under took, she still found time to devote to charity.

On the night of 5 March, 1963, Patsy attended a benefit concert held in aid of Cactus Jack Call's widow. Cactus Jack, a very popular DJ in Nashville, had recently been killed in a car crash. Returning from the concert aboard a piper Comanche plane with Patsy was her manager, Randy Hughes, who was at the controls, and two other country singers, Hawkshaw Hawkins and Cowboy Copas. When the party stopped to refuel they were given warnings of bad weather but, anxious to be home, they decided to continue their journey.

The plane crashed in a field in Tennessee, killing all the occupants, and making Patsy Cline, at the age of thirty, a country music legend. Over 25,000 mourners attended her funeral.

Patsy's career carried on posthumously. Three months after her death her rendition of 'Sweet Dreams' became a hit and, in 1973, she was the first female solo performer to be elected to the Country Music Hall of Fame.

In 1981, by a miracle of modern technology, an album entitled 'Greatest Hits' was released which combined the voices of Patsy and Jim Reeves singing the duets 'Have You Ever Been Lonely?' and 'I Fall To Pieces'. A biographical film of Patsy's life entitled *Sweet Dreams*, which starred Jessica Lange, was produced in 1985, and in 1990, the group Fairground Attraction recorded their own version of 'Walking After Midnight'.

As recently as 1991, Patsy's songs enjoyed a further revival 'Crazy' moved to Number Twelve in the charts and, together with two reissued albums, proved the timelessness of her music.

Clyde McPhatter

Full Name:	Clyde Lensey McPhatter
Born:	15 November, 1933, Durham, North Carolina, USA
Died:	13 June, 1972
Age:	38

Like Hank Williams and Johnny Ace, Clyde McPhatter's early musical background was religious. His father was a Baptist minister and young Clyde's sweet, falsetto voice was to be heard singing in the church choir. Later he formed his own group, The Mount Lebanon Singers. In 1950, he joined a rhythm and blues group, The Dominoes, as co-lead singer. The Dominoes soon rose to the position of the most popular R&B vocalists in the United States, and it was Clyde's soaring voice and vocal acrobatics that brought them the most renown.

In 1953, having made great contributions to The Dominoes, including training Jackie Wilson to replace him, Clyde had a disagreement with Billy Ward, the originator of the group, and he left. That same year a new group was formed, specifically for Clyde, called The Drifters. The line-up for this new group was Clyde as lead tenor, fellow gospel singers The Thrasher Wonders singing tenor and baritone, and Bill Pinkney singing bass. The Drifters, with their emotional gospel sound, were the most successful black vocal group of the fifties. They included among their R&B hits 'Money Honey' (1953), 'Such A Night' and Clyde's own composition, 'Honey Love' (1954). Their very distinctive arrangement of Irving Berlin's 'White Christmas' (1955) took them to success in the US pop charts.

Following the success of these recordings Clyde was drafted into the Army. On his demobilization he decided not to rejoin The Drifters and began a solo career.

Despite a string of minor hits including 'A Lover's Question' (1958), he met with only limited success. Rock 'n' roll music had arrived on the scene and Clyde couldn't adapt his distinctive vocal sound to appeal to the new generation of fans. His career was proving a major disappointment to him and he began to drink.

In the late 1960s Clyde took the decision to move to England, where he was still very popular. He produced one or two minor hits but was unable to recapture his former success, eventually sinking into alcohol dependency.

In 1972, while on a trip to New York, Clyde died of a heart attack as a result of the abuse he had inflicted on his body with his alcoholism. He was thirty-eight.

King Curtis

Real Name:	Curtis Ousley
Born:	7 February, 1934, Fort Worth, Texas, USA
Died:	13 August, 1971
Age:	37

Throughout the fifties and sixties, King Curtis was the undisputed king of session saxophonists. Highly respected by his fellow musicians, he was a master of rock 'n' roll, jazz, soul and blues.

Born in Fort Worth, Texas, where his father played guitar with the local church, King learned to play the saxophone as a child. On a visit to relatives in New York he, like Billie Holiday before him, made his début at the legendary Apollo Club in Harlem. Here, surrounded by other consummate musicians, King realised where his future lay and, by the age of twenty, he had moved to New York permanently.

In 1958, King began recording solos on Coasters' albums. The Coasters were an amusing black vocal quartet. They had been brought together by Leiber and Stoller, a innovative songwriting team who specialised in 'comic strip' songs. King's successes with this group included 'Yakety Yak', 'Charlie Brown', 'Poison Ivy' and 'The Chipmunks Song'.

Later in the year, Alan Freed, a disc jockey who played a major part in introducing rock 'n' roll to the public, took King with him as orchestra leader on the Alan Freed Big Beat show. Also on the sixteen-week tour were Jerry Lee Lewis, Chuck Berry and Buddy Holly. Freed was later involved in a payola scandal that effectively ruined his career, but King formed an instant rapport with Buddy Holly and went on to record with him.

Following this collaboration, King returned to his musical roots and became deeply immersed in rhythm and blues and jazz music. The sixties were hectic years for him: he worked exhaustively, recording several solo albums and even producing several pop songs. 'Soul Twist' and 'Beach Party' were the best of these. There are many fine examples of his work, perhaps the most memorable being 'King Curtis Plays The Great Memphis Hits' (1967) and 'Live at the Fillmore West' (1971).

A certain amount of mystery surrounds King's death. On the night of Friday 13 August, 1971, King, a big man and renowned for his short temper, was involved in a street fight with a young Puerto Rican, Juan Montanez. Both men sustained numerous stab wounds but King's proved fatal. Montanez later stood trial for his murder but the cause of the argument between the two men has never been established. What is certain is that King's death, at the age of thirty-seven, deprived the world of a great musical talent.

King's funeral was a well-attended affair. He had worked with many of the greats of the music world and they gathered together to pay him tribute.

Elvis Presley

Full Name:	Elvis Aaron Presley
Born:	8 January, 1935, Tupelo, Mississippi, USA
Died:	16 August, 1977
Age:	42

There is little doubt that Elvis Presley was not only the most adulated idol rock music had seen, but also the first. His music range covered gospel, country and western, rhythm and blues and rock 'n' roll, and he also enjoyed light opera – in fact, the only form of music he did not like was jazz.

James Dean had been at the forefront of the teenage rebellion, but by the time Elvis came to fame, Dean was dead, leaving the way clear for a far greater and truly innovative leader for the younger generation.

Elvis was born in Tupelo, Mississippi. He was one of twins but his brother, Jesse Garon, was stillborn. Elvis later said he had been told that 'when one twin dies, the other grows up with all the qualities of the other . . . If I did, then I'm lucky'. The Presleys were so poor that when a complication arose following the birth, Elvis's mother, Gladys, had to receive charity medical care.

The Presleys were not unusual in their poverty. The south in 1935 was still in the throes of the worst economic recession of its history. Work was very scarce and Vernon Presley, Elvis's father, was often unemployed. Gladys and Vernon had married young but, being the children of sharecroppers, they were used to privation. However, Gladys wanted a better life for her son, so Vernon undertook work wherever he could find it.

Music played an important part in southern communities. Hillbilly and honky-tonk musicians, with their songs of love, poverty, retribution and violence, often provided the only relief these poor folk received from the relentless struggle of their lives. Religion and its music also featured strongly in southern life and Elvis's parents were deeply religious. They attended the Assembly Church of God and Elvis was steeped in gospel music from an early age.

Gladys adored her only son. She raised him to be a polite, God-fearing child, but she indulged him when she could. They had formed a close bond after Elvis's birth, and this was strengthened when Vernon Presley was sent away to serve a prison sentence, leaving Gladys to care for the boy on her own.

From an early age Elvis loved to sing and, at the age of ten, he won a singing contest with his rendition of 'Old Shep'. For his eleventh birthday he wanted a bicycle, but his parents couldn't afford one and gave him a guitar instead. Elvis soon picked up the rudiments of guitar-playing by listening to all his heroes on the radio. Hank Williams was the major country singer at that time and Elvis idolised him. But his was not the only voice that Elvis listened to: he also admired the sweet voice of blues singer Johnny Ace and the light operatics of Mario Lanza.

Finding employment was difficult in the Tupelo area, and Vernon, in an effort to improve the family's prospects, moved them to Memphis when Elvis was thirteen. Their living conditions were still poor, and Elvis had to take odd jobs to augment the family income, lawn-mowing and cinema-ushering, but it was worth it to him as he loved Memphis. Here he was, at the heart of country music, surrounded by a rich variety of sound, hillbilly, gospel and country, and, of course, blues, for Memphis was the site of the legendary Beale Street, home of the blues. Elvis, with his innate love of music, was in his element.

Extremely polite (he had been taught by his mother to call men 'sir' and ladies 'ma'am'), Elvis was shy in high school. Only an average student, his great love was football. However, Gladys was over-protective and, fearing for the safety of her only son, she discouraged his participation in sports. Elvis turned his attention to his second love, music, and began to perform during his years in high school. He had already decided to emulate his hero Hank Williams and become a country singer.

With his heavy-lidded, sensuous eyes and the half-curled pout on his lip, Elvis was sensationally good-looking. Already an eye-catching dresser, he favoured black slacks, silky shirts and flashy jackets, eschewing the blue denims and overalls which to him signified poverty. He had already adopted the slicked-back pompadour hairstyle with sideburns which was to characterise his look.

On graduation from L.C. Humes High School in 1953, Elvis took a job driving a truck. This left his evenings free for him to play music or sing with a gospel group. He was very popular with the girls, they liked his style of dressing, handsome looks, southern drawl and polite manners. But it was his dedication to his mother that gave him his first break in the music business. As a birthday present for her he made a recording of 'My Happiness' at Sam Phillips' Memphis recording studios. Phillips, the producer of Sun Records, had been looking for a white singer with a black sound for a long time. When he heard Elvis singing, he called him in and suggested that he cut a few tracks with bass player Bill Black and guitarist Scotty Moore in accompaniment.

One day, in 1954, the three were fooling around in the studio together, and the sound they inadvertently produced was wild and original and exactly what Phillips was looking for. He cut the result 'That's All Right Mama' and persuaded the radio station WHBQ to play it on its *Red Hot and Blue* show.

Elvis's singing was a raw explosion of sexuality. Although he considered himself a ballad singer, he sang and moved with the natural rhythm and abandon of the gospel singers. Audience reaction to the first play of 'That's All Right Mama' on the radio was phenomenal and Elvis was immediately called in for an interview. However, knowing that his record was due to be played that night, an embarrassed Elvis had taken refuge in the cinema. It fell to his parents to locate him and get him to the radio station.

The first cutting of 'That's All Right Mama' and its 'B' side, 'Blue Moon Of Kentucky', was for 5,000 records, and they sold immediately. Sam Phillips signed Elvis, Moore and Black to a contract and sent them out on a tour of the southern states to gain experience and increase public awareness. Billed as Elvis Presley, The Hillbilly Cat, and The Blue Moon Boys, they played wherever they were invited, but their real targets were Nashville's Grand Ole Opry and the *Louisiana Hayride* show.

It was quickly obvious that Elvis, with his gyrating body movements and frenzied rock 'n' roll music, had something very special to offer. The teenagers who turned out in number to see him perform went crazy, shouting and screaming. But Elvis and The Blue Moon Boys were not always greeted so enthusiastically: the audience at The Grand Ole Opry were too staid for their youthful exuberance and the talent booker suggested that Elvis return to truck driving! Elvis and The Blue Moon Boys also failed an audition for *Arthur Godfrey's Talent Scouts* – the show on which Patsy Cline made her début singing 'Walking After Midnight' – before finally landing a weekly spot on KWKH's show, *Louisiana Hayride*. It was on *Louisiana Hayride* that Elvis made his local television début, too.

During this time, with Elvis away from home, Gladys worried incessantly about her only son. She felt he was overworking and she had premonitions of disaster which, on at least one occasion when his truck caught fire, were proved correct.

In 1955, Elvis came to the notice of 'Colonel' Tom Parker. The Colonel (a self-styled title) was a country music manager and promoter. Aware of Elvis's growing popularity in the south and realising his enormous potential, the Colonel began negotiations to take over his management.

In the beginning Elvis was basically a country ballad singer, but as his popularity increased, he developed a more rockabilly style, introducing the famous Presley hiccup. In Jacksonville, Florida, the fans rioted for the first time at one of his concerts, screaming and trying to rip off his clothes. Colonel Parker now entered into earnest negotiations for control of Elvis's career. Gladys didn't like the Colonel but he enlisted her sympathies by agreeing with her that Elvis was overworked and assuring her that he would make changes. After lengthy discussions, Vernon Presley signed a contract with the Colonel on Elvis's behalf (Elvis was still legally under age).

The Colonel was a shrewd businessman, and as soon as Elvis was legally bound to him he began to negotiate with RCA to buy out Elvis's contract with Sun Records. When the deal was completed Elvis promptly spent his $5,000 advance on his first Cadillac – colour pink.

In 1956, Elvis recorded 'Heartbreak Hotel' for RCA. Backing on this record was augmented by Chet Atkins (guitar), D.J. Fontana (drums) and Floyd Cramer (piano). The record release received maximum coverage as it coincided with Elvis's first national television appearance on *Jackie Gleason's Stage Show*.

Elvis exploded on to the nation's television screens, causing viewing figures to soar and starting a raging controversy over his blatantly sexual hip gyrations. He was greatly in demand for all the major variety programmes and appeared weekly on such shows as Milton Berle's, Steve Allen's and Ed Sullivan's.

'Heartbreak Hotel' rocketed to the top of the US hit parade and remained there for eight weeks. It was also Number One in the country and western charts and Number Five in the rhythm and blues chart. Before long it had crossed the Atlantic and entered the charts in Britain.

Controversy over Elvis's sensual hip gyrations continued to rage and Colonel Parker capitalised on it to build his popularity with the younger generation. He introduced mass-marketing of Elvis memorabilia. There were Elvis Presley T-shirts, bobby socks, hairbrushes, combs, pens and bubblegum – anything that a teenager might use was imprinted with Elvis's name.

With the fans' adoration came mass hysteria and riots. The younger generation loved Elvis's rebellious look, his outrageous style of dressing and most of all the uninihibited performance of his music. Parents saw him as a threat to authority and public morals but teenagers adopted him as their hero. Elvis had, by his very existence, created a generation gap.

Within nine months, he was a megastar and a millionaire. Although it might seem as though fame had come effortlessly to him, it must be remembered that, although supported by the love of his parents, he had suffered years of penury as a child and, in pursuit of his star, he had paid his dues as a struggling musician at the beginning of his career.

'Blue Suede Shoes' and 'Money Honey' followed 'Heartbreak Hotel' as singles. Both moved instantly into the charts and Elvis was able to buy his parents a new house in Memphis on the proceeds. He revered his mother and wanted to compensate her for all the hardships she had endured throughout her life. For her part, Gladys thought the world of her son and was proud of his achievements, but she was beset by anxiety when she saw how little freedom the adoration of his fans left him.

In the summer of 1956, 'Hound Dog', with its 'B' side, 'Don't Be Cruel', was released to become Elvis's biggest-selling US single. His popularity had spread internationally and RCA released his début album, entitled simply 'Elvis Presley'. It made record sales for RCA and Elvis celebrated by giving his mother a pink Cadillac.

Hollywood now began to take an interest in the

phenomenom known as 'Elvis the Pelvis'. The Colonel, in his element, began negotiations with the major studios, Twentieth Century Fox, Paramount and MGM, eventually settling on Twentieth Century Fox for Elvis's screen début. His first film was a Civil War western, *Love Me Tender* (1956). Like the films Elvis was to make, *Love Me Tender* was merely a vehicle for his singing talent: the storyline was irrelevant and none of his co-stars were major names. Elvis's name and brooding presence were all that was needed to pull in the fans.

Love Me Tender was a huge success and Elvis was scheduled to star in a second film, *Loving You*. However, before filming began he returned to Memphis to spend some time with his family. While he was there he dropped into the Sun studios and joined in a recording session with Carl Perkins and Jerry Lee Lewis. An album of this session was released after his death and, to everyone's surprise, the songs weren't rock 'n' roll but gospel and religious.

Loving You, his second film, was released in 1957 and he was lined up for a third, *Jailhouse Rock*. During the break between films he returned to Memphis, this time to buy a beautiful mansion in the suburbs. Graceland, standing in thirteen peaceful acres of ground, not only ensured complete privacy for Elvis, it also offered him a home base among people he understood and who understood him. Shy by nature, he was out of his depth in Hollywood, where he didn't understand the double standards by which the film world operated.

During this period Elvis was still turning out the hits. 'Hound Dog' (written by Leiber and Stoller), 'Too Much', 'All Shook Up', 'Teddy Bear' and the title song from *Jailhouse Rock* all did very well. His album, 'Elvis's Christmas Album', a selection of seasonal carols and hymns, remained a bestseller for two decades, despite some criticism of the black influence he introduced to such traditional material.

The success of his first three films elevated Elvis to the ranks of the Top Ten movie stars. In December, 1957 he received his draft orders for the US Army. However, Paramount Pictures intervened with the Draft Board, and Elvis was granted a deferment to enable him to complete the filming of *King Creole*. This, of course, gave rise to a barrage of protest about his 'special treatment'.

In March, 1958, despite a mass teenage protest, Elvis was inducted into the US Army as a private. Sadly, in August, while he was still completing his basic training, his beloved mother, Gladys, died. She had been suffering from hepatitis which weakened her heart and died of heart failure. Elvis was devastated, but he was obliged to return to the Army to finish his training.

After his training, Elvis was sent to Germany for a tour of duty. His father and grandmother, still suffering from the shock of Gladys's death, accompanied him. This was permitted as Elvis was the sole supporter of his family.

Colonel Parker, not wanting his protegé's fame to slide, carefully fostered Elvis's mystique during his absence. He had shrewdly seen to it that there was enough material recorded to keep Elvis in the public eye throughout his army stint. Over the two-year period, Parker judiciously released new singles at regular intervals, both in the United States and in Great Britain, where Elvis was now equally popular.

In 1959, Elvis met a fourteen-year-old American girl, Priscilla Beaulieu, the daughter of a US Air Force Captain stationed in Germany. Priscilla was petite and pretty with long brown hair and big blue eyes. Her parents, won over by Elvis's polite southern charm and good manners, were persuaded to allow their daughter to go out with him.

Much to Elvis's dismay, Vernon Presley was also dating, a blonde divorcée named Dee Stanley. Elvis felt that it was far too soon after Gladys's death for Vernon to become involved with another woman, but his advice fell on deaf ears.

Time hung heavily for Elvis during his stay in Germany. His fame and fortune made him different from the other conscriptees. Living off base, he felt lonely and isolated and his feelings for the young Priscilla intensified. It was in Germany that Elvis began to practise the martial art of karate. It filled in his spare time and offered him a spiritual discipline which appealed to his religious nature.

In March, 1960, Elvis returned to the United States for his demobilisation. Back home in Memphis he went straight into the studio for a recording session. The Colonel, anxious to get Elvis's career back on track, also negotiated a spot for him on the Sinatra television show for a fee of $125,000.

But it was soon apparent that the Elvis who had emerged from the Army was not the rebel who had entered. As John Lennon later said, 'he died the day he went into the army'. Elvis's image had now matured into that of a God-fearing, law-abiding, all-American boy who, having done his patriotic duty and served his country, was acceptable even to the older generation.

Hollywood awaited his return and Elvis began work on *GI Blues*, a light-hearted, song-filled comedy. This film was much more family-orientated, and although Elvis was disappointed with it, it greatly increased his popularity with both the younger and older generations.

For the duration of 1960, Elvis worked hard, commuting between Hollywood and Tennessee. With him went a group of young men he had gathered around himself, known as the Memphis Mafia. They were comprised of old school friends, Army buddies, the occasional relative and simply people that Elvis simply liked. It was their job to ensure his privacy, provide companionship and security and generally ease his path through life.

Elvis's next recording, 'It's Now Or Never' (1960), was a complete breakaway in style for him. It was an adaptation of the classic 'O Sole Mio', and it not only consolidated his success with the older generation, it also became his biggest-selling single ever.

Vernon, meanwhile, had married Dee. Elvis didn't attend the wedding, but eventually he became reconciled to his father's decision, and Vernon and Dee moved into a house in the grounds of Graceland.

To console himself, Elvis plunged into his work. His next film project was *Flaming Star*, a western in which he played a half-breed Indian. The fans loved it, but Elvis was ready for a new challenge. He had always had a sense of inner spiritualism, a feeling that he had been chosen to walk a certain path in life, and now he recorded an album consisting solely of religious songs, 'His Hand In Mine'. The initial sales of the album were disappointing and Elvis went back to the studios to make another film, *Wild in the Country*.

Certain that he had the ability to be a good actor if he was offered the right parts, Elvis became depressed by the mediocre material Colonel Parker selected for him. But the Colonel seemed to know what the public wanted and Elvis couldn't argue with the money he was making. On the music side, the hits kept flowing, bringing him international celebrity (except in East

Germany, where he had been named Public Enemy Number One).

In 1962, Elvis persuaded Priscilla Beaulieu's parents to allow her to complete her education in Memphis. He hoped that by bringing Priscilla to live at Graceland he would be able, in her formative years, to mould her into his version of the ideal woman. Elvis didn't care for career-minded women or those who swore. He wanted a woman like his mother who would find her fulfilment in staying at home and caring for her husband and family.

Priscilla moved in with Vernon and Dee Presley, but even her presence at Graceland couldn't provide for all of Elvis's needs. To keep his weight down for his film roles, he had begun to take dexedrine. Then he added other prescription drugs, stimulants and sleeping pills, and the more he added, the more he felt he needed to try.

Elvis thought that he had found his ideal woman in Priscilla. She was young, her adult character as yet unformed, and she adored him. He could envisage that eventually they would marry and have children, with Priscilla being the perfect stay-at-home wife. Meanwhile, Elvis had wild oats to sow. In Hollywood, surrounded by a bevy of beauties, his name had been linked with many starlets and models. During the making of *Viva Las Vegas* (1964), Elvis became romantically involved with his co-star, Ann-Margret. Ann-Margret was a sexy, red-haired, Swedish-born singer and dancer, and she had no intention of giving up a promising career to be a housewife. She and Elvis agreed to go their separate ways although they remained lifelong friends.

Throughout the sixties Elvis churned out an average of three films a year. He still had ambitions to tackle a more serious role but Colonel Parker wasn't taking any chances: he knew that musicals were the big money-makers for Elvis (and, synonymously, himself). He reminded Elvis that his two straight roles, in *Flaming Star* and *Wild in the Country*, had not done well at the box office, and persuaded Elvis to rely on his, Parker's, judgement, which had proved very reliable so far.

Although relationships between Elvis and the Colonel were often strained, Colonel Parker controlled the business side of his career and Elvis was generally satisfied with this arrangement. He lived an opulent lifestyle and he knew the films paid for it. His singing career had declined (he had not had a Number One hit since 1962), but the sales of his film soundtracks compensated financially. In the early sixties, after The Beatles had arrived on the scene, sales in Britain dropped and Elvis was content to follow the Colonel's advice.

But making three films a year, and recording the tracks, proved exhausting for Elvis. When he was home in Memphis he relaxed and indulged in the junk food that he loved: Coca-Cola, cheeseburgers, baconburgers, french fries and buckets of ice-cream. Despite his karate training, his weight fluctuated and he resorted to crash diets, as well as to amphetamines, to control it. He now took a significant amount of pills to govern most aspects of his life – uppers, downers, pills to sleep and stimulants – often taking them in combination. He carried with him a medical manual which gave details of all these prescription drugs, their composition, dosage and side effects.

At Graceland, Elvis was free to pursue the lifestyle he enjoyed. With the 'boys' he would drive his magnificent collection of cars around the grounds, race go-karts and motorbikes, watch films, visit the amusement park (where he loved the bumper cars) and shoot. Hunting, fishing and shooting were what a southern male was supposed to be all about and Elvis loved to shoot. He had a large collection of guns which he had been known to use to blast a television set or shoot up an hotel room.

Priscilla remained at Graceland with Dee and Vernon, joining in Elvis's social life when he was home for breaks between films. Surprisingly, much of his leisure time was also spent reading. There had always been a dominant spiritual side to Elvis's character – after all, he had been raised on hellfire and brimstone preaching – and in the mid-sixties he entered a new religious phase and began taking an interest in metaphysics and the philosophies of other cultures. His reading matter included the teachings of Buddha, Siddhartha, Kahlil Gibran's works and Cheiro's Book of Numbers.

In 1964, he employed his own personal *guru* in the form of Larry Geller. Geller's official position was hairstylist, but he was a deeply spiritual individual and he added a new dimension to Elvis's life, introducing him to a wider spectrum of learning and deeper devotion.

Elvis did not consider the prescribed medication he took, now expanded to include amphetamines, dexedrine, percodan, placidyls, quaaludes, seconals and tuinals, to be drugs. Drugs to him were marijuana, LSD, cocaine and heroin. True, he had dabbled with LSD and marijuana in an attempt to heighten his spiritual consciousness, but he did not judge himself an addict. So when the Federal Bureau of Narcotics, through the assistance of Richard Nixon, presented him with a Special Agent's Badge to add to his collection, he was delighted to accept it.

In 1967, Elvis released an album of gospel hymns entitled 'How Great Thou Art'. To his great joy, the album sold well and he received his first Grammy Award for the year's Best Religious Recording. But he was still discontented with his film career, and he had constant difficulty keeping his weight down. In an attempt to get his life firmly back on track, Elvis decided the time was right for him and Priscilla to marry.

The wedding took place on 1 May, 1967, at the Aladdin Hotel, Las Vegas. Finally, Priscilla's years of patience and loyalty were rewarded. Nine months to the day later, their joy was complete when their daughter, Lisa Marie, was born in Memphis.

The years of bland, mediocre films were over. In 1968, Elvis's contract with MGM expired and a new life began to unfold before him. Colonel Parker had negotiated a television special for the relaunch of Elvis's singing career. *From Elvis in Memphis* was broadcast in December, 1968, drawing a massive viewing audience and, totally deserved, rave reviews. An album containing the numbers from the show enjoyed enormous success and stands as one of Elvis's finest pieces of work. The socially-conscious 'In The Ghetto' was released as a single and sold over a million copies, as did 'Suspicious Minds', another number from the album. Elvis was Number One in the charts again. His star was in the ascendant. The king of rock 'n' roll was back!

Once more in the world he loved, and feeling in charge of his own destiny, Elvis embarked on a series of concerts at the International Hotel, Las Vegas, and his material included many of his early hits plus some new songs. Elvis's stage presence was as magnetic as ever, and the programme was a triumph of showmanship. His entrance was heralded by the stirring sound of 'Thus Spake Zarathustra', the theme music from the Stanley Kubrick's film *2001: A Space Odyssey*. He erupted on to the stage, resplendent in a bejewelled and fringed white suit and swirling white cape. A documentary film of these live shows, *Elvis: That's the Way It Is* was released to tremendous acclaim.

Elvis then embarked on his first live tour of the United States in over ten years. But his marriage was floundering. The strain of preparing for the live shows in Las Vegas, plus the added pressures of separation due to his punishing tour schedule, took their toll. Also, as his confidence in his own ability to entertain was rebuilt, Elvis began to enjoy the excitement and glamour of his stardom and the adulation of his fans, leaving him little time to be a husband and father.

Security around Elvis and his family was necessarily tight. He had received several death threats and, with the assassination of the Kennedy brothers and Martin Luther King and the murder of soul singer Sam Cooke fresh in his mind, Elvis feared for the safety of his family. Priscilla felt the constraint of these security measures. Elvis was always surrounded by his entourage so they had little time alone together. Elvis had also become more dependent on drugs to control his weight and to energise him for the live shows, and this, too, affected their married life.

Priscilla remained at Graceland while Elvis was away on tour and the couple began to drift apart. They disagreed on the upbringing of their daughter. Elvis was away so much of the time that when he was home he tended to over-indulge Lisa Marie. Priscilla felt that she needed more fulfilment in her life. She dispensed with the heavy make-up and flashy clothes that she had worn to please Elvis in the early days of their relationship, and began to learn the martial arts karate and Tae Kwan Do.

In 1972, Priscilla and Elvis separated. It was rumoured that Priscilla had conducted an illicit affair with her karate instructor, and that Elvis, with his puritanical streak, could not tolerate the indiscretion. Elvis, of course, had not been known for his faithfulness, but such are the double standards of men.

The divorce, in 1973, hurt Elvis badly. In fact, it is generally agreed that it was the beginning of the end for him. His health began to deteriorate, he was obviously consuming a great quantity of drugs and as a result he looked fat and bloated. His performances began to suffer as well. On occasion, the electrifying rock 'n' roll star would appear, but more often Elvis's performances were completely lacklustre, his songs reflecting the melancholy of his mood. There were still prolific recordings, however, and a movie, *Elvis On Tour*, which won the Golden Globe Award for the Best Documentary of 1973.

Following the divorce, Elvis and Priscilla, in the interests of Lisa Marie, settled their differences and became close friends. Elvis already had a new girlfriend, a former Miss Tennessee, Linda Thompson. Linda was good for Elvis. He had always had a quirky sense of humour and she was able to make him laugh. She also became popular with his entourage, the Memphis Mafia, and accompanied Elvis on tour, caring for him and worrying about his health. But although Linda was there most often, many girls came and went in Elvis's life after his divorce. Generous to a fault, he showered them with cars, clothes and jewellery.

In 1975, Elvis was hospitalised for a stomach complaint and added a new drug, cortisone, to his already extensive list. One of the unfortunate side effects of cortisone is excessive weight gain, and with Elvis's already corpulent frame, this was a major problem: even his diet pills could no longer keep him thin.

Once released from hospital, Elvis went back on the

road. Colonel Parker had made some financial deals that were more to his benefit than Elvis's, and Elvis, who was spending almost twice what he earned, needed the money. His tours and records produced a high income but his outgoings were much higher. There were fifteen people on his payroll and then there were expenses like clothes, cleaning, laundry, telephone calls, lawyers, taxes, upkeep on the cars and aeroplanes, guns and ammunition, drugs . . . an almost endless list.

Elvis still had an ambition to return to films and to prove that he could be a serious actor. In 1974, thanks to Colonel Parker, he missed an excellent opportunity. Barbra Streisand was producing a remake of the James Mason, Judy Garland classic, *A Star is Born*, and offered Elvis the co-starring role. Unfortunately, 'co-starring' was a word that the Colonel did not like to hear: either 'his boy' got the star billing or he was out. Streisand decided that he was out.

By 1976, it was apparent that Elvis was extremely ill. His stage appearance was grotesque, his hair ineptly dyed to maintain a youthful image and his paunch thinly disguised by voluminous and garish costumes. He was in and out of hospital for treatment and, accustomed as he was to performing at night and sleeping in the day, he required the windows to be covered in foil to keep out the light. His intake of drugs was supplemented with injections and he was totally out of control.

His relationship with Linda had mellowed into friendship. Like Priscilla, Linda found the constrictions of life with Elvis and the Memphis Mafia too limiting, and she moved out of Graceland. Elvis had already found a new love, Ginger Alden, a shy, pretty girl, twenty years his junior.

Being in love again gave Elvis a new lease on life for a

short time. He went back on tour and his fans welcomed him appreciatively. But life on the road was boring and tedious and Elvis's heart wasn't really in his work. He was exhausted by the long hours and, in April 1977, the tour had to be postponed due to his ill health. He was admitted to hospital for another short rest before resuming his arduous schedule.

Colonel Parker's promotion of Elvis as a commodity increased the pressure on him to continue working, and added to the considerable psychological stress he suffered just being 'Elvis'. Only with a constant supply of medication could he keep going, and even then he was just functioning as normal. He began to lose his grip on reality and his stage appearances were a shambles. He stumbled and stammered, slurring his speech and often losing track of what he was saying. But his fans responded loyally, interpreting his actions as intentional.

In the summer of 1977 it became imperative for Elvis to return to Graceland for a rest. Back at home he became reclusive, reading his religious books and playing with Lisa Marie, who was visiting. He was outraged when three former members of his Memphis Mafia, Red and Sonny West and Dave Hebler, published a book entitled *Elvis: What Happened*? The three, who had been fired for no apparent reason that they could see, retaliated by portraying Elvis as a man obsessed by guns, drugs and religion. Elvis saw this as the ultimate betrayal.

On 16 August, 1977, Ginger Alden discovered Elvis's body lying on his bathroom floor. Attempts to resuscitate him proved futile and he was rushed to Memphis Baptist Hospital where he was pronounced dead on arrival. The official cause of death was heart failure, but the autopsy report contained a long list of medical complaints: glaucoma, hypoglycaemia, an enlarged liver, a twisted colon, blood clots in the legs and respiratory ailments. Ten different drugs were discovered in his body. As if all that wasn't enough, there were also rumours that Elvis had terminal cancer.

Thousands of fans watched as Elvis's body was carried from the hospital along Elvis Presley Boulevard (named after him in 1972), to Graceland, where he was to lie in state. The 900-pound copper coffin was placed in the main foyer of Graceland beneath a crystal chandelier. Twenty-five thousand fans filed past to pay their last respects to their idol, now lying at peace in a white suit with a blue shirt and white tie. The grounds outside were a sea of floral tributes, sent from all over the world. Memorial T-shirts and badges were already on sale among the crowds. Then tragedy struck: a speeding car ploughed into the crowd, killing two young girls instantly.

One hundred vans were required to transport the mass of flowers to the Forest Hill Cemetery where Elvis was to be laid to rest beside his mother. A service was held in the music room of Graceland for relatives and friends. Priscilla, Lisa Marie and Vernon sat in the company of Linda and Ginger, Colonel Parker and Ann-Margret, all united in their grief. Then a nineteen-Cadillac cortège took the king on his final ride.

'Way Down', one of Elvis's final recordings, was on its way up the charts at the time of his death. It went on to become a million-dollar single, the first of a steady flow of Elvis records which continued to sell well over the next decade.

In the autumn of 1977, there was an attempt to steal Elvis's body from the cemetery, necessitating a reburial. He and his mother now rest quietly together in the meditation garden at Graceland with Vernon Presley, who died in 1979.

In 1980, Elvis's doctor was indicted on a charge of over-prescription of drugs to Elvis and others. He was suspended from practice for three months and put on probation for three years.

The 'Elvis business' has continued to grow apace over the years. There are Elvis impersonators, Elvis lookalike contests and endless memorabilia: ashtrays, coasters, key chains, anything guitar-shaped, postcards, bumper stickers, bubblegum, even wine – and Elvis didn't drink.

Of course, Colonel Parker got into the act. He adopted the slogan 'Always Elvis', which he used to market and promote various commercial ventures. Anyone who knew Elvis, however slightly, wrote a book. Publications include Priscilla Presley's *Elvis and Me*, Jerry Hopkins' *Elvis* and Larry Geller's *If I Can Dream*. In 1992, Dee Presley told her version of the truth in *The Intimate Life and Death of Elvis*.

In the first year after Elvis's death, RCA sold two million records. Much previously unreleased material has been discovered and a television series based on Elvis's early rock 'n' roll years was produced.

Despite the fact that toward the end, it seemed as if all of Elvis's actions were self-destructive, his death, similar to that of JFK, will remain a fixed point in the memories of many people. Elvis was a legend in his own time. His legacy was the enormous impact that his music made on the rock 'n' roll years. With his genius, he liberated an entire generation.

The list of his Gold Records is impressive. Among them are:

'Elvis', 'Elvis's Golden Records', 'Elvis's Christmas

Album', 'Elvis Presley', 'Elvis's Gold Records Vol.2', 'Elvis's Gold Records Vol.3', 'How Great Thou Art', 'Elvis – A Legendary Performer Vol.1' and 'Elvis – A Legendary Performer Vol.2.

Johnny Burnette

Born: 25 March, 1934, Memphis, Tennessee, USA
Died: 1 August, 1964
Age: 30

Johnny Burnette was born and raised in Tennessee. He was a contemporary of Elvis Presley and their lives crossed on more than one occasion. They attended the same school, L. C. Humes High School, and briefly worked for the same company. Although Johnny was one year older than Elvis, he spent most of his career in Elvis's shadow.

Like Elvis, Johnny wanted to be a singer when he left school. He worked for a time as a Mississippi bargeman and as a boxer before forming his own group. With his brother, Dorsey (on bass), a neighbour, Paul Burlison (lead guitar) and himself as vocalist and guitarist, they became Burnette's Rock 'n' Roll Trio and were soon regular performers at the Hideaway Club in Memphis.

In 1955, the trio auditioned for Sam Phillips at Sun Records. But Phillips had already signed Elvis Presley and, to the trio's chagrin, they were rejected because they sounded too similar.

However, inspired by Elvis's success, they moved to New York where they fared rather better. Supporting themselves with odd jobs they auditioned for the *Ted Mack Amateur Hour*. They were the winners for three consecutive weeks, although they ultimately lost the final. However, it was enough: Coral Records signed them up and they went into the recording studios.

Johnny was an outstanding rockabilly singer and their first single, 'Tear It Up' (1956), did very well, but they were disappointed with the success of their subsequent tracks.

After a tour of the north-eastern United States they secured a spot in Alan Freed's movie *Rock Rock Rock* singing 'Lonesome Train'. This, too, was released as a single, but it didn't attract much attention. Discouraged by their lack of success, Dorsey Burnett left the trio in 1956, then Paul Burliston in 1957, so Johnny Burnette went solo; Burlison returned to Memphis and the Burnettes tried their luck in California.

In California, the brothers began songwriting together. Their first successes were three numbers written for the teenybopper hero Ricky Nelson, 'Waiting In School', 'Believe What You Say' and 'A Little Too Much'. But they both still had aspirations to be solo artists and gradually they began to establish their reputations. In 1960, Johnny had a Top Ten hit with 'Dreamin''. His next single, 'You're Sixteen', eclipsed the success of his first and sold over a million copies, but he had no further hits. In an attempt to make a comeback, he changed record labels and singing styles but still success eluded him.

Eventually he formed his own company, 'Magic Lamp', so that he would have the freedom to develop new projects. But, in 1964, when Johnny was only thirty, he fell overboard and drowned while out fishing on his boat at Clear Lake, California.

Dorsey moved into country music and enjoyed a respectable career, singing and writing songs for Glen Campbell and Jerry Lee Lewis. Ironically, in 1973, at the age of forty-one, he was voted the Academy of Country Music's Most Promising Newcomer. Sadly, he died of a heart attack at the age of forty-six.

The Burnette Brothers' legacy has been carried on by their sons. Dorsey's son, Rocky, had a major hit with 'Tired Of Toein' The Line' (1980), and Johnny's son, Billy, joined Fleetwood Mac in 1989.

Sam Cooke

Real Name:	Samuel Cook
Born:	22 January, 1935, Clarksdale, Mississippi, USA
Died:	11 December, 1964
Age:	29

Sam Cooke, although born in Mississippi, was raised in Chicago. He was one of eight children of a Baptist minister, Charles Cook. As a minister, Charles expected his children to participate in church affairs, and Sam, with three of his siblings, formed the Singing Children. As a teenager, he sang with the Highway QCs before joining The Soul Stirrers in 1950.

The Soul Stirrers were the most popular gospel group of the day and Sam became their lead tenor. Gospel music was the dominant church music of black America and Sam's clear, soulful voice was ideally suited to it. From his debut, for which his sensitive singing brought him a standing ovation, he quickly began to develop his own distinctive style.

With The Soul Stirrers, Sam cut a few discs for Specialty Records but, seeking a wider audience, he also recorded a couple of pop numbers using the pseudonym

Dale Cook. Although these attempts were not a major success, Sam gained confidence and useful experience from them and he left Specialty to sign with Keen Records.

His recording of 'You Send Me', a song written by his brother Charles, was released in 1957, and stayed in the Number One position in the pop charts for two weeks, selling over a million copies. Sam made his début on national television on the *Ed Sullivan Show* – coincidentally, Buddy Holly and The Crickets made their initial appearance at the same time and place.

Sam's career was now well and truly launched and a string of hits followed. Some were sentimental ballads such as 'I Love You For Sentimental Reasons', others commercial pop, like 'Only Sixteen' and 'Wonderful World', and yet others dance numbers, 'Everybody Loves To Cha Cha Cha', for example. A distinctive feature of all the recordings was Sam's immaculate vocal style.

In 1960, Sam's contract with Keen came to an end and he signed a lucrative deal with RCA, becoming their second black artist. His appeal to the black community, with his gospel and rhythm and blues music, had always been strong, but now, with the release of the gospelly 'Chain Gang', Sam bridged the gap between black and white music and rocketed to international stardom.

A tour of the Caribbean (the first of three) in 1960, was a sell-out success. It also influenced a whole new generation of West Indian singers, amongt them Bob Marley.

Another of Sam's gifts was his aptitude for business. In 1961, with his old friend J. W. Alexander, he formed a company for recording and writing music. Sam was a strong exponent of black rights and this company gave him the opportunity to produce songs which were geared to encouraging desegregation. Over the next three years, Sam produced a number of ballad and dance recordings. 'Cupid' (1961), 'Twisting The Night Away' (1962) and 'Another Saturday Night' (1963), mostly written by Sam himself, did well commercially and increased his popularity.

By the beginning of 1964, Sam was a hero of black America. Cassius Clay, the world heavyweight boxing champion, set the seal on his fame by declaring him 'the greatest singer in the world'. But it was not only Sam's voice that made him a symbol of black liberation – it was also his renowned business acumen. In addition to his successful recording company, he had acquired a management company and a publishing organisation, proving that it was possible for blacks to achieve success in commercial ventures.

It therefore seems difficult to understand the chain of events that led to his bizarre death at the age of twenty-nine. Sam had a reputation for being a very kind person and, like Elvis Presley, he was interested in spiritual teachings. He had been happily married to his childhood sweetheart since 1959, yet it was alleged that in December, 1964, he took a young girl back to a motel room in Los Angeles and attempted to rape her. The manageress of the motel claimed that when his victim fled to call for help, Sam turned on her, the manageress, and attacked her. She then shot and cudgelled him to death in self-defence. Was this the simple truth? Many believe there was a cover-up. Could it have been a case of mistaken identity? Or was it a white plot to discredit a successful black businessman? All these theories were advanced and perhaps the truth will never be known. The coroner's verdict was justifiable homicide.

Sam was buried in Chicago, where thousands of his fans jostled and shoved to have a final look at their dead hero as he lay in his glass coffin. Due to the enormous crowd, pandemonium broke out and the doors and windows of the funeral home were smashed.

Following Sam's death, his recording of the oddly prophetic 'A Change Is Gonna Come' was immensely popular. So, too, was 'Shake', another posthumous release which Otis Redding later sang as a tribute to Sam. 'Chain Gang', however, probably remains Sam's greatest triumph. It was a watershed for modern music and from it came the music we now regard as soul. Sam Cooke was undoubtedly the father of soul music, and was also largely responsible for the transformation of black music.

In 1986, twenty-two years after his death, Sam Cooke was inducted into the Rock 'n' Roll Hall of Fame at their first annual dinner. The Soul Stirrers, the first gospel group Sam belonged to, joined him there in 1989.

Gene Vincent

Real Name: Eugene Vincent Craddock
Born: 11 February, 1935, Norfolk, Virginia USA
Died: 12 October, 1971
Age: 36

Although he never attained the stardom of Elvis Presley, Gene Vincent is still regarded as one of rock 'n' roll's greats. When he was sixteen, Gene joined the US Navy where he served as a despatch rider. But his Navy career came to an end when he was involved in a motorcycle accident in which he injured his leg. He spent many months in hospital, but irrevocable damage had been done to his leg, and he was left with a permanent limp.

On his twenty-first birthday in 1956, Gene, like Jerry Lee Lewis and Roy Orbison, married a teenage girl. Like the other marriages that Gene contracted, it didn't last very long.

He had begun singing during his long convalescence, and now he found that his rockabilly could earn him a living on the local radio station, WCMS. 'Sheriff' Tex Davis, a disc jockey at WCMS, impressed with his singing, arranged for Gene to cut some demos, then submitted them to Capitol Records, who were looking for a singer to rival RCA's Elvis Presley. A Capitol executive, Ken Nelson, heard the demos and offered Gene a contract.

Accompanied by guitarists Cliff Gallup and Willie Williams, bassist Jack Neal and drummer Dickie Harrell, Gene recorded his first single. The 'A' side was called 'Woman Love' and the 'B' side, written by a fellow patient of Gene's in hospital, 'Be-Bop-A-Lula'. It was the 'B' side that caught the public's imagination and shot Gene and His Blue Caps (as his back-up was now known) to the top of the hit parade.

Gene and the boys made their debut live television appearance on *The Perry Como Show* prior to the release of their first album, 'Blue Jean Bop'. Unfortunately, the cracks were already beginning to appear in Gene's life. By the end of 1956, The Blue Caps had lost two of their founder members, Willie Williams and Cliff Gallup, and the line-up remained unstable for the rest of their existence. Also, Gene's injury was playing up. His leg was in a plaster cast and when he and the Blue Caps were offered a cameo appearance in the film *The Girl Can't Help It*, his cast had to be disguised as a shoe.

A dispute with his management – the first of many – kept him off the road for a few months and Gene used this time to get further hospital treatment. Back on the road, he exchanged the plaster cast for a metal brace which he was to wear all his life. His limp, along with his slicked-back hair, had become his trademark.

Gene's next recordings, 'Lotta Lovin' and 'Wear My Ring' (1957), did not reach the heights of 'Be-Bop-A-Lula' but they did enjoy enough success to warrant Gene undertaking a tour of Australia with Eddie Cochran and Little Richard. Gene was greeted rapturously by his fans, but the general behaviour on the tour was so appalling that various hotels, hearing of the drinking and wild parties, were wary of accepting their bookings. One hotel manager asked for a deposit of $50,000 against damages.

In 1958, Gene and the Blue Caps made another 'teen' movie, *Hot Rod Gang* before embarking upon an exhausting tour of the United States and Canada. Gene's behaviour became increasingly erratic. He was drinking heavily and he was beset by financial problems. The taxman was hounding him and he owed the Blue Caps back wages. When his Musicians' Union card was withdrawn for unprofessional conduct Gene, with a new bride for company, disappeared from the scene for a short while.

Ever a performer, Gene bounced back in 1959. However, he couldn't recapture his early popularity in the United States. A tour of Japan was followed by a trip to England, where he was still very much a star. Britain had not seen enough of the American rock 'n' rollers, the fans greeted Gene enthusiastically, and he decided to stay.

Jack Good, the producer of Britain's first youth-orientated television shows, *Boy Meets Girl*, *Six-Five Special* and *Oh Boy*!, had changed the approach of presenting rock 'n' roll to the masses, introducing live audiences. When he saw Gene he knew he was on to a winner and set about remodelling his image. In the United States a clean-cut image was essential – anything radical was frowned upon – but Good capitalised on Gene's mean, good looks, dressing him in black leather and adding a gold medallion for effect. He persuaded Gene to emphasise his limp, even going as far (so legend has it) as to call out from the wings one night. 'Limp, you bugger, limp!' Gene's career was temporarily revitalised and he became a regular performer on *Boy Meets Girl*.

In April 1960, Gene teamed up with his old friend Eddie Cochran for a tour of the United Kingdom. The tour was long and arduous, and when it was decided to extend it, Gene, Eddie and his fiancée, Sharon Sheeley, interrupted the tour for an Easter break. On the way to Heathrow Airport, their car was involved in an accident. Eddie Cochran was killed, and Gene was admitted to hospital suffering from a broken collar-bone, broken ribs and further injury to his leg. Suffering from a much more pronounced limp, and deeply affected emotionally by his friend's death, Gene tried to pull his life together.

By May, he was back at Abbey Road Recording Studios to cut 'Pistol Packin' Mama'. His recording career, however, seemed to be over. But Gene was a consummate performer, and he maintained a good following throughout his tours of Britain, Europe and South Africa. He was also very popular on the club circuit, appearing once at Liverpool's Cavern Club on the same bill as the yet-to-be-famous Beatles.

As the sixties progressed, Gene's popularity declined. Elvis Presley had eased him aside in the United States and now The Beatles and The Rolling Stones were doing the same to him in Britain. Marriage number three, in 1963, had been superseded by number four in 1965 and Gene had financial problems. In an attempt to revive his flagging career, he produced a mix of country and rock music in his album 'I'm Back And I'm Proud' (1970). It was acclaimed critically but the public's interest wasn't rekindled and they didn't buy it.

His personal life was falling apart fast. As ever, he was plagued by ill health and he was drinking heavily. He also had a serious weight problem. His fourth wife had left him and was claiming maintenance. He suffered from depression and his recurrent management problems had brought him to financial ruin.

In a final desperate attempt to regain stability and control of his life, Gene returned to the United States. While there he collapsed and died of a perforated ulcer. Gene Vincent was a sad victim of his own lifestyle. He sought fame and fortune, but died, at the age of thirty-six, alone, in relative obscurity, burnt out and broke. But he is still imitated and his memory lives on in his music. In 1976, Ian Dury paid tribute to him with his recording 'Sweet Gene Vincent'.

Jack Good, the impresario who had been instrumental in remoulding Gene and promoting his career in Britain, announced, in 1992, that he was to retire from the world of rock 'n' roll. No longer the sound of music for him, instead, amazingly, the silence of a religious order in Texas.

Bobby Darin

Real Name:	Walden Roberto Cassotto
Born:	14 May, 1936, New York City, USA
Died:	20 December, 1973
Age:	37

Bobby Darin's father died before he was born, leaving his mother, with the help of the welfare department, to raise her family alone. They were very poor and young Bobby's earliest ambition was to be rich and famous. He had a premonition that he would not live beyond thirty years of age and he wanted to pack as much as possible into his life.

By the time he was in high school, Bobby could play the piano, drums and guitar. He won a scholarship to Hunter College but dropped out after only a term to pursue a career in showbusiness.

His first step in search of fame was to change his name. Cassotto didn't have the magic ring to it, Bobby thought, so he chose another one from the telephone directory. He began his career writing songs for other artists, and singing in New York clubs and coffee houses. A recording, for Decca, of Lonnie Donegan's 'Rock Island Live' made hardly a ripple. However, in 1958, Bobby,

Atlantic Records' first white singer, recorded one of his own compositions, a novelty rock number entitled 'Splish Splash'. It was a big hit and Bobby had his first Gold Disc.

Two other major hits, 'Queen Of The Hop' (1958) and the teen ballad 'Dream Lover' (1959) consolidated his position as a teen idol. But Bobby was a very versatile performer and he sought wider recognition.

He followed 'Dream Lover' with a jazzy interpretation of 'Mack The Knife' (1959) from Brecht and Weill's *Threepenny Opera*. It zoomed to Number One in the charts and earned Bobby two awards, the Grammy Awards for Best Single Record of the Year and Best New Performer of 1959.

Now that he had emerged as an all-round entertainer, with adult as well as teen appeal, Bobby became known for his up-tempo rearrangements of standard songs. 'La Mer' (1960), which earned him his fifth Gold Disc, and 'Clementine', an update of an old miners' song, were but two.

His next target was success on the nightclub and cabaret circuit. In 1960, Bobby opened at the Sahara in Las Vegas. By the end of that year he had added the American Variety Club's Personality of the Year to his list of awards.

Marriage to Hollywood starlet Sandra Dee signalled the beginning of his film career, which was to be very prolific. He appeared in *Pepe* and *Heller in Pink Tights* (both 1960) before co-starring with his wife in *Come September* (1961). The instrumental theme from *Come September* was credited to the Bobby Darin Orchestra, showing yet another facet of Bobby's talent.

Sandra Dee and Bobby were regarded as all-American sweethearts. She, the girl next door, and he, the boy from the Bronx made good. On their second anniversary Bobby even cancelled a lucrative engagement so that they could spend the evening together.

Light musical comedy wasn't enough of a challenge for Bobby. After three films with his wife, he appeared in *Pressure Point* with Sidney Poitier and *Hell is For Heroes* with Steve McQueen. In 1963, his dramatic portrayal of a shell-shocked GI in *Captain Newman, MD* won him a nomination for an Academy Award.

And the hits were still flowing, from the jazzy 'Bill Bailey', through the rhythm and blues-orientated 'Multiplication' to the country sound of 'Things', which again was one of Bobby's own compositions.

As a result of rheumatic fever in his childhood, Bobby had suffered from heart trouble for much of his adult life. He gave freely of his time to charity and, in 1964, his contributions were recognised when he was voted National Heart Ambassador for the American Heart Association.

Sadly, the perfect all-American marriage ended in 1967 when Bobby and Sandra Dee divorced. Bobby married for a second time in 1971, but this, too, ended in divorce after only a few months.

Once again Bobby added a new dimension to his career, moving into folk music. His version of Tim Hardin's song 'If I were A Carpenter' took him back into the charts. Coincidentally, Tim Hardin's only big hit, 'Simple Song Of Freedom' (1969) was written by Bobby.

A very outspoken, politically-aware person, Bobby campaigned tirelessly for Robert Kennedy's presidential nomination. He supported him at rallies, singing protest ballads and freedom songs. Kennedy's assassination was a severe blow to Bobby and afterwards he abandoned the establishment for the life of a hippy in a caravan. He formed his own record label and produced an album, 'Born Walden Roberto Cassotto', which featured protest songs and poetry all written, arranged, produced, designed and photographed by himself.

In 1971, Bobby emerged from his hippy period a more mature and polished performer. He signed a recording contract with Motown and went back on the nightclub and cabaret circuit. His health, however, wasn't good and he was admitted to hospital for the replacement of two heart valves. On his recovery he launched his own television series, *The Bobby Darin Show*, also returning to the screen for a role with Patricia Neal in *Happy Mothers' Day*.

In December, 1973, Bobby was admitted to the Cedars of Lebanon Hospital in Hollywood to have a heart valve repaired. But the operation proved too taxing for his heart and he died following surgery, aged thirty-seven. The boy from the New York ghetto had survived his childhood premonition by seven years, and achieved the fame he sought, but this talented and versatile artist would have been capable of much more if he had lived a normal lifespan.

Buddy Holly

Real Name:	Charles Hardin Holley
Born:	7 September, 1936, Lubbock, Texas, USA
Died:	3 February, 1959
Age:	22

Although his professional career was tragically short, Buddy Holly, with his large, dark-rimmed glasses and boy-next-door looks, was a hero to millions of teenagers. They could relate to his lyrics of simple, uncomplicated love, which reflected their own dreams and hopes. In two short years he laid the foundations for many groups that were to follow: The Beatles chose their name in homage to The Crickets and The Rolling Stones' cover of 'Not Fade Away' was their first British hit.

Buddy Holly was born in Lubbock, the biggest city in west Texas, and the heart of the cotton-growing area. Lubbock sits on a plateau in the midst of the great western plains of Texas. Few people outside the state had heard of Lubbock before Buddy Holly put it on the map, and now the rest of the world is more familiar with his name than the citizens of his birthplace.

Buddy's father, Lawrence Holley, like Elvis Presley's

father, had moved his family in search of work during the Depression. He and his wife, Ella, had four children of whom Buddy was the youngest. In Buddy's early years he was surrounded by music. His mother and brothers and sister were all very musical. The Holley family were religious, too. They attended the Tabernacle Baptist Church and the music of the church was an important influence in Buddy's life.

Academically, Buddy didn't shine – perhaps his poor eyesight was to blame. But at the age of five he won his first talent competition, singing and accompanying himself on a toy violin. Buddy's mother taught him to play the piano, and when he was in high school his parents presented him with his first acoustic guitar. Through listening to country music on the local radio station, Buddy taught himself to play it. The king of country and western music, Hank Williams, was his idol, and Buddy liked to imitate him, singing 'Lovesick Blues'.

Another great country music enthusiast and budding musician was Buddy's friend, Bob Montgomery. The two practised their guitars together. By 1953, while they were still in high school, they had formed a duo. Buddy and Bob played their music at school dances, supermarket openings and anywhere else they could find an audience.

One night in April, 1955, Buddy and Bob went to hear a new singer who was performing at the Cotton Club in Lubbock. Elvis Presley, dubbed The Hillbilly Cat, was just at the beginning of his career but already he was playing rockabilly, a fusion of country and rock 'n' roll, and it had a profound effect on Buddy.

Buddy and Bob adapted their music to this innovative sound and soon had a regular spot on the local radio station, KDAV, one of the first stations to play rock 'n' roll in Lubbock. The Buddy and Bob show was born.

Larry Welborn, a bass player, now joined the line-up and they began to play to a wider audience, appearing at concerts. At first, they opened for Elvis Presley, Bill Haley and The Comets and other big names of the day.

At a concert in Lubbock in 1956, a talent scout from Decca Records of Nashville heard them play. He offered Buddy a recording contract, but as it excluded Bob Montgomery Buddy was reluctant to accept. However, Bob Montgomery persuaded Buddy to accept. He felt that his own future was in country music (he did indeed go on to become a successful songwriter and producer in his own right) whereas Buddy's star lay with rock 'n' roll.

Nashville was not a success. RCA had capitalised on Elvis Presley's unique style, but Decca was tradition-bound. They insisted that Buddy record country music. One of the singles cut in this period was an early version of 'That'll Be The Day'. This was dismissed by Decca producer Owen Bradley as being one of the worst songs he had ever heard! Decca did not renew Buddy's contract and legend has it that Buddy was so disgusted with the treatment he received that he punched Owen Bradley in the face before storming back to Lubbock.

Money was a prime consideration for Buddy now. It had cost him a lot to travel backwards and forwards to Nashville, and he had had to borrow money to buy his Fender Stratocaster guitar which, along with his dark-rimmed glasses, was to become his trademark. Disillusioned and frustrated, Buddy turned to an independent record producer, Norman Petty.

Petty, a former musician himself, had set up a recording studio in Clovis, New Mexico, to experiment with new ideas. He suggested that Buddy get a backing group together before they went into the studio. Buddy assembled his group, Jerry Allison on drums and Niki Sullivan on rhythm guitar. Joe B. Mauldin later joined as the group's bass player.

The first two tracks they cut were 'I'm Looking For Someone to Love' and 'That'll Be The Day'. As Buddy had previously recorded the latter for Decca he was prohibited from releasing it under his own name. Petty solved the problem by suggesting that the group change its name prior to the record's release. Buddy consulted an encyclopaedia, which fell open at the 'insects' section, and 'The Crickets' came into being.

Petty also took over the management of the group and set about finding a record company. Brunswick Records signed Buddy and The Crickets and Coral Records offered Buddy a solo contract. Both were subsidiaries of Decca, which tickled Buddy. 'That'll Be The Day' was released in May, 1957 and by the end of the year it was Number One on both sides of the Atlantic. Introducing Buddy's inimitable hiccupping vocals, it was one of the most influential songs in the early days of rock.

Buddy and The Crickets were now in great demand. Tours were an important part of the rock scene and The Crickets were booked for a major tour of the United States. First, they needed to polish their image: their 'country boy' garb was far too laid-back. Out went the casual shirts and jeans, and in came smart suits and ties. Buddy even swapped his metal-framed glasses for more serious black-rimmed ones.

The Biggest Show of Stars for '57 included performers of the calibre of Chuck Berry, Clyde McPhatter, Paul Anka and The Everley Brothers. At times racial tension on the road was high: there were theatres where blacks could not appear; equally, there were those where whites were not welcome, but rock 'n' roll was beginning to erode the barriers between the two.

In December, 1957, Buddy and The Crickets made their national television debut on the *Ed Sullivan Show* singing 'That'll Be The Day' and 'Peggy Sue'. 'Peggy Sue' was written by Buddy and originally entitled 'Cindy Lou'. It had been renamed in honour of Allison's girlfriend. One month later they were back on the *Ed Sullivan Show* with their new single 'Oh Boy'.

With three hits in the Top Fifty, their popularity was firmly established. Buddy and The Crickets undertook a worldwide tour – without Niki Sullivan, who had left to pursue a solo career. The tour began in Australia and then proceeded to Great Britain. Surprisingly, Buddy was already more popular in Britain than he was back home, and the fans greeted him rapturously. Some of the national newspapers were not overly enthusiastic at this invasion of energy and sound from across the Atlantic but, compared to Elvis Presley, with his sexual hip gyrations, and Jerry Lee Lewis, the wild man of rock, The Crickets seemed almost tame. For many British teenagers this was the first experience of live rock 'n' roll and they loved the raw, vibrant sound of it, turning out in great numbers to see their idol.

In April, 1958, the inventive 'Rave On' was released to a disappointing reception and Buddy began to consider new challenges. Any decision he might have made was taken out of his hands in June, when he met a lovely Puerto Rican girl, Maria Elena Santiago, in New York. Maria Elena worked for as a receptionist for Southern Music, where her aunt was an executive. For Buddy it was love at first sight. He proposed immediately and was accepted.

The couple met with initial opposition from their

families. Maria was a Catholic and Buddy's family were strict Baptist. Racial and religious discrimination was very strong in Texas, and both families advised caution. But Buddy was determined, and the couple were married in August, 1958.

Following a short honeymoon, they returned to New York where they had decided to live. This created a certain feeling of separation between Buddy and The Crickets, who preferred to remain based in Texas. Further difficulties arose because Buddy had begun to take more of an interest in the business side of his career, and he felt that there was a discrepancy between the money The Crickets earned, and the money they were actually paid by Petty. Petty had absolute control over their financial affairs at that time and friction grew between him and Buddy. Maria Elena was knowledgeable about the music business and felt she could offer Buddy any guidance that he needed, so Buddy severed all connections with Petty. In an attempt to recover some of the money that he suspected Petty of having misappropriated, he instigated legal proceedings.

The Crickets had been persuaded to remain with Petty, which caused a further rift between them and Buddy. It seemed the right time for Buddy to pursue a solo career.

In October, 1958, Buddy went into the recording studio in New York to experiment with a new sound: vocals backed by a full string section. The resulting 'It Doesn't Matter Any More', written by the young Canadian, Paul Anka, was a major breakthrough for a rock 'n' roll singer. Sadly, it was to be Buddy's final soaring contribution to the recording world.

Marriage suited Buddy and he was full of creative energy. The only cloud on his horizon was his financial situation. Much of his money was tied up in the complex legal proceedings against Petty and Maria Elena was expecting a baby. When Buddy was offered the name position on the Winter Dance Party tour, it seemed the answer to all his problems.

The tour began on 23 January, 1959. The weather, predictably for the mid-west of America at that time of year, was bitterly cold. The tour party often found themselves travelling on buses that broke down or had no heating. Buddy was exhausted by the first day of February. He decided to charter a plane to carry him from Mason City, Iowa to the next venue so that he could at least get a good night's sleep. Ritchie Valens and J. P. Richardson, The Big Bopper, decided to accompany him on that fateful night.

Weather conditions were very bad and the pilot of the single-engine Beechcraft Bonanza was inexperienced. Nevertheless, Buddy decided to press on. Tragically, the plane crashed within minutes of take-off, killing all those on board. Don McLean, in his album 'American Pie' (1972), which was dedicated to Buddy, described that day as 'the day the music died'.

Buddy was buried in his native Lubbock, an electric guitar engraved on his headstone. He had passed into the world of legend and in the minds of his fans he will be forever young.

His music, particularly in Britain, has remained popular. Paul McCartney, who had been profoundly affected by Buddy's tour of Britain in 1958, purchased the rights to his songs.

In 1978, a biographical film, *The Buddy Holly Story* was released. It starred the remarkable Buddy Holly lookalike, Gary Busey, who was nominated for an Academy Award and a Golden Globe Award for his performance. The picture won an Oscar for the Best Original Song Score. Gary Busey became so entangled in the Buddy Holly legend that, in 1990, he paid $242,000 for one of Buddy's acoustic guitars.

In 1980, the proceeds from a memorial concert were used to erect a statue of Lubbock's most famous citizen in the Civic Centre. A television programme celebrating Buddy's life and contribution to rock 'n' roll was broadcast on the fiftieth anniversary of his birth.

The Crickets continued to record and perform together, although they never achieved the same measure of fame. Thirty years after their death, relatives of Buddy Holly, J. P. Richardson and Ritchie Valens gathered together in Port Arthur, Texas to unveil commemorative statues of the rock singers.

A musical entitled *Buddy*, opened on the London stage in 1990 and is still running, playing to large audiences. And so it goes on.

Buddy Holly's influence on the rock scene was tremendous. With Norman Petty, he pioneered new recording techniques, using experimental overdubbing and multitracks. He pulled rock 'n' roll into the mainstream with orchestral backing, and proved that artists could write and arrange their own material as well as produce it. Such is Buddy's legacy.

The Big Bopper

Real Name: Jiles Perry Richardson
Born: 24 October, 1930, Sabine Pass, Texas, USA
Died: 3 February, 1959
Age: 28

Another victim on the cold dark night in February when Buddy Holly died was J.P. Richardson, otherwise known as The Big Bopper.

Jiles Perry Richardson, grew up in Beaumont, Texas where he was a popular figure at school and on the football field. Finding his name too much of an embarrassment, Jiles had become Jape (for J.P.) somewhere along the way.

He took up playing the guitar during his army stint and on his discharge he went to work as a disc jockey at the Beaumont radio station, K-TRM. J.P. was a big, warm-hearted man and the name by which he called himself, The Big Bopper, became his radio persona. In 1957, he set a record for continuous on-the-air broadcasting, five days, two hours and eight minutes, playing nearly 2,000 records!

That same year, Mercury Records signed him to a

recording contract. J.P. was a prolific songwriter and many of his compositions reflected his humorous nature. His novelty rock number 'The Purple People Eater Meets The Witch Doctor', released in 1958, was overshadowed by its 'B' side, 'Chantilly Lace', which sold over a million copies.

Both sides of his next single, 'The Big Bopper's Wedding' and 'Little Red Riding Hood' were successful, and J.P., putting together a stage act that incorporated his humorous radio personality and his musical talents, signed up for the Winter Party Tour.

On the night of 3 February, 1959 J.P. persuaded Waylon Jennings to give up his seat on the single engine Beech Bonanza Buddy Holly had chartered to fly to Fargo, North Dakota. The rest is history. J.P. Richardson, aged twenty-eight, perished on that cold night in 1959, along with Buddy Holly and Ritchie Valens, all three forever frozen in time.

Much of the Big Bopper's fame arrived posthumously through songs that he had written for other artists, the biggest hit being 'Running Bear', which he wrote for his friend, Johnny Preston.

Eddie Cochran

Real Name:	Ray Edward Cochrane
Born:	3 October, 1938, Albert Lea, Minnesota, USA
Died:	17 April, 1960
Age:	21

In company with Buddy Holly, Eddie Cochran was one of the first rock 'n' roll guitarists to write and play his own material. Although he was born in Minnesota, he was brought up in California, which he always regarded as his home. Eddie was a natural musician and he could play the guitar before he was twelve years old. By the age of sixteen he was playing professionally.

He teamed up with another singer, Hank Cochran, and went on the road. Although the two were not related, they toured as The Cochran Brothers. In 1955, they saw Elvis Presley perform and it had a profound influence on Eddie. This was the kind of music that he wanted to play and he changed his style from hillbilly to harder rock.

Hank Cochran preferred the more traditional country sound and the Cochran Brothers split. Hank returned to Nashville, where he became a successful songwriter – one of his well-known compositions was Patsy Cline's

1961 hit, 'I Fall To Pieces'. Eddie began a collaboration with a young aspiring songwriter and drummer, Jerry Capeheart. Between the two of them, they were to produce some of Eddie's finest work.

Still only eighteen, Eddie was cast in the 1956 rock 'n' roll film, *The Girl Can't Help It*. Also in the cast was Gene Vincent, who became a good friend of Eddie's. Eddie's performance of the number 'Twenty Flight Rock' was electrifying. As well as making him a teenage idol, it brought him a recording contract with Liberty Records. Another film followed, but music was Eddie's first love. He cut a single, 'Sittin' On the Balcony' (1957), and to publicise it joined the Biggest Show of Stars for '57, along with Buddy Holly (who also became a close friend), Chuck Berry and The Everly Brothers.

The following year, Eddie had his first Gold Record with 'Summertime Blues'. Co-written with Jerry Capeheart, this song reflected all the hopes and yearnings of teenage life and was a resounding success on both sides of the Atlantic.

Scheduled to join the 1959 Winter Dance Party tour with his friend Buddy Holly, Eddie was prevented from doing so by the film *Go, Johnny, Go*'. When Buddy's plane crashed, killing him, The Big Bopper and Ritchie Valens, Eddie was devastated. He and Ritchie Valens had been filming together only days before. Afterwards, Eddie avoided flying whenever he could. He recorded John D. Loudermilk's song 'Three Stars' as a tribute to his friends, but ironically it was not released until after his own death.

Eddie's personal life, unusually for the music business, was harmonious. His girlfriend, Sharon Sheeley, was also a songwriter and understood the vagaries of the business. They had been introduced by Phil Everly (Sharon had been his girlfriend), and following Eddie's next single, 'C'mon Everybody', the couple worked together to produce 'Somethin' Else' (1959).

'C'mon Everybody' proved much more popular in Britain than in the United States, and Eddie decided to consolidate his popularity there. To the rapture of his ecstatic fans, Eddie undertook a tour of Great Britain with his friend Gene Vincent.

Eddie was the darling of the British teenagers. They loved his music and his all-American good looks, turning out in number for his live television and radio appearances. The tour was such a resounding success that it was decided to extend it for a further ten weeks. First, though, Eddie had recording commitments in the United States. With Sharon Sheeley, now his fiancée, and Gene Vincent, he decided to fly back to the States for the Easter break.

En route to London Airport their car blew a tyre and crashed into a lamp post. All three were rushed to hospital. Gene Vincent was treated for broken ribs and collar-bone and further injury to his bad leg. Sharon Sheeley suffered a broken pelvis. Eddie Cochran had been thrown through the windscreen and had brain injuries. He never recovered, dying the next day in hospital at the age of twenty-one. He was buried quietly at Forest Lawn Cemetery in California.

Eddie's record 'Three Steps To Heaven', which was in the charts at the time, rocketed straight up to Number One in the UK charts. He had had three major hits before he died.

Over the years, Eddie's records have remained popular. Previously undiscovered material has been released and various artists have covered his biggest hits. In 1987, he was elected to the Rock 'n' Roll Hall of Fame. In

1988, 'C'mon Everybody' was used on the soundtrack for an ad for Levi's 501 Jeans, to commemorate the fact that Sharon Sheeley had been wearing jeans on her introduction to Eddie.

Marvin Gaye

Real Name:	Marvin Pentz Gay
Born:	2 April, 1939, Washington DC, USA
Died:	1 April, 1984
Age:	44

Marvin Gaye was a great artist and performer. He sang rhythm and blues, pop and soul, but his great ambition was to be a crooner, a black Frank Sinatra. The young Marvin Gaye was wonderfully handsome. In his later years, his looks ravaged by his cocaine habit, he grew a beard and took to wearing a woolly cap to disguise his balding head.

His relationship with his father, who was a Pentecostal minister, was always complex and troubled. The Pentecostal religion was very strict, a real fire-and-brimstone religion. Marvin Gay Snr travelled, preaching the scriptures, and young Marvin accompanied him, often singing at the services.

Despite his religion, Mr Gay was a violent man. His wife and children were afraid of him and he beat Marvin often. Life in the poor section of Washington was hard, but Marvin still sought to please his father. Not a brilliant scholar, he nevertheless worked hard at school and sang at church meetings. He participated in sports, particularly enjoying boxing, which he felt made him attractive to girls. But music was his main interest, and he could play the piano, drums and guitar by the time he was in high school. He didn't like to sing in public except at church because, in the tough area where he lived, it was considered effeminate.

When Marvin dropped out of high school in the hope of pursuing a musical career, Mr Gay insisted that his son either got a job or joined the Armed Forces. Marvin, feeling that a uniform would attract girls, chose the latter course.

The United States Air Force, however, was not at all to his liking. Instead of flying, he peeled potatoes! Always a non-conformist, Marvin rebelled against the stifling military life. Eventually, the Air Force realised that he was not officer material, and he was granted an honourable discharge after only one year's service.

Back on civvy street, Marvin joined a doo-wop group, The Marquees. But he wanted to be a solo artist and, frustrated by his lack of personal success with the group, he left to join Harvey Fuqua and The Moonglows. Marvin's father had by this time retired from the church and gone into seclusion, and Harvey Fuqua replaced him in Marvin's life as a father figure.

In 1960, The Moonglows disbanded and Marvin went with his mentor, Harvey Fuqua, to Detroit, where Berry Gordy was fast establishing himself as a recording tycoon with his Motown company, so named for Detroit's nick-name, Motor City.

Initially, Marvin worked as a session musician but, in 1961, Gordy, building up his label, signed him as a singer. It was at this point that Marvin added the final 'e' to his name, to escape the modern connotation of the word 'gay'. His first single 'Let Your Conscience Be Your Guide' and the follow-up album, 'The Soulful Moods of Marvin Gaye' did not make the charts, and Gordy put Marvin to work writing for other artists.

Marvin, with his sweet soul voice and innocent good looks, was very attractive to women and he had a reputation as a womaniser. It caused some surprise, therefore, when he married Gordy's sister, Anna. Anna was a beautiful woman, seventeen years older than Marvin and experienced in the music business. She encouraged him to persist in his desire for a career as a solo artist and, in 1962, her encouragement paid off.

The single 'Stubborn Kind Of Fellow', with backing vocals by Martha and The Vandellas, went into the charts and Gordy, to capitalise on it, sent Marvin on the road with the Motown Revue tours. The tours were a nightmare for Marvin. When they visited the southern states, they encountered extreme prejudice, and were often not able to find a restaurant which would serve blacks. The hours were long and arduous, and Marvin, who had refused to attend Motown's Artist Development department (a charm school programme), felt upstaged by the slick performances of the other acts. But black music was being put on the map, and The Marvelettes, The Supremes, The Temptations, Stevie Wonder and Marvin himself had all become household names.

In 1962, Marvin recorded 'Hitch Hike', a dance number which was popular with teenagers, following up with a tribute to his wife, 'Pride and Joy'. Now Gordy decided the time was right to endow Marvin with a new pop image. He teamed him with a young unknown singer, Mary Wells, for the duet 'Together'. By the time the song was released, Mary Wells had become a big name with 'My Guy', and teenagers, believing that she was romantically involved with Marvin, rushed to buy the record.

But Marvin was still not satisfied. He wanted to write and produce his own work, and he felt that Gordy was manipulating him and stifling his artistic independence. It was not until 1965 that Marvin finally made his big breakthrough with the single 'How Sweet It Is (To Be Loved By You)'. This took him into the top bracket of Motown's singers and allowed him more freedom to choose his own material.

Now more financially secure, Marvin and Anna adopted a son, Marvin. However, Marvin's career was very demanding and he didn't have much time to spend as either a husband or a father. He had a large fan following and he needed to tour and make personal appearances to keep it going. The personal appearances took their toll. Marvin had always been a shy person, and the courage he needed to appear nightly often came from cocaine.

Another album, released in 1965, 'A Tribute to the Great Nat "King" Cole', displayed the beauty and clarity of Marvin's voice. The seal of success was set on his career when he appeared on nationwide television on the *Ed Sullivan Show*.

Tammi Terrell entered Marvin's life in 1967. She was a young, lovely and very talented singer who had recently signed with Motown. Gordy decided to team her up with Marvin. Their duet 'Ain't No Mountain High Enough' marked the beginning of a very successful partnership. Tammi brought out the best in Marvin's voice and personality, and on stage the two emanated a special chemistry, although their relationship was always purely professional.

But Marvin's marriage was in difficulty: there was the age factor, and Marvin was constantly inundated with females clamouring for his attention. To make matters worse, Anna was unfaithful.

Marvin continued to record as a solo artist. In 1969, he became a megastar with his version of the Gladys Knight and The Pips hit 'I Heard It Through The Grapevine'. This single was the biggest-selling record in the history of Motown. The Tammi Terrell/Marvin Gaye partnership also went from strength to strength. Blended together, their voices gave a rich and powerful sound and their duet 'Your Precious Love' (1967) was their most successful. Tragically, at a concert in Virginia, Tammi collapsed in Marvin's arms. She had been complaining of headaches for some time and, following her collapse, a brain tumour was diagnosed. Struggling with ill health, Tammi tried to carry on recording with Marvin. She fought a courageous fight but even surgery could not save her. Sadly, in 1970, at the age of twenty-four, she died. Marvin, was devastated by her death, joined 3,000 other mourners at the graveside of the beautiful young singer.

Marvin's life fell apart. He sank into depression, and couldn't work. His marriage was over, although neither he nor Anna wanted to end it. His solo career disintegrated and he retreated temporarily from the world. During this period of self-imposed exile, Marvin abandoned his debonair look, grew a beard and returned to his great love, sport. Motown, who had little unreleased material in stock and wanted to keep Marvin's name in the public eye, announced, quite untruthfully, that he was working.

It was a more serious and meaningful Marvin who returned to the music world. Concern about the atrocities of the Vietnam War, poverty and pollution were apparent in his work. His voice had mellowed and his style was soulful and moody. His first self-produced album,

'What's Going On' (1971), was a mammoth success in the United States, although the issues it raised were too limiting to give it the same appeal to the British public. However, fellow musicians and critics declared it a classic.

Marvin felt that it was time for a change of direction in his career, and acting seemed a logical progression. Gordy thought that Marvin would be a natural to portray Sam Cooke in a film. But Marvin was superstitious about playing a soul singer who had been shot dead. Other projects fell through and Marvin decided to write a film soundtrack.

He moved his family to Los Angeles and began work on the music for 'Trouble Man'. Unfortunately, when the film was released it didn't enjoy the success Marvin had hoped for. Once again, he agreed to cut an album for Motown. Although still married to Anna Gordy, Marvin had fallen in love with a young girl seventeen years his junior, Janis Hunter. 'Let's Get It On' written and sung by Marvin for his new love, was a steamy, lyrical tribute.

Hurt by this, Anna Gordy instituted divorce proceedings which forced Marvin into financial crisis. To escape from this pressure he undertook a European tour, which was a tremendous success. But on his return to the United States he was hounded on all sides. Anna sued him for back child support, his musicians took him to court for unpaid wages and the taxman was after him.

He had married Janis Hunter following his divorce, but theirs was a very volatile relationship. Finally, mentally and emotionally exhausted, Marvin was admitted to hospital for a rest. His second marriage seemed to be over: Janis had taken their children and moved in with another singer. When the tax authorities got into the act and demanded over two million dollars in back taxes, it was too much for Marvin. He retired to life in Hawaii. His drug addiction was common knowledge by now, and his friends were very concerned for his health.

Emaciated and depressed, Marvin attempted to kick his cocaine habit and improve his health. From a financial viewpoint he needed to be well enough to honour a prior commitment to another European tour. He was well received in Britain and on the Continent but, unable to break his drug addiction, it was apparent that he was often completely stoned on stage.

Returning to take up residence in the United States, Marvin was obviously a very ill man. After receiving death threats, he had also become paranoid about his own safety and always carried a gun. Despite the fact that his relationship with his father was as problematical as ever, he returned to the family home in Los Angeles to be cared for by his mother. An attempt to cleanse himself of drugs was doomed and he was soon snorting as much cocaine as ever.

On 1 April, 1984, Marvin and his father became involved in a violent argument. Mr Gay shot Marvin twice, once in the heart and once in the shoulder, then left the house, taking the gun with him. When the paramedics arrived on the scene, they refused to enter until the gun had been found fearing for their own safety, and Marvin was left to bleed to death.

Mr Gay was charged with murder but pleaded self-defence and the charge was reduced to manslaughter. He was given a six-year suspended sentence and five-years' probation. Mrs Gay posted his bail and then sued him for divorce, citing 1 April as the first day of separation.

Ten thousand people attended Marvin's funeral service

at Forest Lawn Cemetery, resting place of the stars. Tributes were received from his many friends, Berry Gordy, Harvey Fuqua, Smokey Robinson, Stevie Wonder and Diana Ross among them. Marvin's body was cremated and his ashes scattered into the sea.

He left no will, only very tangled financial affairs. He owed alimony and child support arrears to both wives as well as a substantial sum in taxes. But he also left his music, and his fans are enjoying it to this day.

In 1985, Lionel Ritchie wrote a tribute to Marvin Gaye entitled 'Missing You', which became a hit for Diana Ross. His memory has been honoured with a star on Hollywood's famous Walk of Fame.

Rick Nelson

Full Name:	Eric Hilliard Nelson
Born:	8 May, 1940, Teaneck, New Jersey, USA
Died:	31 December, 1985
Age:	45

Ricky Nelson was born into a theatrical family. His father, Ozzie Nelson, had been a big band leader in the 1930s and his mother, Harriet, had been the band's lead singer. In the 1940s they became well-known when they starred in a radio comedy, *The Adventures of Ozzie and Harriet*. After eight years the programme was transferred to television, where it enjoyed a fourteen-year run. Both Ricky and his elder brother, David, appeared on these shows, playing themselves.

When Elvis Presley burst on to the music scene in the 1950s Ricky, like every other teenage boy, decided that he wanted to be a pop singer. He had an opportunity, however, that many others did not. His father arranged for him to sing the Fats Domino hit 'I'm Walking' on their television show, and his career was launched. As he was a very good-looking boy, it didn't matter to his teenage fans that he didn't sing it very well, and it didn't matter to the show's producers, either, because Ricky greatly improved their viewing audience.

Using his father's influence, Ricky got an inside at Verve Records and cut a single, 'I'm Walking', with 'A Teenager's Romance' on the 'B' side. Both were smash hits, as were the two other recordings he made for Verve, 'You're My One And Only Love' and 'Honey Bop'. But Verve did not have the foresight to sign Ricky to a contract, and when a dispute arose over royalties, he moved to Imperial Records.

To ensure maximum publicity for Ricky's records a regular music spot was incorporated into the television programme. Between 1958 and 1960, while Elvis Presley was safely tucked away in the Army, Ricky was the teenagers' heart-throb, turning out one Gold Record after another.

At the age of seventeen, he followed in his father's footsteps and formed his own band. With strong instrumental backing from James Burton, a guitarist who later played with Elvis Presley, James Kirkland (bass), Gene Garf (piano) and Richie Frost on drums, and supported by excellent material, Ricky established himself as a prolific hit-maker.

His fans adored his boyish good looks and, up to 1963, he made a string of teen-orientated records. Johnny and Dorsey Burnette, recently arrived in California, wrote 'Waiting In School' (1958) for him. Sharon Sheeley, later to become Eddie Cochran's fiancée, wrote 'Poor Little Fool' (1958) and Gene Pitney penned 'Hello Mary Lou' (1961).

In 1959, Ricky broadened his horizons, appearing in the film *Rio Bravo* with John Wayne and Dean Martin. The critics praised his acting ability but Ricky couldn't shake off his teen pop star image. He didn't make another film for eighteen months, when he appeared with Jack Lemmon in *The Wackiest Ship in the Navy*.

During this period Ricky was still having success with his recording career, but he had added country style ballads to his rock song repertoire.

On his twenty-first birthday, in 1961, Ricky announced his intention to drop the 'y' from his Christian name and to sing more adult music. But his fans were not interested in this departure. A change of record label, from Imperial to Decca, in 1963, did not help. Even his marriage in 1963 to Kristin Harmon, who joined him as his wife on the *The Adventures of Ozzie and Harriet*, did not bring him a more mature following. Rick seemed doomed to remain an adolescent forever.

In 1966, the bubble burst, *The Adventures of Ozzie and Harriet* came to an end after fourteen years on television. Beatlemania had created a whole new musical era and Rick moved into country music. Forming The Stone Canyon Band in 1970, he became one of the first exponents of country rock music.

But his fans refused to allow him to grow up. At a rock revival concert in 1971, at Madison Square Gardens, New York, Rick was booed when he tried to introduce some new material to his act. Hurt and frustrated, he wrote and produced the album 'Garden Party' (1972), confounding his critics when it became a million-seller, his first since 1961. Sadly, it was his last major success.

In 1977, his singing career was in the doldrums. His personal life was in ruins, too. His wife had divorced him and taken the four children. Rick returned to acting. He appeared in several television series and films but his heart wasn't in it and he took his singing back on the road. A nostalgia rock tour of Britain, in 1985, was a great success and revived some interest in Rick's work.

Hoping to achieve the same result in the United States, he undertook a tour of the south.

On Monday 30 December, following a performance in Guntersville, Alabama (where Rick's last number was Buddy Holly's 'Rave On'), Rick, his fiancée, Helen Blair, and five members of The Stone Canyon Band boarded a charter plane to fly to their next venue in Dallas. The plane, once owned by Jerry Lee Lewis, was not in very good condition. After take-off, the pilot radioed that smoke was seeping into the cockpit. He attempted an emergency landing on a highway and all seemed well when the plane landed intact. But it burst into flames on the ground, killing all seven passengers.

Rumours abounded that the fire had been caused by Rick and his party freebasing cocaine. It was also reported that a medical examination had discovered traces of marijuana, cocaine and painkilling drugs in his body.

A memorial service was held at the Forest Lawn Memorial Park in California, and a show featuring Rick, Fats Domino, Johnny Cash, Jerry Lee Lewis and Roy Orbison, which had been recorded before his death, was aired on American television as a tribute to Rick. Rick Nelson became frozen in time, the 'teenage idol' depicted in his 1962 hit of that name. His twin sons, Matthew and Gunnar, have carried on the family name and musical tradition with their duo, Nelson.

John Lennon

Full Name:	John Winston Lennon
Born:	9 October, 1940, Liverpool, England
Died:	8 December, 1980
Age:	40

John Lennon's childhood was very unsettled. His father, Fred, was a merchant seaman and often away, and his mother, Julia, was left to rear her son alone much of the time. When Julia fell in love with someone else and moved in with him, she sent John to live with her sister, Mimi.

The feelings of insecurity that John carried with him all his life sprung from this early background. All around him he saw children raised in a family unit but neither of his parents seemed to want him. When Julia and Fred divorced, John's father disappeared from his life for many years.

His Aunt Mimi loved John, however, and took good care of him. They formed a bond that remained strong throughout their lives. Even as an adult, and no matter where he was in the world, John still telephoned Mimi every day.

Mimi and her husband, George Smith, lived in Liverpool,

where John attended Dovedale Infant and Primary School. From his earliest days he showed signs of rebellion: he was ill-mannered, stole and got into fights. Despite this he was good at English and Art. Drawing caricatures of the teachers and other pupils was one of his talents, and while they were usually funny they sometimes revealed a cruel streak in John's character.

When he moved on to Quarry Bank High School his behaviour did not improve. He was rude to the teachers, played truant and misbehaved in class. His aunt, a bit of a disciplinarian, could do nothing to discourage this rebelliousness. However, John was very popular with his fellow students. He had a good sense of humour and enjoyed joking and playing tricks.

When his Uncle George, of whom he was very fond, died, John's behaviour at school worsened. He failed all his 'O' Levels but, because of his artistic talent, he was accepted into Liverpool Art College in 1957.

Like many other teenagers of his generation, John had discovered rock 'n' roll. In 1956, Elvis Presley was a big star. The wild sound that he produced, based on the blues music of black America fused with the white sound of country and western, was sweeping Britain. Little Richard, Buddy Holly, Bill Haley and The Comets and Jerry Lee Lewis were also strong influences on John. But Elvis, with his hit song 'Heartbreak Hotel', was his hero.

James Dean, the young star of *Rebel Without a Cause*, had presaged the teenage rebellion that Elvis and others had followed enthusiastically. John Lennon loved it all, the Teddy Boy style of dressing, the music and, most of all, the rebellion against authority. He grew his hair and adopted the long jackets and tight jeans of his heroes.

Another influential figure in John's life was the jazz

musician Lonnie Donegan. Donegan and his group had shown that it was possible to make music on a shoestring. They used cheap acoustic guitars, banjos, improvised bass and played washboards with metal thimbles. The music was called skiffle and was very popular with the youth of the day. John wanted to join a skiffle group and tried to persuade his aunt to buy him a guitar. But Mimi was against it: she didn't like the new music, she didn't like long hair and she wanted John to pay more attention to his schoolwork.

Meanwhile, John's mother had reappeared in his life. She and John were very similar in many ways. They shared a love of music and both had a quirky sense of humour. Julia did not want to upset her sister by buying John a guitar, but when he ordered one, she paid for it. Mimi was not at all pleased, warning John that he would never be able to make a living playing the guitar. Later in life this advice caused them both much amusement.

With some friends from primary school, John formed his skiffle own group, The Quarrymen. John was the leader and the group played wherever they could, mostly at youth clubs and school dances. Although John still lived with Mimi, he became a regular visitor to Julia's house, where he practised his guitar and played the banjo.

In 1957, John met another teenager interested in rock 'n' roll. Paul McCartney was much more serious about his music. He came from a very musical family and had been actively encouraged to learn the guitar. Although the McCartney family were not well off, money had been found to buy Paul his first guitar. Paul, a natural musician, quickly picked up the music of Elvis, Buddy Holly and Little Richard.

John and Paul became friends and Paul joined The

Quarrymen. Paul's school was next door to John's art college and they were able to meet often. Paul, with his superior musical ability, helped John with his guitar-playing, teaching him the chords. Soon they were writing songs together.

In 1958, to John's sorrow, Julia was knocked down by a car and killed. She and John had become close and he was very upset. He suppressed his feelings, but Paul, whose own mother had died in 1955, understood the depth of his grief and helped him cope with it, strengthening their friendship.

George Harrison was a friend of Paul's. He had attended the same primary school as John, but he was younger and the two had not been friends. George, who worked as a butcher's boy, loved rock 'n' roll and wanted to join the group. John, who had developed a cynical streak following Julia's death, was often quite cruel to George, but eventually he relented and allowed him to become a regular member of The Quarrymen.

When the Quarrymen won the heat of a talent contest for rock 'n' roll groups, John thought they were on their way to success. He changed the group's name to Johnny and The Moondogs and was very disappointed when they did not win the final.

Allan Williams, the owner of a coffee bar in Liverpool, arranged for them to audition for the famous agent Larry Parnes, who offered them a tour as a backing group. Once again they decided to change their name. Looking to their favourite rock 'n' roll group, Buddy Holly and The Crickets, for inspiration, they chose the name of another insect, the beetle. John, with his mastery of words, altered the spelling to embrace the idea of 'beat' music, and they became The Silver Beatles.

Neither John's Aunt Mimi or Paul's father were very

Elvis Presley

(Glenn A. Baker Archives/Redferns)

Alma Cogan
(David Redfern)

Gene Vincent
(Richie Howells/Redferns)

Charlie Parker
(William Gottlieb/Redferns)

Mario Lanza
(Glenn A. BakerArchives/ Redferns)

ight: Eddie Cochran
(Glenn A. Baker Archives/Redferns)

below: King Curtis
(Glenn A. Baker Archives/Redferns)

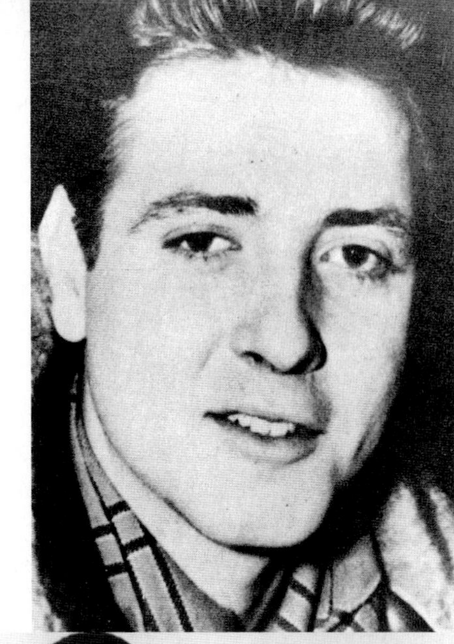

Mama Cass *(David Redfern)*

above: Andy Gibb (original member of The Bee Gees) *(Michael Putland/ Retna Pictures)*

right: Sandy Denny (Fairport Convention) *(Michael Putland/Retna Pictures)*

above: The Supremes *(left to right:* Florence Ballard, Mary Wilson and Diana Ross) *(S & G/Redferns)*

below: Karen Carpenter *(David Redfern)*

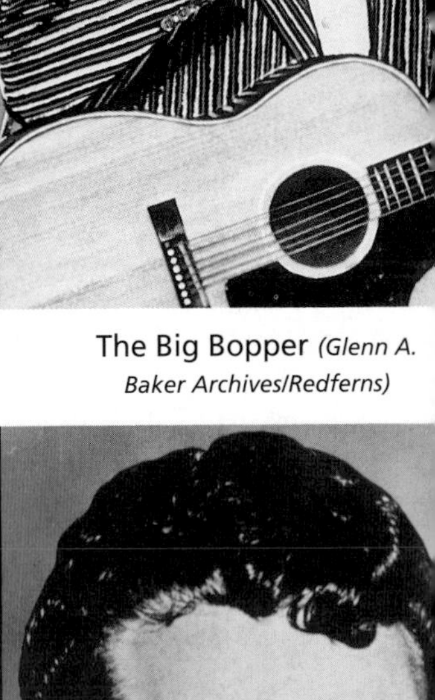

Patsy Cline *(Glenn A. Baker Archives/Redferns)*

The Big Bopper *(Glenn A. Baker Archives/Redferns)*

Billie Holiday *(William Gottlieb/Redferns)*

Buddy Holly *(S & G/Redferns)*

Stevie Ray Vaughan
(David Redfern)

Jim Croce *(Glenn A. Baker Archives/Redferns)*

John Bonham (Led Zeppelin) *(Richie Aaron/Redferns)*

Phil Lynott (Thin Lizzy) *(Fin Costello/Redferns)*

pleased at this turn of events, but they were eventually persuaded to give their permission for the boys to go off on tour to Scotland. The Scottish tour was not a great success and the boys returned to Liverpool and the coffee bars. The group still did not have a permanent drummer, but when they were offered a club booking in Hamburg, Germany, they asked Pete Best to join them. The next hurdle was to persuade Aunt Mimi and Paul's father to agree. John was persistent – he felt this was going to be their big break – and eventually permission was granted.

Hamburg was not at all what they expected. They had very basic living accommodation and were expected to work for very little money. Often they could only afford to eat cornflakes. As a result of the long hours and the lack of food, they had their first encounter with drugs, taking pep pills to keep themselves going.

However, the long hours of playing were good experience for the group and they developed a reputation as good, professional musicians. They put a lot of energy into their performances and attracted a large following. Hoping for better working conditions, they moved to another club in Hamburg, the Top Ten. It was a big blow when they were reported to the police because George Harrison was under age for work in Germany and the others did not hold work permits, and they had to go home.

Back in Liverpool John became very depressed, but he was not down for long. He dropped the 'Silver' from their name and managed to get them a booking at the Casbah.

In 1961 they had their first booking at the Cavern, a jazz club in a Liverpool cellar. Word had spread that they were worth listening to and young people began to come from near and far to hear this hot new group, The Beatles.

In April they were invited back to the Top Ten in Hamburg. This time George was old enough, and the others made sure that they had all the necessary permits. Their pay and living conditions had improved, too. In Hamburg, they cut their first record as a backing group for the singer Tony Sheridan. The number was 'My Bonnie Lies Over The Ocean', and it was an important step in their career.

That summer The Beatles returned to the Cavern, more popular than ever and with their record in demand. Here they were approached by Brian Epstein, a wealthy young man who, unhappy in his career and looking for a new challenge, wanted to take over the management of the group. He overcame their misgivings about his lack of managerial experience with his enthusiasm and they agreed to sign with him.

The first thing Epstein did was to smarten up their image. He insisted that they wear suits and ties on stage and told John to stop play-acting and to show more respect for the audiences. After many rejections Epstein arranged an audition with Decca Records in London. But the lads failed the audition and returned to Hamburg for a stint at the new Star club.

Meanwhile, Epstein secured an offer from EMI for them to record a single. However, George Martin at EMI did not think that Pete Best was a drummer of sufficiently high calibre and Epstein asked him to leave the group. He was replaced by Richard Starkey, who was to become better known as Ringo Starr a drummer from a group called Rory Storm and The Hurricanes. The Beatles line-up was now complete.

In August, 1962, John married Cynthia Powell, an

art student he had been dating since art college. Paul McCartney was the best man, and following the ceremony, he and John went off to perform at a concert. John's son Julian was born the following year, but by then John had little time to be either a father or a husband. Furthermore, Epstein felt that it was in the best interests of the group for John's marriage to remain a secret. He didn't think that the teenage fans wanted to see their idols married, and therefore unavailable.

In September, 1962, The Beatles cut their first record, 'Love Me Do', with John playing the harmonica, at the Abbey Road Recording Studios. The single sold slowly at first, but by December it had reached the Top Twenty. Rumour had it that Epstein had helped it along a little by purchasing 10,000 copies for his shop.

Their next recording was another of John and Paul's compositions, 'Please Please Me'. This single was destined to be a big hit. The Beatles made their national television debut on the show *Thank Your Lucky Stars*, and instantly, they *were* stars. Adults and teenagers alike loved their music and the energy and enthusiasm that they put into it. They were perceived to be ordinary boys from ordinary homes, young men with a cheeky attitude to whom audiences could relate. John, always irreverent, liked to crack jokes. On one occasion, at a Royal Command Performance, he called from the stage: 'Will the people in the cheaper seats clap your hands. All the rest of you, rattle your jewellery'.

The Beatles were in demand everywhere. There were concert tours, television appearances and their records sold like hot cakes. 'Please Please Me' went straight to the Number One position in the charts and so did their next releases, 'From Me To You' (April, 1963) and 'She Loves You' (September, 1963). Everywhere they went they were met by screaming crowds. Beatlemania had arrived.

In February, 1964, the lads began their conquest of America. They appeared on the *Ed Sullivan Show*, drawing an enormous viewing audience and cutting the crime rate drastically in US cities while they were on air. By April they had control of the US charts with the top five records.

Back in Britain, they rose to new challenges. Their first film, *A Hard Day's Night* received critical acclaim and two Academy Award nominations. The album from the film, the only album ever made which consisted exclusively of Lennon/McCartney songs, was also a great success. John demonstrated his literary talent – and his quirky sense of humour – with the publishing of his book, *John Lennon in his Own Write*, which was a bestseller. At a literary lunch in his honour, he made an erudite speech: 'Thank you very much. You've got a lucky face.'

Already household names in Britain and the United States, The Beatles expanded their horizons with a worldwide tour. Even the disclosure of John's marriage could not dent their popularity. As 1965 progressed, it seemed that The Beatles could do no wrong. Their film *Help* was released; John's second book, *A Spaniard in the Work* was published, and they all became MBE's. They later admitted to smoking marijuana in the toilet while waiting to receive their honour at Buckingham Palace.

John had come much further than he had ever expected. He was very wealthy and generously shared his good fortune with those he loved. He bought his Aunt Mimi a house and provided his errant father, with whom he was now reunited, with an income. He and Cynthia bought a large mansion with a swimming pool and garaging for the many expensive cars he collected.

But John was discovering that fame and fortune have their price. The Beatles were so famous that that they could not appear anywhere without being mobbed by screaming fans. There were riots at their concerts and, like Elvis Presley, they received death threats. At home, they were confined to their fine houses and grounds, and on tour, they were obliged to accept a police escort when they left the confines of their hotel rooms.

Worst of all, John felt he was no longer able to express himself freely. The Beatles had been the darlings of the media, but when John told a reporter that The Beatles were 'more popular than Jesus', and added that his disciples 'were thick and ordinary', it was a mistake. When they toured the United States, they found they had lost much of their popularity, particularly in the south. John, following Epstein's advice, apologised for his remarks, but the damage had already been done.

Another aspect of his career that John didn't like was the business side. Inevitably, an endless number of record company executives, lawyers and accountants were required to take care of The Beatles and their fortune. John couldn't tolerate them and contemptuously dubbed them 'men in suits'.

The tour of the United States in 1966 was their last tour, and John returned home to spend some time with his wife and son. He wasn't idle for long, however, and was soon involved in various different projects: a film, songwriting and recording.

Flower power was at its peak in 1967 with hippies preaching the power of love, peace and drugs. In the early part of the year The Beatles released 'Penny Lane' and 'Strawberry Fields Forever', but it was the unique album 'Sergeant Pepper's Lonely Hearts Club Band', featuring 'Lucy In The Sky With Diamonds' and 'With A Little Help From My Friends' that set them firmly in the middle of the drug controversy. Paul McCartney admitted that he had taken LSD, causing the BBC to ban a number from the album in case it encouraged drug-taking among The Beatles' fans. But as an album, 'Sergeant Pepper's Lonely Hearts Club Band' has stood the test of time and is considered one of the best in rock history.

John had by this time become somewhat eccentric. Already an habitual drug-taker – he used speed to improve his performance in the studio – he decided to sample LSD. He and Cynthia had been drifting apart for some time and their marriage was in trouble. Unhappy in himself, John, together with the other Beatles, sought help from the Indian *guru*, Maharishi Mahesh Yogi. But there was another blow awaiting him: Brian Epstein, who seemed to have lost the direction of his life when The Beatles stopped touring, died of an overdose of sleeping pills.

John had become involved with an avant-garde, politically-aware, Japanese-American artist, Yoko Ono, and was now living with her. Yoko was a major influence in John's life but she was not very popular with either John's fans or the other Beatles. The Beatles had always had an agreement that no wives or girlfriends should be present during recording sessions, but now John insisted that Yoko was there.

The Beatles were also having management difficulties. Following Epstein's death, they had established the Apple Publishing Company to release their records. It had been mismanaged, however, and they were losing money. Also, their original contract with EMI had been badly negotiated by Epstein, and they received only a tiny percentage of their earnings. There were other financial difficulties to be resolved so it was agreed that they would seek professional assistance. Paul proposed his father-in-law, a show business lawyer, but John, George and Ringo favoured Allen Klein, an American agent recommended to them by Mick Jagger, and a dispute began.

Although The Beatles continued to record together, cracks were beginning to appear in their relationship. John and Paul no longer collaborated much and were often heard to argue. Despite this 'The White Album' (1968) and 'Yellow Submarine' (1969) were released and sold well.

Cynthia had divorced John, leaving him free to marry Yoko Ono in 1969. John and Yoko became involved in some very bizarre projects. They campaigned for world peace by planting acorns and conducting a seven-day 'sleep-in' at an Amsterdam hotel. In 1968 they were arrested for possession of illegal drugs. It allegedly took forty policemen to take the two into custody, and, not surprisingly, the press were out in force to witness the event. The Beatles had become fair targets in the police war against drugs.

Following John's marriage to Yoko, The Beatles recorded 'The Ballad Of John And Yoko' before cutting 'Abbey Road', which was to be their final album. Appropriately enough, the last track was called 'The End'.

In 1970, Paul McCartney took the first legal steps towards disbanding the group. For John it was the end of an era, but his natural talent began to re-emerge, and in 1971, John Lennon and The Plastic Ono Band (formed in 1969) produced the hauntingly beautiful 'Imagine', John's most successful solo work.

The city of New York attracted him. He loved the freedom and anonymity of it and he and Yoko decided to settle there. Once again, John was involved in controversy. He had returned his MBE to the Queen as a protest against the Biafran War in Nigeria. Now he criticised the US government for their involvement in Vietnam, and the British government for sending troops to Ireland. He was very sincere in his beliefs, but they did little for his popularity. Richard Nixon did not take at all kindly to this criticism of his regime. When John applied for permission to remain in the United States on a permanent basis, Nixon tried to block it. And the US Immigration and Naturalisation Office served John with a deportation order because of his 1968 drug conviction.

In spite of all this, John continued his campaign for world peace, making controversial political statements through his songs at the same time as appealing for the right to hold a green card.

There were still financial and legal problems outstanding from the break-up of The Beatles. John, George and Ringo were in dispute with Allen Klein; he was suing them and they were counter-suing. John and Yoko had split up and John became very depressed. With his Chinese secretary, May Pang, for company, he spent a few bleak months in Los Angeles. Although he produced the lovely song 'Whatever Gets You Through The Night' during this period, otherwise John's creativity seemed to have deserted him.

But January, 1975 was a momentous month for John. He was reconciled with Yoko, and The Beatles' dispute was legally resolved. Finally, it looked as though he could get on with his life.

On 9 October, 1975, John's thirty-fifth birthday, Yoko

gave birth to John's second son, Sean. It was a miracle, for Yoko had been told that she could bear no more children. John was overwhelmed. He determined that this time around he would not miss the joy of fatherhood and announced his intention of retiring. Yoko, meanwhile, had discovered that she had a good head for business and decided to take over their affairs. John, always a firm supporter of equal rights for women, backed her decision and they swapped roles.

There followed a very fulfilling period of life for John. He had completely forsworn drugs and enjoyed being away from the synthetic world of the pop star. He undertook all the domestic tasks – baking, cleaning and every element of childcare – and entertained his Aunt Mimi over the phone with stories of his life as a househusband.

In 1976, he was finally granted permanent residency in the United States. Yoko's handling of their complex business affairs was also thriving, and in 1980, she bought up many of the apartments in the Dakota, the building in which they lived.

They were also enjoying the benefits of travel, and on holiday in Bermuda John began songwriting again. 'Double Fantasy', an album inspired by a flower he had seen in Bermuda, was released in October, 1980 and reached the top of the album charts on both sides of the Atlantic. Just when it seemed that John was back in the music business for good, tragedy struck.

On the night of 5 December, 1980, John stepped out of his car in front of the Dakota building. A 'fan', Mark Chapman, approached and spoke to him, then pulled a gun and shot him five times. John died shortly afterward in hospital.

There seemed no logic or reason behind John Lennon's

senseless death. Mark Chapman suffered from mental illness. He is believed to have shot his idol, John, because he thought John had betrayed his genius. Chapman is now serving a twenty-year prison sentence.

Crowds gathered outside the Dakota for days to mourn John's death, and messages flooded in from all over the world to comfort Yoko in her grief. In commemoration of John's passing, Yoko called for a ten-minute worldwide silence and nearly half a million people gathered in New York to participate. John's compositions 'Imagine', 'Happy Christmas (War Is Over)' and 'Give Peace A Chance' went straight into the charts. In 1982, 'The John Lennon Collection' was released and, in 1984, Yoko released 'Milk And Honey', an album of the songs John had been working on at the time of his death.

Awards and the inevitable compilation albums, films and biographies have followed. John Lennon was awarded a star on Hollywood's Walk of Fame in 1988, and in 1989, as one of The Beatles, he was inducted into the Rock 'n' Roll Hall of Fame.

Julian Lennon, John's son by Cynthia, is a singer/songwriter in his own right, his music often echoing that of his father. Sean, John's son by Yoko, joined his half-brother on the concert stage in 1989 and performed solo at a John Lennon tribute concert in 1990.

In New York's Central Park there is a small piece of ground dedicated to John's memory that will be 'Strawberry Fields Forever'.

Stuart Sutcliffe was another early member of The Beatles. He was a friend of John Lennon's from art college and joined the group to play bass. He accompanied them to Hamburg in 1960, but when the rest of The Beatles returned to Liverpool, he stayed there with his fiancée. In 1962, at the age of twenty-one, Stuart died of a brain haemorrhage, caused, it is believed, by an injury sustained in a fight.

Phil Ochs

Born: 19 December, 1940, El Paso, Texas, USA
Died: 9 April, 1976
Age: 35

Folk music has always been the music of the common man, but in the sixties it developed increasingly political overtones. Profound political and cultural changes were sweeping through the world and anyone who could play a guitar or a banjo jumped on to the bandwagon and spread the word. The trend had begun on college campuses, but by the time Phil Ochs reached New York, it had moved into the bohemian Greenwich Village coffee houses.

Phil came from an ordinary middle-class family in Texas. He attended a military academy before realising that his aspirations lay elsewhere. It was at Ohio State University, where he was studying journalism, that he began songwriting. His first attempt was a political commentary in support of Fidel Castro, 'Ballad Of The Cuban Invasion'.

By 1961, Phil had moved to New York where he joined Bob Dylan and Tom Paxton, among others, on the topical song magazine *Broadside*. He was soon a familiar name in the Greenwich Village clubs and a major contributor to the protest movement of the sixties. And there were certainly plenty of things to protest about: war, fall-out, civil rights and unemployment among them.

In 1964, Elektra Records signed Phil to a contract and the 'singing journalist', as he had become known, produced 'All The News That's Fit To Sing', an album full of protest songs. It also included an effective adaptation of Edgar Allan Poe's poem 'The Bells'. Phil's next album, 'I Ain't Marchin' Any more' (1965) was also packed with protest songs and included a strong attack on racial discrimination.

But 1966 saw Phil, like Bob Dylan, striving to reconcile his political beliefs to a more commercial market. 'Phil Ochs In Concert' had a more romanticised sound and was his most acclaimed album. Joan Baez, the sweet-voiced folk singer, herself a great supporter of nuclear disarmament and civil rights, scored a hit in Britain with a track from the album, 'There But For Fortune'. However, it didn't bring Phil great commercial success: he was still better known for his biting political satire.

'Pleasures Of The Harbor' (1967) was more rock-orientated, a sound that Phil sustained and built on for the remainder of his recording career. But he was disillusioned by America's involvement in the Vietnam War and his own inability to attract audiences outside the folk market. He became increasingly mentally unstable, at one point even changing his name to Che Guevara Wordsworth.

In 1976, at the age of thirty-five, finally overwhelmed by manic depression, Phil committed suicide at his sister's home in New York. A double compilation album of his work, 'Chords Of Fame', which was released posthumously, gives a fair representation of his work.

Billy Fury

Real Name:	Ronald Wycherly
Born:	17 April, 1941, Liverpool, England
Died:	28 January, 1983
Age:	41

Billy Fury was born, raised and educated in Liverpool, home of the Merseybeat. He was a contemporary of The Beatles, having attended school with Ringo Starr, so perhaps it is not surprising that he felt his future lay in the music world. He had begun writing songs, and accompanying himself on the guitar, at a very early age. A bout of rheumatic fever had left his health impaired, but he built up his strength working on the Mersey tugboats.

In 1958, when Marty Wilde was appearing in Liverpool, Billy decided to show him some of his compositions. While in the theatre he had the good fortune to encounter Marty's agent, Larry Parnes. Parnes, affectionately known to his artists as 'Mr Parnes, Shillings and Pence', was a powerful force on the British rock 'n' roll scene. As an agent he included many of the top pop stars of the day in his stable, each with a carefully-selected stage name: Tommy Steele (Thomas

Hicks), Marty Wilde (Reg Smith), Georgie Fame (Clive Powell); only Joe Brown had refused to bow to the inevitable and retained his original name.

Sensing the young man's potential, Parnes promptly changed his name to Billy Fury and began to build his career. Billy was a shy, sensitive young man with the brooding, attractive good looks of James Dean. He also had a good voice, could play the guitar and was a prolific songwriter, so it was not a difficult task for Parnes.

Billy's first record for Decca, 'Maybe Tomorrow' (1959), was well received. Dressed in a gold lamé suit, he had developed a very erotic stage act, grinding his hips in Elvis-like gyrations. He attracted a certain amount of criticism from the media – even *New Musical Express* once described his act as 'downright disgusting'. But exposure on Jack Good's television shows *Boy Meets Girl* and *Wham* secured Billy's success as a teen heart-throb.

Together, Billy and Good produced a rockabilly album, 'The Sound Of Fury'. Although it was later to be acclaimed a rock 'n' roll classic, Decca didn't feel this was the right direction for their young star. They thought that Billy was better suited to the strong ballads that were so popular in the US charts.

In 1961, Billy's career really took off when he successfully covered Marty Robbins' hit 'Don't Worry', the hauntingly beautiful 'A Thousand Stars' and Tony Orlando's 'Halfway To Paradise'. Over the next couple of years, he consolidated his success as a balladeer, but his fellow Liverpudlians, The Beatles, with their unique sound, were overtaking him in popularity. In 1965, he had his final major hit with 'In Thought Of You'.

Billy had been struggling for some years with his ill health. On occasion he had been forced to cancel bookings and abandon tours. Now he decided that it was an opportune moment to retire and pursue his other interests, breeding racehorses and animal conservation.

In the early seventies, Billy came out of retirement briefly to join the club circuit and appear in a film, *That'll Be The Day*, which starred David Essex and was based on Billy's own career. Billy appeared in a cameo role as an ageing rock 'n' roll singer, Stormy Tempest.

In 1981, he re-emerged once again from retirement and returned to the recording studio. A new contract with Polydor Records produced a string of minor hits, including 'Love Or Money' and 'Devil Or Angel'. But his ill health followed him and, in 1983, at the age of forty-one, he died of a heart attack. His song 'I'm Lost Without You' was reverently played at his funeral, and an album, 'The One And Only', completed shortly before his death, was released posthumously. Sadly, 'Forget Him' the single from the album, was Billy's last foray into the charts.

Ritchie Valens

Real Name:	Richard Steven Valenzuela
Born:	13 May, 1941, Los Angeles, California, USA
Died:	3 February, 1959
Age:	17

Ritchie Valens came from a poor Mexican-American family in Pacoima, California. His mother had been left to raise the family on her own and they struggled to make their living by fruit-picking and other temporary employment.

Brought up surrounded by the richness of Spanish music, Ritchie was music-obsessed from an early age. Determined to play the guitar, he overcame the handicap of being left-handed and learned to play with his right hand. His first love was *chicano*, (Mexican-Californian) music, but when he heard Little Richard, rock 'n' roll took pride of place and Ritchie dreamed of being a rock musician like his hero.

In high school he joined a group called The Silhouettes. Originally he was the guitarist, but as his popularity grew, he took over as the lead singer. In 1958, Bob Keene of Del-Fi Records heard the handsome young Chicano singing at a concert and promptly offered him a contract as a solo artist.

Ritchie shortened his surname to Valens and made his first recording, his own composition 'Come On, Let's Go'. This was successful enough to warrant sending him on his first rock 'n' roll tour, on which he not only gained useful experience, but also had the opportunity to meet other rising young rock 'n' roll stars such as Eddie Cochran, with whom he formed an immediate friendship.

Ritchie's next single, 'Donna', written for his high school sweetheart, Donna Ludwig, rocketed to the top of the charts. The 'B' side, Ritchie's arrangement of 'La Bamba', a Mexican wedding song, was an equal success, and his career seemed assured. He made a cameo appearance in Alan Freed's film *Go, Johnny, Go* and began recording some tracks for a new album.

In early 1959, Ritchie joined the Winter Dance Party, a group of rock 'n' roll musicians touring the mid-western United States. Other headliners on the bill were Buddy Holly, The Big Bopper (J.P. Richardson), Dion and The Belmonts and the saxophonist King Curtis.

Conditions on the tour were dreadful. The weather was bitterly cold, and there was no heating on the buses, which often broke down in the snow. Only the enthusiasm of their young fans kept the artists going. On the night of 3 February, the bus broke down yet again and Buddy Holly decided to charter a plane to Fargo, North Dakota, their next venue.

Ritchie had always had a premonition that he would die on an aeroplane and so he avoided flying whenever possible. However, on this fateful occasion, he persuaded guitarist Tommy Allsup to give him his seat. The plane crashed on take-off, killing all those on board and fulfilling Ritchie's prophesy.

It had been generally believed that Ritchie was twenty-one, and only after his death was it revealed that he was only seventeen. But although his career was short, Ritchie Valens contributed greatly to the American music culture, enriching it with Latin rhythm and pioneering the way for other Chicano musicians. And 'Donna' has become a classic of American pop.

'Ritchie Valens', a collection of the work he had recorded prior to his death and which included some of his instrumentals, was released posthumously in July, 1959, emphasizing the tragedy of his early demise.

In 1986, a film was made of Ritchie's life. Starring Lou Diamond Philips, it was entitled, appropriately enough, 'La Bamba'. The film's music was supervised by Hispanic-American group *Los Lobos* who reached Number One with the title track. In 1990, Ritchie Valens was honoured with a star on Hollywood's Walk of Fame.

Otis Redding

Born: 9 September, 1941, Dawson, Georgia, USA
Died: 10 December, 1967
Age: 26

In the southern bible belt of the United States, the church has provided many fine musicians, Hank Williams, Johnny Ace, Clyde McPhatter, Sam Cooke and Marvin Gaye, to name but a few. Otis Redding was also the son of a minister, and the church was where he found his voice. His early love of music was greatly influenced by the gospel, folk and blues music of the south that he heard all around him.

He began singing as a child, often imitating Little Richard, but as he grew older, Sam Cooke became a much greater influence on the development of Otis's own unique soul voice.

In 1959, Otis joined a rhythm and blues group, Johnny Jenkins and The Pinetoppers, serving as driver and part-time singer. At one of their recording sessions in the Stax Studios, Memphis, Otis persuaded Stax boss Jim Stewart to allow him to cut a ballad of his own, 'These Arms of Mine'. Recognising the record's commercial potential, Stewart released it and watched as it climbed into the R&B chart of 1963.

Otis followed this with a string of R&B hits, including 'That's What My Heart Needs', 'Pain In My Heart' and 'Chained And Bound'. Theoretically, he was signed to Atlantic Records, but he continued to have the backing of the excellent Stax house band, Booker T and The MGs. In 1965, he produced the deep soul ballad 'I've Been Loving You Too Long (To Stop Now)'. It was the moment Otis had been waiting for, his breakthrough into the pop charts. Otis consolidated this success with another of his own compositions, the up-tempo 'Respect'. Two years later, Aretha Franklin had an even greater success with this number, topping the charts and selling over a million copies.

European audiences, who were at that time enjoying the black soul music of Ray Charles and James Brown, gave Otis a rapturous welcome in 1966. His emotive interpretation of The Rolling Stones' '(I Can't Get No) Satisfaction' and The Beatles' 'Day Tripper', included in his programme with his own hits, were highly acclaimed. He returned to the United States on the crest of his popularity and determined to make more impact on American white audiences.

In 1967, the Monterey Pop Festival was a major event. Rock and pop musicians from all around the world gathered together, attracting massive audiences and producing some of the finest sounds the crowds had ever been privileged to hear. Otis, one of the few black performers present, reigned supreme as the king of soul. With all the suffering of black America in his voice, Otis beseeched his audience, 'We all love each other, right? Let me hear you say yeah', to which he received a rousing response. He, Janis Joplin and Jimi

Hendrix all erupted on to the international music scene and reached superstar status at this festival.

Now, having caught the attention of a young white audience, and having been acclaimed as the champion of soul music, Otis determined to make the crossover into rock music. He embarked on a tour of the United States, flying from venue to venue in a private jet.

On a cold December night, ignoring warnings of bad weather conditions, Otis and his backing group, The Bar-Kays, took off to fly to a gig in Madison, Wisconsin. Just outside Madison, the plane crashed into a frozen lake, leaving only one survivor, Ben Cauley, at twenty the oldest member of The Bar-Kays.

Otis finally achieved the success he had been seeking, but not until after his death. His own composition '(Sittin' On) The Dock Of The Bay', recorded two weeks before his death, became his biggest hit, reaching the Number One position in the charts and selling over a million copies. In all, he had nine posthumous chart hits, and his album 'Otis Blue' (1965) is regarded as one of the greatest soul albums of all time.

He also left behind a musical legacy. In 1980 his sons, Dexter and Otis Redding III, and a cousin, Mark Locket, formed a soul group called The Reddings to carry on his name and his music.

In 1989, Otis Redding was inducted into the Rock 'n' Roll Hall of Fame by none other than Little Richard, the legendary star Otis had began his career by imitating.

Tim Hardin

Born: 23 December, 1941, Eugene, Oregon, USA
Died: 29 December, 1980
Age: 41

The son of classical musicians, Tim Hardin had an early introduction to music. His more famous relative, however, was the gunslinger and outlaw John Wesley Hardin, who killed forty men before dying himself at the age of forty-two.

Tim, following his discharge from the United States Marines, settled in Boston, where he became well known in the folk clubs. Part of the Bob Dylan/Tom Paxton/Phil Ochs school of folk singer-songwriters, he naturally gravitated to New York's Greenwich Village.

In 1966, he signed a contract with Verve Records and produced the albums 'Tim Hardin' and 'Tim Hardin II'. But he was more successful with his songwriting than with his recording career, and these two albums remain the best of Tim's work. Rod Stewart had a hit with his 'Reason To Believe' and Bobby Darin with 'If I Were A Carpenter'. Ironically, Tim's only chart hit was a Bobby Darin composition, 'Sing A Simple Song Of

Freedom' (1969). Sadly, this virtually signalled the end of his career.

In 1970, with an expensive drug habit and harassing business problems, Tim moved to Britain. But his creative muse seemed to be deserting him. 'Bird On A Wire' (1971) was a collection of unoriginal pieces, and 'Painted Head' (1973) was unimpressive. Tim couldn't kick his drug addiction and it was proving very expensive.

Returning to America in 1980, he began work on a new album but died of a drug overdose before it could be completed.

Brian Jones

Real Name:	Lewis Brian Hopkin-Jones
Born:	26, February, 1942, Cheltenham, Gloucestershire, England
Died:	3, July, 1969
Age:	27

Although Brian Jones, wishing to appear the same as the other Rolling Stones, claimed a working-class background, in reality he came from a comfortable middle-class family in Cheltenham. His father, who was Welsh, was an aeronautical engineer and very involved with the local church. His mother was a piano teacher, and Brian and his sister Barbara, were taught to play at an early age.

Brian instinctively realised that music would be an important aspect of his life and, at the age of twelve, he added the clarinet to his list of musical accomplishments. At sixteen, he took up the guitar.

From early childhood Brian suffered from asthma attacks, which hampered his participation in school sports. Academically, however, he did well, shining particularly in English. His father quite naturally hoped that Brian would follow in his footsteps and attend university. With this thought in mind he steered him towards scientific studies for his 'A' Levels. But Brian was already heavily into music. Like many teenagers in the fifties, he had joined a skiffle group and thumped away on a washboard, but his great love was American jazz and blues music. An incredibly gifted natural musician, he taught himself to play the saxophone when he discovered the hauntingly expressive alto saxophone tones of Charlie 'Bird' Parker.

Brian had also become increasingly rebellious. He felt that his future lay with his music and not with the stuffy, conventional way of life advocated by his father. He refused to go to university and for the next few years he just drifted, taking any jobs that would allow him to spread his time between music and girls. He was a very handsome boy and had always been popular with girls – he was said to have fathered his first illegitimate child at the age of fifteen. A trip to Scandinavia further liberated him sexually, and he gained a reputation all over Cheltenham as a womaniser.

In 1960, Brian began to spend much of his time with a local girl, Pat Andrews. He was still drifting from job to job but it was music that dominated his life. He had discovered American Blues music and loved to frequent the local jazz clubs.

Throughout 1960 and 1961 he continued to live in Cheltenham, working when necessary and generously sharing his charms among the local girls. Pat, by now the mother of his son, was still on the scene but Brian didn't want to be tied down.

In 1962, on a visit to London, Brian played the guitar publicly for the first time with Alexis Korner's Blues Incorporated at the Ealing Blues Club. This experience made such an impression on Brian that he decided to move to London, leaving Cheltenham and Pat behind him. Pat followed him with the baby and moved into his flat, but their living conditions were so dreadful that she returned to Cheltenham within the year.

In London, Brian became a frequent visitor to the Ealing Blues Club, where he enjoyed the company of other young musicians.

Deciding to form his own R&B group, Brian recruited a piano player, Ian Stewart, and a guitarist, Geoff Bradford, and Mick Jagger joined them as a singer. With Mick Jagger came Keith Richard and Dick Taylor and the group was set to go. They named themselves The Rollin' Stones, after a song by Muddy Waters, the American blues singer and guitarist much admired by Brian. By 1963, the line-up was complete and featured Brian on rhythm guitar, Keith Richard on lead guitar, Mick Jagger on vocals, Bill Wyman on bass, Charlie Watts on drums and Ian Stewart on the piano, Dick Taylor having dropped out. Brian was the leader and inspiration behind the group, and he believed that one day they would achieve the stature of The Beatles.

Brian, Jagger and Richard moved into a flat together. Money was very tight and they lived a hand-to-mouth existence, relying on whomever was working to pay for their food. Brian, acting as manager, secured a regular spot for the band at the Crawdaddy Club in Richmond. The club featured traditional jazz, and the Rollin' Stones, playing in their own unique style, soon enjoyed great popularity. The raw energy of their R&B renditions attracted young people and encouraged audience participation.

Andrew Loog Oldham, who at one time had been a press officer for The Beatles, spotted them here and, realising their enormous potential, signed them to a contract. Assuming management of the group, he set about creating a new, sexy, pop image for them. His initial attempt to polish them up met with failure, and eventually he realised that a contrasting image to that of the clean-cut Beatles would work best, and the long-haired, unkempt look became their trademark.

Oldham's next move, which created tension between him and Brian, was to try to ease Ian Stewart out of the line-up. Oldham didn't think Stewart suited the new image: his face didn't fit and his hair wasn't long enough. However, he did concede that Stewart could remain as road manager and back-up on recordings as long as he remained in the background. Oldham also insisted that a 'g' be added to their name, and so they became The Rolling Stones.

The early days were a struggle, but Brian worked tirelessly for the Stones' success. He wanted to be a star, with all the trappings: fame, money and the adoration of the girls. Even with his long hair, or perhaps because of it, Brian was particularly attractive to young girls, and they flocked around him. He was the snappiest dresser of the group and by far the most popular at this point in their career.

Their first single 'Come On' was released in June, 1963, and their second, a Lennon McCartney number, 'I Wanna Be Your Man' followed in November. Both singles enjoyed some success in the United Kingdom but it was their third single, the Buddy Holly cover 'Not Fade Away', released in 1964, that reached the Top Ten, and they were on their way to the stars. By the end of this year, they were enjoying enormous popularity and all the benefits that accompanied it. The more successful they became, the more outrageous their behaviour, and stories of their exploits were legion. Sex and drugs were readily available to them and Brian, already famed for his sexual appetite, was willing to try anything. Oldham, realising the financial benefit of this publicity, encouraged their 'bad boy' image.

The Rolling Stones were now as popular in the United States as they were at home. Riots followed their concerts everywhere, hysterical fans mobbed them, grabbing their clothes and pulling their hair. The more adulation they received, the more exaggerated their already sexually provocative performances became. Brian and Mick were peacocks, strutting the stages of the world, preening their long locks and basking in the adoration of the younger generation. Their popularity did not extend to the older generation, or to the media, who constantly reviled them.

During the years between 1964 and 1967, the Stones worked flat out, touring the world and producing one smash hit after another. Brian was still the most popular with the girls, but Jagger, as the singer, and because of his raunchy style, began to receive the lion's share of the publicity. Brian, undoubtedly the better musician, resented this. In addition, he was suffering health problems and his behaviour became erratic.

Although Brian enjoyed the fruits of the Stones' stardom, spending a small fortune on clothes and girls, he still had difficulty coming to terms with Oldham's commercial promotion of the group. Oldham's concept clashed with his musical integrity and relationships between the two were very strained. Furthermore, the long tours exhausted Brian and aggravated his asthma, and he became increasingly dependent on drugs and alcohol.

Jagger, meanwhile, had formed a musical partnership with Keith Richard and now further alienated Brian by officially taking over the leadership of the group. Slowly, despite the fact that he had been the originator of the Stones, Brian was eased out of his prominent position.

Further signs of strain began to show. There were very tangled relationships within the group. In 1965, Brian had met a beautiful Italian model, Anita Pallenberg, and began what was to develop into a serious relationship. But in 1967, on a Moroccan holiday, Anita left Brian for Keith Richard. Brian was devastated by this and found it hard to recover. It was later rumoured that during the filming of *Performance* Anita also had an affair with Jagger. Marianne Faithfull was another girl who was reputed to have played musical beds with the group, her tally competing with that of Anita Pallenberg.

The loss of his girlfriend to Richard compounded Brian's sense of isolation. He was still musically creative but he began to miss recording sessions, sometimes turning up too drunk or drugged to participate.

In 1967, media and police harassment greatly increased. Brian, Jagger and Richard were all arrested on drugs charges. Drugs had always formed a part of the music world, but until the mid-sixties they had been mild – speed, amyl nitrate, marijuana and only occasionally cocaine. As the sixties progressed, the abuse of heroin and LSD was becoming widespread. The police, determined to crack down on this problem, saw The Rolling Stones, the bad boys of rock, as convenient scapegoats, a theory that was even supported by *The Times* newspaper.

Brian was sentenced to nine months in jail, but his medical condition was so precarious that he was released on bail to receive treatment at a clinic. On appeal, his sentence was set aside, and he was fined and placed on probation. But the stress of the situation had been too much for Brian and he continued to consult a psychiatrist.

Unable to face life in the flat where he had been arrested, he moved into another flat while he looked for a house in the country where he thought he would be happier.

May, 1968 saw Brian's last live appearance with the Stones in a concert at the Empire Pool, Wembley. On 20 May he was once again arrested for the possession of cannabis. This persecution by the police contributed further to his fragile mental state and he began to withdraw into himself. When the case came to trial he was found guilty, but as he was still on probation for his previous offence he was only fined.

He was still contributing to the group's recording sessions but his behaviour was unpredictable and his health very fragile, and these contributions were minimal. Leaving the others to complete their latest album without him, Brian flew off to Tangiers and immersed himself in learning the Moroccan pipes of Pan. An album of the work that he collated at this time was released posthumously.

The Rolling Stones were once again on top form now, with Brian or without him. After several disappointing recordings, they had three great successes; 'Jumpin' Jack Flash', 'Honky-Tonk Woman' and its 'B' side, 'You Can't Always Get What You Want'.

In June, 1969, Brian finally decided to leave the Stones. He had become disenchanted with the musical direction of the group and felt personally isolated from them. On his return from Tangiers he had fallen in love with, and purchased, Cotchfield Farm, a house set in eleven acres of lovely Sussex countryside. Cotchfield Farm had once been the home of A.A. Milne, the creator of Winnie the Pooh, now it was to be a haven for Brian. He vowed to stay off drugs and set about improving his health. He began to compose again and considered the possibilities of forming a new group, with an emphasis on American contemporary blues music.

But on a warm summer evening in July, 1969, after he had taken an evening swim, Brian's girlfriend discovered his unconscious body at the bottom of his outdoor swimming pool and his asthma inhaler on the side. She and a friend tried, unsuccessfully, to resuscitate him, but when the doctor arrived Brian was declared dead. The coroner's verdict was misadventure, drowned under the influence of drugs and alcohol.

His funeral was held in his native town of Cheltenham. Masses of flowers and wreaths covered the cemetery as hundreds of people gathered to mourn. Conspicuous by their absence were Andrew Oldham, Mick Jagger, Keith Richard and Anita Pallenberg.

A Rolling Stones concert, scheduled long before the group heard the appalling news of Brian's death, took place on 5 July in Hyde Park. Enormous crowds gathered for this event, the biggest open-air concert ever held in Britain, and it served as a fitting memorial to Brian Jones.

In 1971 The Rolling Stones, through their own company, released Brian's final work, 'Brian Jones Presents The Pipes of Pan at Joujouka'.

Ian Stewart died in 1985, at the age of forty-seven, of a massive heart attack. The album 'Dirty Work' (1986) was dedicated to his memory.

Jimi Hendrix

Full Name:	James Marshall Hendrix
Born:	27 November, 1942, Seattle, USA
Died:	18 September, 1970
Age:	27

Jimi Hendrix, with his wild music, flamboyant personality and psychedelic clothes, was born for the sixties. A mixture of Negro and Cherokee blood, he was the first major black rock star and the most creative guitarist of his day. It was said that Jimi Hendrix had redefined the art of guitar playing.

Born while his father was away serving in the Army, his mother named him Johnny Allen Hendrix. His parents had a very rocky marriage and four years later, on his father's return from the services, Johnny's name was changed to James Marshall Hendrix.

Jimi's mother died when he was sixteen, but by then his parents were already divorced, and he and his brother, Leon, were living with their father. Al Hendrix was a landscape gardener, but in his spare time he loved nothing more than to listen to music and play the saxophone. He encouraged Jimi in his love of music, and when Jimi was twelve, he presented him with a guitar. Although he was left-handed, Jimi taught himself to play the guitar – upside down! Without any formal teaching, he learned to play music from the records of Muddy Waters, B.B. King, Chuck Berry and other greats, spending all his spare time practising.

More interested in his music than his schoolwork, Jimi dropped out of school to help his father as a landscape gardener. Anxious not to be drafted into the Army, he then enlisted as a paratrooper.

In 1961, he was invalided out after suffering an injury during a parachute jump. Following his discharge, Jimi went on the road as a backing artist. He worked with great artists such as B.B. King, Sam Cooke and Little Richard, gaining valuable experience. In 1964, he accompanied the Isley Brothers to New York and there he stayed.

New York was the hub of blues, folk and jazz music. Among the master musicians gathered here, Jimi made little impact. Until, that is, he heard Bob Dylan's voice. He decided that if Dylan could make a living by singing, so could he. He formed his own group, Jimmy James and The Blue Flames, and began playing the club circuit in Greenwich Village.

In 1966, Chas Chandler, bassist with The Animals, heard Jimi play at the Café Wha? in Greenwich Village. Chandler, seeking a new direction in his career, wanted to move into management. Recognising the enormous potential of Jimi's talent, Chandler offered to manage him in Britain.

In London, Chandler set about forming a trio. He teamed Jimi up with Noel Redding on bass (Redding was a guitarist but he made the switch to bass with alacrity) and Mitch Mitchell on drums. Together, they were the perfect foil for Jimi's scintillating guitar technique, and

Chandler sent them on the road as The Jimi Hendrix Experience. But not before he perfected their image. He frizzed Jimi's hair, giving him a 'wild man' look, chose violently-coloured clothes, and encouraged Jimi to employ all the guitar tricks he had learned in his days as a side man, plucking the strings with his teeth and playing the guitar behind his back. The resulting stage act was truly outrageous and in every way an experience for the fans.

Fellow musicians were the first to extol Jimi's musical ability, but audiences soon joined in and The Jimi Hendrix Experience took Britain by storm. Their first single, 'Hey Joe' (1966), a blues number, reached the Top Ten, and by the time 'Purple Haze' was released four months later their fame had spread.

The Experience's debut album, 'Are You Experienced?' was a major breakthrough in modern rock guitar music. Jimi could coax the most amazing sounds from his guitar. He had also developed the habit of smashing up or setting his guitar on fire at the end of his act, and audiences throughout Europe were mesmerised.

'The Wind Cries Mary' was the group's third successive Top Ten hit, and Jimi decided that the time was right for him to make a further onslaught on the US rock scene. The place was the 1967 Monterey Pop Festival. Jimi's sexually-charged, inspirational performance, which culminated in his habitual pyrotechnic display, electrified the audience and brought him acclaim as a genius. Legend has it that until this point in time Jimi was so unknown in his native country that a lady in his hotel mistook him for a bellboy! Monterey changed all that.

A successful tour of the United States preceded The Experience's return to Britain. Although some of Jimi's onstage antics outraged the establishment, the media loved him and covered every aspect of his life and personality. With money no object, Jimi freely participated in the rock 'n' roll lifestyle, spending vast sums of money on drugs, parties and women. He was renowned for his incredible sexual appetite and prowess, but he never seemed to have a serious relationship: the most important individual in his life was his guitar.

Back in Britain, Jimi sought ways to expand his musical creativity. He was tired of the carefully-cultivated 'wild man' image, feeling that audiences attended more to see his flamboyant act than to hear his music. And he wanted to devote more of his time to being a serious musician.

Although The Experience were still touring, tensions were building up in the group, partly because of Jimi's behaviour. Drugs had become a regular feature of his life: he sniffed heroin and cocaine, took uppers and downers, dropped LSD and consumed alcohol, all designed to improve his performance. However, he was often totally spaced out. He had always been prone to wild rages, but now he was on occasions uncontrollable. In January, 1968, following a disagreement with Noel Redding, he was arrested in Sweden for smashing up a hotel room and it took three policemen to subdue him. Jimi was fined and obliged to pay damages, and he was no longer a welcome visitor in Swedish hotels.

Despite these difficulties, The Experience spent 1968 working hard. 'Axis: Bold As Love', their second album, remained in the charts for a year, and 'Electric Ladyland' reached the Number One position in the US charts, finally bringing Jimi the recognition he sought in his native country. But the pressures of non-stop work and financial difficulties took their toll. Relationships between Jimi and Redding had deteriorated badly and the group split up temporarily.

In May, 1969, Jimi was arrested in Toronto, Canada and charged with possessing heroin. At his trial, in December of that year, he insisted that the package had been given to him by a fan. He admitted that he had taken LSD, pot and cocaine in his life, but claimed that he had now 'outgrown' drugs. Amazingly, he was acquitted.

Following a tour of the United States, The Jimi Hendrix Experience finally split up for good, leaving Jimi free to pursue his own musical interests. In August, 1969, at the Woodstock Music and Art Fair, where protests about American involvement in Vietnam were uppermost in young people's minds, his unpatriotic performance of 'The Star-Spangled Banner', was the highlight of the festival.

Next Jimi formed his own group, Band Of Gypsies, an all-black trio with Billy Cox on bass and Buddy Miles on drums. Band Of Gypsies was an ill-starred venture. Their first performance, at the Fillmore East, was recorded for an album, 'Band Of Gypsies', but the rights and proceeds of this album had to be signed over to one of Jimi's ex-managers to honour a contract. Their second appearance, at a peace rally in New York's Madison Square Gardens, was a shambles. In front of 19,000 people, Jimi stopped playing and left the stage, telling the audience, 'I'm sorry, but we just can't get it together'.

Meanwhile, he was following another one of his dreams by pouring money into the creation of an ideal recording studio, Electric Ladyland. Here, he hoped to be able to work with fellow musicians, experiment with jazz, and get some of the music he heard constantly in his head on to record. But this state-of-the-art studio consumed more money than Jimi had, and he was forced back on the road. With Mitch Mitchell (ex-Jimi Hendrix Experience) and

Billy Cox (ex-Band Of Gypsies), Jimi undertook a tour of the United States.

Finally, life seemed to be looking up for him. His Electric Ladyland Studios in New York were officially opened and he could look forward to many creative recording hours. But first he was committed to a European tour.

As the tour neared its end, Jimi gave what was to be his final performance at the Love and Peace Festival, Isle of Fehmarn, Germany. Jimi's arrival at the concert had been delayed and he was poorly received, the German audiences booing his appearance. Then Billy Cox, suffering from a bad drug trip, dropped out. The final venue scheduled for Rotterdam, Holland, was cancelled and and Jimi flew to London to be with his girlfriend, Monika Danneman.

On the night of 18 September, Jimi and Monika attended a dinner party before returning to their hotel. The next morning Monika found Jimi unconscious in their room at the Samarkand Hotel. He had taken nine of her very strong sleeping tablets and died, ignominiously, of vomit inhalation due to barbiturate intoxication. The pathologist made no mention of drug addiction.

James Marshall Hendrix was laid to rest in his home town of Seattle, honoured by the attendance of many of his fellow musicians.

Jimi had once jokingly remarked, 'Once you're dead, you've got it made'. This has certainly been true in his case. 'Voodoo Chile', his final recording, was released after his death and shot to the Number One position in the charts. Over 300 previously unreleased pieces of material, some good, some bad, have appeared and, believe it or not, it is thought that there is more still to come.

'Hendrix Year', the twentieth anniversary of Jimi's

death, was celebrated in 1990 with the publication of books, videos and new albums. In January, 1992, the year that Jimi would have turned fifty, he was inducted into the Rock 'n' Roll Hall of Fame. The Jimi Hendrix Exhibition, a collection of photographs, posters and magazines, opened in London on May, its first visit before travelling to all the major European capital cities, across the United States and Canada and to Japan, Australia and Russia. And, of course, there was the obligatory launch of books, videos and CDs.

Jimi Hendrix was a bizarre mixture of creative and destructive forces, but he left behind a rich legacy of innovative guitar techniques for which he will long be remembered.

Harry Chapin

Born: 7 December, 1942, New York City, USA
Died: 16 July, 1981
Age: 38

Like Phil Ochs, and of the same era, Harry Chapin was a folk singer, but more than a folk singer, he was a storyteller. His father was a drummer, and from their earliest days, Harry and his brothers, Tom and Stephen, had a love of music instilled into them.

A member of the Brooklyn Heights Boys Choir, Harry went on to form a musical act with his brothers. The Chapin Brothers disbanded when Tom and Stephen left the country to avoid the draft. After graduating from Cornell University, Harry tried his hand as a film-maker. In 1969, his documentary about boxing, *Legendary Champions* won him an Academy Award nomination. At the time, folk singing as a way of making a commentary on life was fashionable, and so Harry went back into music. With Ron Palmer on acoustic guitar and Tim Scott on cello, Harry presented his work at the Village Gate in New York.

Elektra Records signed him to a contract in 1970 and Harry began work on his first album, 'Heads And Tails'.

One track from this album, 'Taxi' (1972), did particularly well as a single, despite the fact that it was seven minutes in length. A prolific songwriter, Harry kept up a regular output throughout the seventies, but two songs brought him most recognition: 'W.O.L.D.', the story of an ageing disc jockey, and 'Cat's In The Cradle', a song about a neglectful father.

In 1975, with the help of his brother, Stephen, Harry opened a musical revue, *The Night that made America Famous*, on Broadway. Sadly, it didn't run for long, but before closing, it secured two Tony nominations.

Always politically aware, in the nature of a folk singer, Harry became more committed to his ideals as the years passed. He was deeply concerned about world hunger and poverty and, in 1975, he was the co-founder of WHY, World Hunger Year. He was also involved with many other charities, and gave generously of his time and talent, raising over five million dollars for his various causes.

As the seventies drew to a close, and America's involvement in the Vietnam War was terminated, folk singing as political comment gave way to other musical forms. Seeking more commercial success, Harry left Elektra in 1980 and signed with Boardwalk Records. His first album for them, enterprisingly called 'Sequel', produced the hit track of the same name, which was in fact a six-minute sequel to his earlier hit 'Taxi'.

In 1981, on his way to one of the many benefit concerts he still patronised, Harry was killed when the petrol tank of his car caught fire and exploded, depriving the world of a uniquely generous soul. The Harry Chapin Memorial Fund was launched at his memorial service in appreciation of the considerable amount of time and money he had donated to charity.

Janis Joplin

Full Name:	Janis Lyn Joplin
Born:	19 January, 1943, Port Arthur, Texas, USA
Died:	4 October, 1970
Age:	27

Janis Joplin was surely the greatest white blues singer of her time. The raw, uncontrolled quality of her voice reached out to her audiences, giving them of her very soul. Sadly, a lifetime of excess was to deprive the world of her great talent when she was only twenty-seven.

Port Arthur, Texas, a booming oil town, attracted many people of different ethnic origins. Seth Joplin, Janis's father, had moved there to work for a petroleum company, married, and settled. Janis, the eldest of three children, had a childhood similar to that of many other middle-class American children, encompassing school, church, the Girl Guides and summer picnics.

At school Janis excelled, particularly in the creative subjects, English and Art. She was a pretty, blonde child, but as childhood gave way to adolescence, her weight ballooned, her hair turned mousy and she developed acne. As her looks changed, so, too, did her character.

Aware that she was a physically unattractive teenager, Janis deliberately cloaked herself in aggressiveness.

Unwilling, and unable, to blend in with the other girls in high school, Janis became 'one of the boys'. She developed a tough, beer-drinking persona, taking delight in shocking all those about her. But what was acceptable for boys in middle America certainly was not so for girls. She attracted a great deal of animosity from the other students, who took to teasing her and calling her names, of which 'pig' was a favourite. Rumours circulated that Janis was promiscuous. Although it is unlikely that there was any truth to these stories, Janis chose not to deny them, and so became an outcast.

Her talent for painting had been obvious throughout her school years, making art college the logical outcome. However, in the interim period between high school and college, because of her rebellious attitude and behaviour, Janis's parents decided to send her away to visit a relative in Los Angeles. These months changed Janis's life. She discovered Venice Beach, the home of beatniks, and San Francisco. Here rebellion and freedom of expression were the rule of the day, and Janis returned from this trip with a new outward air of *braggadocio* and confidence.

Back in Texas, she attempted to settle into the routine of college life. Always a music-lover, she discovered that she could sing. She had long admired the blues singer Bessie Smith, and adopted her style, although she was also able to impersonate other well-known singers.

In the summer of 1962, Janis went to the University of Texas in Austin. Austin, like San Francisco, had a 'beatnik' culture, where folk music, country and western, and blues thrived. Janis was in her element. She taught herself the autoharp and sang around the clubs, adapting her style to suit her audience.

Yet university life was not much better than high school had been. Janis refused to conform to the morés of middle America or to the traditions of campus life. While other girls wore dresses and saddle shoes, she wore jeans and went barefoot. Shiny, clean, curled hair was the fashion, but Janis's hair hung in a limp, stringy mass.

She began to drink hard alcohol to assuage the self-doubt and pain caused by the cruelty of her classmates. She also became the life and soul of the party, pretending an insouciance she didn't possess, and behaving in a deliberately provocative manner.

The final blow came in 1963, when Janis was voted 'Ugliest Man on Campus'. Feeling she had endured all the humiliation she could tolerate, she packed her bags and hit the road for San Francisco. In San Francisco the 'beat' culture was on the way out, flower power on the way in. Janis landed up in North Beach, the area of San Francisco made famous by Jack Kerouac, and home of bohemians. She began singing a mixture of blues and country and western around the coffee houses, allowing all the anger and pain of her emotions to permeate her voice.

In pursuit of the ultimate experience, Janis experimented with drugs. Grass was easily available but she also indulged in speed, smack, methadrine and her old faithful, booze. Her motto was 'stay stoned and have a good time'. Still Janis was discontent. She craved acceptance and belonging but thought herself unattractive to men because of her bulky body and acne-scarred skin. She embarked on a series of affairs in an effort to prove her desirability.

By the summer of 1965, she was a mess, heavily dependent on methadrine and unable to function on a normal level. Scared, Janis returned to Port Arthur, determined to kick her habit. But life in a small town was not to her liking and she soon returned to singing.

In 1966, an old friend persuaded her to return to San Francisco as lead singer for a blues band, Big Brother and The Holding Company. Big Brother comprised David Getz on drums, guitarists James Gurley and Sam Andrew and Peter Albin on bass.

Janis found that San Francisco had changed during her year's absence. Rock music was firmly established, and Bob Dylan, The Beatles and The Byrds were all big names. Hippies and flower children had flooded into the Haight Ashbury district and peace reigned. Janis loved it.

As she and Big Brother began to adjust to each other and develop a rapport, she began to change. She greatly admired Otis Redding and was influenced by his style. Her own voice became louder, her movements in front of the band wilder. Janis also adopted a more feminine way of dress, wearing beads, jangly bracelets and silky, flowing gowns. She had also been introduced to LSD.

In 1967, Janis and Big Brother were asked to perform at the Monterey Pop Festival. For three days the best rock musicians in the world gathered together to perform before rapturous audiences. Otis Redding, the king of soul, was there; so, too, was Jimi Hendrix, with his innovative guitar-playing and pyrotechnics. Acid rock, the music of the acid-dropping generation, had come of age.

Janis's energetic foot-stamping and raucous screaming of 'Love Is Like A Ball And Chain' were greeted with frenzied enthusiasm by the crowds, and a legend was born.

Following the festival, Janis and Big Brother signed with a new manager, Albert Grossman. Grossman was a highly successful and powerful businessman. Among his clients he numbered Bob Dylan, Peter, Paul and Mary, and Mike Bloomfield. But he had one stipulation: he would not tolerate heroin abuse. Janis readily agreed. Although it is not known whether she had any intention of complying with this condition, what is certain is that it was only a short time before her anxieties drove her back to drugs.

Janis had slimmed down and her appearance improved. Her performance was much more confident, but insecurity was still the keynote of her life. She confused sex with love, not being able to believe, despite the evidence of her fans' adulation, that anyone could love her for herself alone.

Big Brother's début album under Grossman's management, 'Cheap Thrills', was recorded at a live concert. The 'four gentlemen – and one great, great broad' as they were introduced, looked set for great success. But Grossman felt that the instrumental backing was woefully inadequate for Janis's powerful and raunchy voice, and announced that she was going solo.

In 1969, with her new band, The Kozmic Blues Band, Janis went on a tour of the United States. Life on the road was an endless round of airports, bars, shows, hotel rooms and more bars, and Janis became heavily dependent on alcohol and drugs. In an effort to disguise her drug-taking with alcohol, she kept a bottle of Southern Comfort to hand but it fooled nobody. And her heavy drinking was causing excessive weight gain. Even a European tour, during which drugs were not readily available, did nothing to stem the downward slide.

Even so, Janis was still in demand – her presence, and the energy of her performance, electrified her fans. She exhorted her audiences to get out of their seats and show their love for her by screaming, yelling and dancing. The police had great difficulty maintaining order at her concerts, and in 1969, she was arrested in Tampa, Florida, for the use of obscene language to a police officer.

By now Janis's drug consumption was beginning to overpower her performance. Frequently she appeared on stage stoned and drunk, and her audiences began to dwindle. They wanted to see the raucous, stamping Janis of old, the Janis who compared performing with sexual gratification, not the pale shadow they were being offered.

Janis made many efforts to kick her habit, but the pressures of touring and wrestling with her insecurities always drove her to regression. In the middle of one of these drug-free periods of her life, Janis met a law student, David Niehaus. She had always been famous for the number of her sexual partners, but until this time she had not formed a serious relationship. However, this one was not to be. The pressures of work caused Janis to revert to drugs and Niehaus disappeared from her life.

In 1970, Janis formed a new group, The Full Tilt Boogie Band. The line-up included Brad Campbell (ex-Kozmic Blues Band) on bass, John Till on guitar, Clark Pierson on drums and Richard Bell on piano. Janis plunged enthusiastically into her debut with this band, with whom she hoped to reflect the changing sound of music in the seventies.

Happy and confident with her new sound, Janis once again withdrew from drugs, increasing her consumption of alcohol to compensate. She had also become involved with the singer/songwriter, Kris Kristoffersen. Kristoffersen, fighting his own battle with the demons of alcohol, wasn't ready to be tied down, and Janis went on the road with The Full Tilt Boogie Band.

The promise of the tour was unfulfilled. The days became, for Janis, an alcohol-induced haze. Her familiar bottle of Southern Comfort accompanied her everywhere, and her moods fluctuated wildly between abject despair and performance-inspired confidence.

Back in California, she met Seth Morgan. Morgan, the son of a wealthy family, was a student at Berkeley University. Janis was often away in Los Angeles, where she was working on a new album, 'Pearl', but the couple spent as much time as possible together. Morgan was only twenty-one to Janis's twenty-seven, but the subject of marriage came up early in their relationship. Morgan was an excellent influence on Janis: with him she came off drugs and cut down on her drinking.

In view of this, the circumstances of her death are all the more bizarre. On 18 September, 1970, Jimi Hendrix died in London from a drugs overdose. This should have served as a warning to Janis but, as she remarked to a friend, 'two rock stars can't die in the same year'. She was under pressure in the recording studio and she resorted to heroin for respite.

In the early hours of 4 October, 1970, at the Landmark Hotel in Hollywood, Janis injected herself with a lethal dose of very high-quality pure heroin. Ironically, had she not been free of drugs for those months, or had the quality of the heroin been lower, Janis's body would probably have tolerated it. But the wild woman of rock, the third of the young musicians who came to fame in Monterey, was dead. Her body was cremated and the ashes scattered over the coast of northern California, the scene of her greatest triumphs. Touchingly, her old flame, Kris Kristoffersen, composed and sang in her memory 'Epitaph (Black And Blue)'.

'Pearl', released after she died in its unfinished state, remains Janis's finest work. Her version of Kristoffersen's number, 'Me And Bobby McGee', also released posthumously, became her biggest-selling single.

Following her death, Janis has enjoyed much commercial success and critical acclaim as a result of posthumous releases and the inevitable compilations. In 1979 *The Rose*, a film starring Bette Midler, was released, purportedly based on her life.

Janis Joplin, like Jimi Hendrix, was the victim of the excesses of the rock 'n' roll lifestyle. But it is fair to say that Janis packed more men, more drugs, more booze and more living into her short life than most of us could handle in two lifetimes.

Jim Croce

Born: 10 January, 1943, Philadelphia, Pennsylvania, USA
Died: 20 September, 1973
Age: 30

Jim Croce loved music from the moment of his birth, and by the time he was six he had already mastered the piano accordion. After high school he attended Villanova University, where he was very involved musically, acting as a disc jockey on a folk programme and playing guitar with several rock bands.

Set on following his musical star, Jim and his wife, Ingrid, also a folk singer, moved to New York, working at various odd jobs while playing around the coffee houses. They never really felt at home in New York, however, and soon moved to Los Angeles. Capitol Records signed them up and they released one record, aptly entitled 'Jim And Ingrid Croce' in 1969. Sales of the album were, unfortunately, very disappointing and the Croces returned to Pennsylvania.

Over the next few years they lived pretty similar lives to any other middle American family, Ingrid raising their son and making pots while Jim drove a truck and worked as a telephone linesman to earn a living. But Jim had never stopped writing music or performing. His unique appeal stemmed from the contents of his songs, songs that reflected the lives, loves and hopes of the average working man.

In 1972, it appeared that Jim's time had finally arrived. One of his old college friends, Tommy West, and his partner, Terry Cashman, were in record production. They took Jim to New York to record, with acoustic guitarist Maury Muehleisen providing the backing. The result was 'You Don't Mess Around With Jim'. Both the title track and 'Operator' went immediately into the Top Ten and remained there for some time. Finally, Jim began to receive the recognition he had been struggling to achieve since the early sixties.

Fame didn't change Jim Croce. He had always been, and would remain, essentially a man of the people, performing, in his denims and boots, the songs that reflected their lifestyle.

Jim's next album 'Life And Times' (1973), was also a great success. One of the tracks 'Bad, Bad Leroy Brown' shot to the Number One position in the charts and Jim went back into the studio to record another album, 'I Got A Name'.

Sadly, he didn't live to see its release. On a September night in 1973, Jim, Muehleisen and four others, on a tour of the southern states, boarded a charter plane at Natchitoches en route to their next venue. The plane crashed into a tree on take-off, killing all those on board.

'Time in A Bottle' was used on the soundtrack of *The Last American Hero* and became Croce's second Number One. All Jim's previous recordings also continued to sell well. Surely Jim Croce must rate as one of the unluckiest singers of all time: after so many years of hard work, he lost his life just at the moment that his dedication was beginning to be rewarded.

Florence Ballard

Born: 30 June, 1943, Detroit, Michigan, USA
Died: 21 February, 1976
Age: 32

Poor, pretty Florence Ballard – fate really dealt her a rough hand. Born in Detroit, the car-manufacturing centre of the United States, Florence was a true child of Motor City, USA. Her parents, Jesse and Lurlee Ballard, had moved north to escape the poverty trap of the south, and Jesse worked for Chevrolet.

Florence was one of thirteen children, so making ends meet was a problem for the Ballards. Nevertheless, Florence's was a very happy childhood; the family were close and Jesse's love of music bonded them further. It was he who taught Florence to sing, and she sang in the church, at school and at talent contests, sometimes with her schoolfriend, Mary Wilson.

In 1959, when Florence was fifteen, she was approached by the manager of a male vocal trio, The Primes, and asked if she would be interested in forming a sister group. Delighted, she, Mary Wilson and Diana Ross (both fourteen) and Betty McGlown became The Primettes.

A friendship quickly developed between Florence, Mary and Diana. They were very close in age, shared similar backgrounds and had many interests in common. Florence assumed the leadership of the group from the beginning, her rich, gospel-style singing and luminous beauty making her the natural choice.

For a time life was very good. Where The Primes (later to become the Temptations) performed, the Primettes supported. When the girls were not at school or working, they practised their harmonies and embellished their home-made costumes.

In 1960, The Primettes won a prestigious talent contest and their future seemed assured. But fate intervened: first, Betty dropped out to get married; then an event occurred which destroyed Florence's innocence and haunted her throughout her life. Coming home from a dance one night, she was raped. Supported by her family, she survived the trial, which was a major ordeal for her, but her personality underwent a profound change. No longer a self-assured, outgoing young girl, she became mistrustful and suspicious of the sincerity of others.

In 1961, when Betty was replaced by Barbara Martin, Florence was once more back as The Primettes' lead. Berry Gordy, the founder of Motown Records, took them under his wing and signed them to a contract. The terms of the contract were very disadvantageous to the girls, as Florence later discovered to her cost, but at the time they were young, and didn't think to employ their own legal representative.

Gordy also decided that they needed a name change, and it was Florence who chose their new name, The Supremes. Their new career didn't get off to an auspicious start. Their first two singles, 'I Want A Guy' and

'Buttered Popcorn' were flops. Then Barbara dropped out and the girls had to re-adapt as a trio.

They joined several Motown tours, which usually included fellow artists of the calibre of Marvin Gaye, Stevie Wonder and Mary Wells. But after three years of performing on the road, and recording, it didn't look as though The Supremes were hit material.

Until this time the girls had taken it in turns to sing the lead, but now Gordy decided that Diana Ross was the most commercially appealing. He handed them over to the songwriting and production team Holland, Dozier and Holland. The single released under this new arrangement was 'Where Did Our Love Go?' (1964), one of twelve top hits for The Supremes.

With a Number One hit under their belts at last. The Supremes were prime candidates for Gordy's charm school. Motown was like a big family, with all the artists mingling and supporting each other when necessary. It varied in another respect from most record companies: Gordy had instituted a charm school programme at Motown, the Artist Development department. This department prepared his singers for stardom, teaching them grooming, make-up, music, dancing, choreography and even etiquette – anything that a performer might need when he or she was appearing as a representative of Motown was included in their instruction.

Fully polished, The Supremes took America and Britain by storm with their slick new act. Hit followed hit in quick succession: 'Baby Love' (1964), 'Come See About Me' (1964), 'Stop! In The Name Of Love' (1965), and so on. The girls appeared on the most prestigious television programmes and were fêted wherever they went.

Being on the road took on new meaning. They were

superstars now, and as such travelled first-class. Limousines waited to transport them to wherever they were playing. They could afford the finest hotels and restaurants, champagne and designer clothes. The world was their oyster.

But trouble was brewing in paradise. Diana Ross, firmly established as lead singer, was also dating Berry Gordy, which gave her the upper edge over the other girls. She gradually moved herself into the prime position, assuming control of the act and seizing the lion's share of publicity. Even the songs that had been Florence's solos became Diana's.

These actions distressed Florence deeply and she became very moody and defensive. She had a very low tolerance to alcohol, which became obvious when she began to drink regularly, no doubt to suppress her feelings of rejection and resentment. The inevitable happened: she began to gain weight.

When it was finally announced that The Supremes were to become Diana Ross and The Supremes, it was more than Florence could bear. The group that she had loved so much, and of which she had orginally been lead singer, was being irrevocably changed. Her behaviour became very erratic and she missed shows. Her heavy drinking caused her weight to balloon, making the contrast between her and the sylph-like Diana Ross more evident.

In 1966, following the two major hits 'You Can't Hurry Love' and 'You Keep Me Hanging On', the tensions in the group reached an unbearable level. Cindy Birdsong was auditioned as a replacement for Florence and Florence bowed out.

Under the terms of her contract, Florence was forbidden to discuss her dismissal. But it was later learned that, in July, 1967, when she signed her release, she had also relinquished all rights and claims to all future income from the group. She received a settlement of $160,000 from Motown, in return for agreeing not to mention that she had been a Supreme. What an irony when the choice of name had been hers!

Florence's personal life, fortunately, was somewhat happier. She had fallen in love with Berry Gordy's chauffeur, Tommy Chapman, and now she married him. Together they set up their own management company and Florence tried to re-establish her career. She signed a contract with ABC Records, but her debut single for them, 'It Doesn't Matter How You Say It', was not a success, and in 1969 she was released from her contract.

The settlement money exhausted, Florence was horrified to discover that she was penniless. She instituted a court case against Motown, Berry Gordy and Diana Ross, claiming that they had conspired to force her to leave the group. The suit was dismissed, plunging Florence even further into debt.

Florence was already the mother of twins, and a third daughter was born in 1971. All she had left from her time with The Supremes was the house she had purchased in the early days of their success, and which she had tried to hang on to for the sake of her children. Now totally destitute, her marriage broken up and her three children dependent on her, she was forced to sell even this, the last symbol of her once great expectations. She moved into a housing project with her mother and a sister, and applied to Aid to Families with Dependent Children for support.

In 1974, the *Washington Post* ran a story about the destitute Supreme, relating her shabby treatment by

Motown, and Florence received new offers of work. But demoralised by the events of the past years and suffering from ill health, she was unable to capitalise on the publicity engendered by the report.

The following year, Florence came into an unexpected sum of money, in settlement of a law suit. She was again able to provide a roof over her family's head, and she and Tommy Chapman attempted a reconciliation. It looked as though Florence was once more in control of her life. But it was too late. She was on medication for weight control and high blood pressure, and in 1976, she was admitted to hospital complaining of shortness of breath and pains in her leg and arm. On 21 February, at the age of thirty-two, Florence died from cardiac arrest caused by a blood clot in the artery.

Her funeral was well-attended – she had been very much loved by all those she knew. Diana Ross gave an emotional speech, and masses of flowers, from family, friends and all the artists at Motown, covered her coffin. The Supremes hit 'Someday We'll Be Together' was played in the church, but ironically, Florence's voice was not heard on this recording. And how tragic it was that although The Supremes were one of the most popular and long-lasting vocal groups in the history of pop music, Florence Ballard died in poverty.

In January, 1988, Lisa Chapman had the honour of representing her mother when the Supremes were inducted into the Rock 'n' Roll Hall of Fame.

Cass Elliott

Real Name:	Ellen Naomi Cohen
Born:	19 September, 1941, Baltimore, Maryland, USA
Died:	29 July, 1974
Age:	32

The group who headlined the 1967 Monterey Pop Festival were The Mamas And The Papas. Just the mention of their hit song, 'California Dreamin', is enough to evoke soft-focus images of girls in beads and free-flowing dresses with flowers in their hair, and long-haired young men in psychedelic clothes. Karma and existentialism had arrived with the flower children, and the music that wafted over the San Francisco Bay area spoke of love, peace, mysticism and LSD.

Cass Elliot's father owned a delicatessen in the Washington area. They were a musical family, but Cass herself didn't begin singing until she went to college. Here she joined The Mugwumps, a folk-rock group, and toured extensively with them.

In 1964 she moved to New York, the hub of the folk movement, and with The Mugwumps played the coffee houses of Greenwich Village. They were not the most successful group of their time but Cass, with her big voice and a great sense of humour, was very popular. She married another member of the group, Jim Hendricks (legend has it that she did so to help him evade the draft), but they soon went their separate ways.

While 'resting' between engagements, Cass also served as a waitress. When another member of The Mugwumps, Denny Doherty, met up with John and Michelle Phillips in the Virgin Islands and decided to join them in forming a harmony quartet, Cass needed little persuasion to abandon waitressing in favour of singing.

As The New Journeymen the group moved to Los Angeles, where they were fortunate enough to quickly secure a recording contract. But they needed a new name to complete their image. Cass pulled one from bikers' jargon and they became The Mamas And The Papas.

John Phillips was a prolific songwriter, and the group's first release, 'California Dreamin'', penned by him, sold over a million copies. Cass brought herself a swanky car to celebrate, the first of many major extravagances.

It was hard for Cass to stand next to the stunningly beautiful Michelle in the line-up. The colourful caftans Cass wore did nothing to conceal the fact that she was a very large lady indeed. But she had a very powerful voice and a magnetic stage presence, and she soon developed a tremendous following. To her fans, she was the personification of the Earth Mother and they loved her all the more for her size.

The group's second single, 'Monday, Monday', which followed just two months later, won them a Grammy and brought them worldwide success. But there was already dissent in the group. Michelle and John Phillips' marriage was very much an on-and-off affair and Michelle left the group for a few months.

Fame had brought them more money than they had ever imagined possible and Cass bought herself a lovely house in the hills that had once belonged to Natalie Wood. She was always surrounded by people and spent money on a lavish scale entertaining them. She was a mystic, a believer in cosmic energy and the aura of personal vibrations. Unfortunately, her intuitiveness did not extend to her choice of her friends, and many of those who gathered around her were spongers and drug-pushers. Cass herself experimented with drugs and drank heavily, retreating to a health farm whenever she needed to drop a little weight.

John Phillips was busy organising the big event of 1967, the Monterey Pop Festival. It was to be the first of its kind, a global rock benefit concert. The big hit of 1967 was one of his compositions, 'San Francisco (Be Sure To Wear Some Flowers In Your Hair)', sung by Scott McKenzie (formerly of The New Journeymen), and Phillips was asked to organise the festival. The Mamas And The Papas were to headline it. Although Cass had become a single mother, her daughter, Owen Vanessa, had opportunely been born a few months prior to the festival and Cass was able to appear.

Their album, recorded live at the event, was a disappointment. Times were changing and the California sound had had its day. Two more hits followed, but by the summer of 1968, the Phillips' marriage was over and the group had split up.

Cass, whose extravagant lifestyle had left her in debt, decided to pursue a solo career. She once said: 'Pop music is just long hours, hard work and lots of drugs', and perhaps the drugs contributed to her weight problem. She had been arrested in 1967, ostensibly for an unpaid hotel bill, but in reality the police were looking for drugs. And she certainly felt that the long hours on tour kept her from her duties as a mother.

Cass had always wanted to sing in musicals, and now she sought a more conventional form of musical career. She could belt out a song with the best of them and her first solo album, 'Dream a Little Dream Of Me', launched her on the cabaret circuit.

An opening at Las Vegas was marred by illness – she had been suffering from an ulcer, her drug intake was heavy and her voice deserted her – but she was not down for long. Her ebullient personality and sense of humour made her a favourite with audiences on both sides of the Atlantic. She particularly enjoyed performing in Britain, where she believed she had lived in a previous life.

In 1971, she was married for the second time, to a German Baron. But this relationship, too, was short-lived. Cass's career had been gaining momentum, but constant dieting and prescription drugs took their toll and began to affect her behaviour.

While she was in London, in 1974, to appear at the Palladium, Cass's heart, weakened by the strain of obesity, gave out. She was five feet two inches tall and weighed over two hundred pounds at the time of her death. The pathologist dispelled the rumours that she had overdosed on heroin, or choked on a ham sandwich when under the influence of drugs, stating firmly that she had died of a heart attack.

Her final album, 'Don't Call Me Mama Any More', was released posthumously, but of course it is as Mama Cass that she is best remembered. Of the other Mamas

And Papas, Michelle Phillips became an actress, John Phillips is still a singer-songwriter, but little is heard of Denny Doherty.

Jim Morrison

Full Name:	James Douglas Morrison
Born:	8 December, 1943, Melbourne, Florida, USA
Died:	3 July, 1971
Age:	27

Jim Morrison, poet, singer, songwriter, visionary, seemed to take pleasure in outraging the establishment. Yet he came from a regimented, military family: his father was an officer in the United States Navy and the family lived the kind of nomadic existence associated with the forces. Jim was the eldest of three children, and his childhood was as ordinary as that of any other child brought up on a military base.

The signs of rebellion were visible by the time Jim was twelve. He used sexually explicit language and, imbued with a macabre sense of humour, was constantly pulling stunts that amused no one but himself. Despite this, he was a good student and a voracious reader, consuming everything from Kerouac to Nietzsche.

His favourite reading matter, however, was poetry; Ginsberg, Whitman, Dylan Thomas and Brendan Behan. He himself had also begun to write poetry, in which a

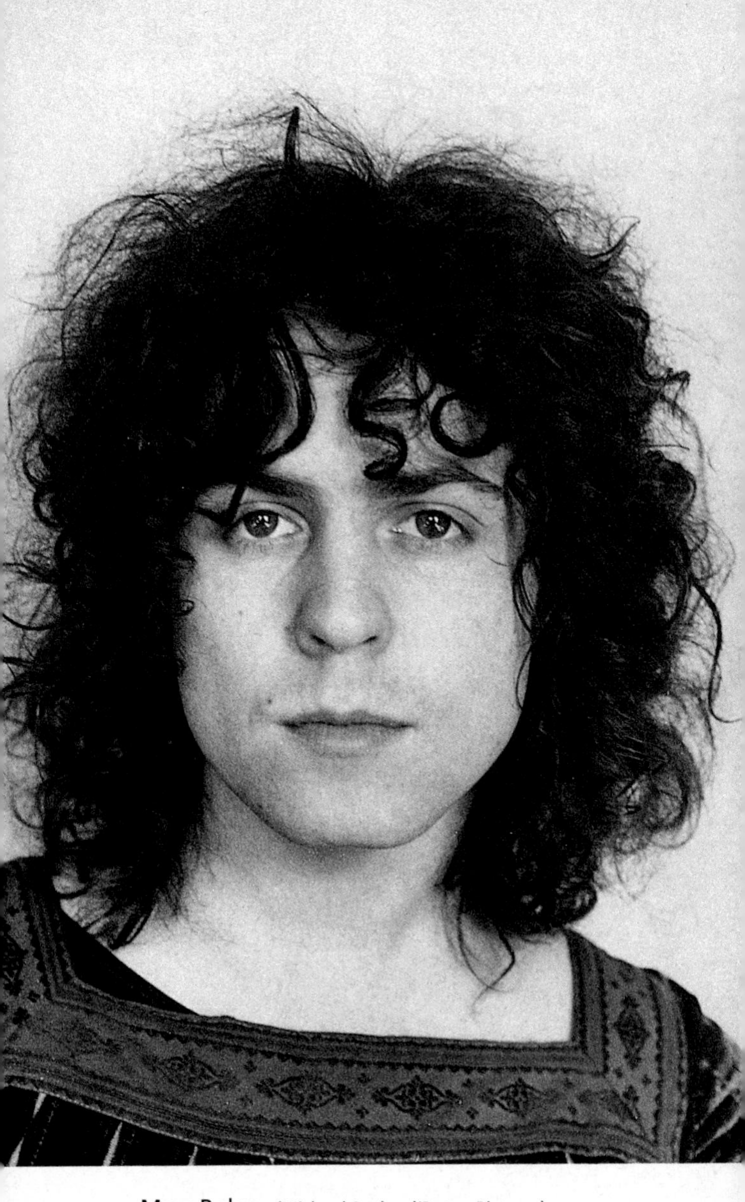

Marc Bolan *(Michael Putland/Retna Pictures)*

John Lennon
(David Redfern)

Brian Jones (The Rolling Stones) *(David Redfern)*

Jimi Hendrix *(King Collection/Retna Pictures)*

Tommy Bolin (Deep Purple
(Fin Costello/Redferns)

Jim Reeves *(Photofest/Retna Pictures)*

Sam Cooke *(Photofest/Retna Pictures)*

Otis Redding *(Photofest/Retna Pictures)*

Jim Morrison *(Henry Diltz/Retna Pictures)*

Peter Tosh (an original member of The Wailers)
(Fin Costello/Redferns)

Janis Joplin *(Glenn A. Baker Archives/Redferns)*

Bob Marley *(Adrian Boot/Retna Pictures)*

Steve Marriott (The Small Faces) *(King Collection/ Retna Pictures)*

Marvin Gaye *(S & G/Redferns)*

Billy Fury *(Richie Howells/Redferns)*

Sid Vicious
(The Sex Pistols)
(J.Tiberi/Redferns)

Keith Moon (The Who)
(Michael Putland/Retna Pictures)

Freddie Mercury
(Richie Aaron/Redferns)

preoccupation with death could be seen. Painting was another of his favourite occupations, but many of Jim's cartoons were of a cruel and obscene nature. He also delighted in taunting or goading his contemporaries into doing the wild things that he enjoyed, pushing them to their limits.

Jim's father was often away and it was left to his mother, Clara, to run the house and raise the children. She and Jim had basic personality differences and Clara simply could not understand his eccentric behaviour. In the late 1950s, Jim adopted an unconventional style of dress, long hair and desert boots, designed, no doubt, to shock his parents. Like Janis Joplin he was an intellectual, but a complete misfit in the conservative, middle-class background from which he came.

Following high school, Jim enrolled at Florida State University to study philosophy and cinematography, both of which fascinated him. He was most at ease with the professors and older students who appreciated his intellect. When his parents moved to San Diego he decided to transfer to UCLA to continue his cinematography studies.

The film school at UCLA was in its heyday, and some of the major directors of the day contributed their time to pass on their skills to a new generation. Yet within a short space of time Jim's interest had moved on to music, and he wanted to start a rock group. He had even chosen the name, The Doors, from Aldous Huxley's quotation of William Blake: *The Doors of Perception*, a reference to a hallucinogenic drug experience.

Jim dropped out of UCLA and moved to Venice Beach. Venice had been the hub of the beat generation in the 1950s and it was still an artistic community. But now beatniks were giving way to hippies, and pot and

LSD were easily available. Jim felt at home in this environment. He was constantly high on LSD, claiming that it enabled him to hear the music in his head that he used to accompany his poems.

An encounter on Venice beach with a fellow UCLA student, Ray Manzaret, was the beginning of Jim's rock 'n' roll career. Manzaret was a keyboard musician. He was overwhelmed by the lyrics of Jim's song, 'Moonlight Drive', and suggested that they assemble a group. Jim couldn't play an instrument so he was nominated vocalist, Manzaret was on keyboards, John Densmore on guitar and Robbie Krieger on drums.

As a teenager, Jim had been inclined to puppy fat. Now he had slimmed down and his hair was long and curly, emphasising the brooding drama of his face. An inner confidence added to the magnetic appeal that he had always held for girls. Throughout high school there had always been a girl in Jim's life. His latest love was Pamela Courson, a beautiful eighteen-year-old with the translucent, freckled skin of the true redhead. But Jim believed in being liberal with his sexual charms and there were always other girls in his life.

The Doors cut several demos and began hawking them around the record companies. But there was no interest and, suffering from rejection, Jim turned to drugs, using grass, acid and coke to blunt the realities of life and to heighten his creativity. Densmore, who was into meditation, tried to persuade him to cut down but Jim was hooked.

Finally, in 1965, Columbia Records signed The Doors to a contract. However, when no studio work was forthcoming, the group began to play gigs, interspersing their own material with standard rock numbers. They spent some time as the house band at the London Fog club, which gave them the opportunity to work on their act and to develop musical unity. But Jim was constantly stoned, and his act was so outrageous that the group were fired. Their contract with Columbia Records was also allowed to lapse.

Jim had a heavy alcohol consumption and was openly taking drugs on stage. He seemed to be on a deliberate path to self-destruction. Nevertheless, The Doors' reputation for drawing in the crowds was such that they were booked into the Whisky-a-Go-Go club. Jim's act became increasingly blatant and sexual. He shouted expletives and stroked the microphone suggestively. At last, one evening, following a heavy drugs session, he was so explosively obscene that The Doors were fired from the Whisky-a-Go-Go – but not before Jac Holzman of Elektra Records had seen them and offered them a recording contract.

Then Jim was called before the draft board. His induction had originally been deferred for his studies at UCLA, but now his time had run out. Legend has it that he used drugs to alter his body rhythms, and that, just to make sure, he declared to the induction board that he was a homosexual. Whatever the truth of the matter, the army decided to pass him by.

The Doors' first album for Elektra, entitled simply 'The Doors', was released in 1967. One track from the album, 'Light My Fire', so electrified the audience at a concert to publicise the album that it was released as a single. Issued in a shortened version – the original was nearly seven minutes long – it zoomed straight to Number One in the charts. The Doors were on their way.

In September, annoyed that they had been excluded from the Monterey Pop Festival where the cream of rock musicians were booked to appear, the group accepted an invitation to appear on television on the *Ed Sullivan Show*. There was only one stipulation: they must exclude the line 'girl, we couldn't get much higher' from 'Light My Fire'. In rehearsal, Jim was obliging and substituted another line. In reality, he had no intention of following this through. Once they were on air he delivered the original line, leaving the show's director in a fury.

In celebration of their first hit, Jim bought himself a skin-tight black leather outfit which served to emphasize the dark side of his nature, wearing it constantly throughout their summer tour of the United States.

With the Vietnam War at its peak, Jim began to write protest songs. The words of these songs were highly topical and inflammatory. His open drug abuse and heavy drinking also added to The Doors' popularity, and wherever they went they were greeted enthusiastically. Jim's stage performances grew increasingly wild, he screamed and shouted, threw things, spat and caressed himself suggestively. The press loved him: he was good copy, and with his intellect he was able to give lucid interviews, although some of his answers were oblique. His magnificent, brooding physical appearance added to his mystique and he was compared to other famous rebels, such as James Dean, Marlon Brando and The Rolling Stones.

The more successful The Doors became, the more Jim seemed to react against the traditional attitudes of the middle class from whence he came. He had alienated himself from his family, claiming that they were dead. He still took drugs, although it was his alcohol consumption that ruled him. And he was sexually promiscuous, although he always returned to Pamela. Officially he lived with Pamela, and referred to her as the keeper of his poems. In many ways they were similar. Pamela was also the child of a military family, both were physically attractive, intelligent and drug-users. Pamela seemed to understand the devils that beset Jim.

These demons were severe. On stage, Jim had become progressively erratic: he often forgot his lines and the blatant sexuality of his act degenerated into the grotesque. The police were always on hand, just waiting for him to make a false move, and he often did so. In 1967, he was arrested in Florida for profanity to a police officer. The following year he upset the police again in Los Angeles.

Like Janis Joplin, he seemed to deliberately provoke the police. And yet there was no love lost between him and Janis. It should have been a true meeting of minds, both were heavy drinkers and drug-abusers, rebellious souls constantly seeking to upset the status quo, but each encounter between them ended in physical abuse.

In March, 1969 in Miami, Jim was arrested and charged with lewd and lascivious behaviour, indecent exposure, open profanity and drunkenness. He was eventually sentenced to sixty days' hard labour and six months in jail, but remained free pending an appeal. As a result, a special clause was written into The Doors' contracts forbidding any obscenity. The police attended their concerts to ensure that the letter of the law was enforced, causing The Doors to lose bookings.

Jim's bizarre behaviour worsened. He even urinated in public, seemingly unaware of the furore he was causing. Relationships between the members of the group deteriorated and Densmore threatened to quit. To appease him, a minder was put on the payroll. It was his job to see that Jim got to shows on time and that he was not too drunk to perform.

For a time the plan seemed to work. Jim was bored

with being a rock star. He became more introspective and returned to writing his poetry. But his actions were very eccentric. Always fascinated by reptiles, he dubbed himself the lizard King, a reference to one of his poems, 'Celebration of the Lizard'. He purchased an extravagantly expensive lizard skin coat to perfect the image. He began to treat his young fans with contempt, realising that they came not for his music but to see his strange behaviour. He would spit at them and, on one occasion, deliberately provoked them to riot.

In 1969, Jim decided to change his image. No longer young and handsome, he was showing the effects of his debauched lifestyle. He was bloated and fat, and his abundant dark tresses were streaked with white. Discarding his leather gear, Jim adopted the Ché Guevara look with dark glasses and a beard. He talked about leaving the group to develop his creative talents.

Throughout 1970, Jim concentrated on the publication of his book of poems, *The Lords and The New Creatures*, and resolving the legal difficulties that had arisen as a result of his lewd behaviour.

During this period he had become involved with the editor-in-chief of *Jazz and Pop* magazine, Patricia Kennealy. An intelligent and beautiful young woman with an extensive knowledge of spiritualism and the occult, Patricia fascinated Jim. On Midsummer's Night, 1970, they were married in a pagan Celtic wedding ceremony conducted by a high priestess of Patricia's coven.

However, the relationship deteriorated when Patricia learned she was pregnant. Jim paid for her to have an abortion and by February 1971 he was back with the long-suffering Pamela Courson.

In 1971, The Doors released what was to be their final album, 'LA Woman'. Jim was often incoherent during recording. He had added cocaine to his alcohol abuse, feeling that the drug would heighten his creativity. Jimi Hendrix and Janis Joplin were both dead and he had premonitions of his own mortality.

He and Pamela moved to Paris, Jim in search of his muse. Paris suited him – he walked the streets, visiting the sights and allowing the artistic atmosphere to engulf him. Although he was still drinking heavily, his poetry flowed from him.

In July, 1971, he died mysteriously in the bathtub. His death was attributed to heart failure, but his body was immediately encased in a sealed coffin, giving rise to much speculation. Rumours circulated that he had been snorting heroin, supplied by the ever-faithful Pamela. Pamela herself died of an heroin overdose in April, 1974 and so could not corroborate or refute this allegation.

There are those who maintain that Jim is not dead, that he was tired of his own celebrity and just walked off into obscurity. Be that as it may, the sealed coffin was buried quietly in the Père Lachaise Cemetery in Paris where Oscar Wilde, Edith Piaf, Chopin and Balzac also lie. The inscription carved on his tombstone reads 'Light My Fire – Light My Fire', but it is almost completely obscured by graffiti.

The Doors have long since disbanded but their records still sell as well as they did in the sixties. In 1991, Oliver Stone's film *The Doors*, released to coincide with the twentieth anniversary of Jim's death, sparked off a further spate of merchandising.

Jim Morrison's poetry still reaches across the span of years, and only Elvis Presley's grave draws more visitors than the Lizard King's final resting place. Jim Morrison, like Jimi Hendrix, Elvis Presley and Buddy Holly, has become a member of the 'worth more dead than alive' club.

Mike Bloomfield

Full Name:	Michael Bloomfield
Born:	28 July, 1944, Chicago, Illinois, USA
Died:	15 February, 1981
Age:	36

Mike Bloomfield was the son of a prosperous, Jewish family in middle America. He loved to listen to the music of Muddy Waters and other great blues men, and he learned to play the guitar surrounded by their music.

In 1965, he joined The Paul Butterfield Blues Band, coming to prominence at the Newport Folk Festival, where he provided the guitar backing for Bob Dylan. Mike's virtuoso guitar-playing can be heard on Dylan's 'Highway 61 Revisited'.

In just two short years Mike became the American guitar hero, earning himself a reputation to rival Eric Clapton's. He broke away from The Butterfield Band to form his own blues band, Electric Flag. The line-up of Electric Flag included Buddy Miles – later to join Jimi Hendrix – on drums and Nick Gravenites, who went on to sing with Big Brother and The Holding Company.

Electric Flag made their debut at the Monterey Pop

Festival in 1967, but their first album, aptly titled 'A Long Time Comin', was not released for several months, by which time they were already thinking of disbanding.

When the group split up in 1968, Mike drifted off to San Francisco to pursue a solo career. For a couple of years he wrote film soundtracks, including *Medium Cool* (1970) and *Steelyard Blues* (1973). In 1975, he was back with Electric Flag for a reunion. They released an album, 'The Band Kept Playing', but it wasn't a success and once again they split up.

Mike was dancing to the tune of a drug habit by now. He retreated to San Francisco where he played the clubs, occasionally scoring a second-rate film to pay for his habit.

Several minor blues albums remain from this period in testament to his great talent. But in 1981 the drugs won out, and Mike was found dead in his car, from a heroin overdose. His final album, released just before his death, was appropriately called 'Living In The Fast Lane'.

The Paul Butterfield Blues Band was the most important white blues band of the sixties. Under Paul Butterfield's leadership, the band perfected the contemporary Chicago blues style and rose to fame during the height of the folk era. Success at the Monterey Pop Festival followed before the band split up in 1972. Paul moved to Woodstock to pursue a solo career but, plagued by ill health, he died at the age of forty-four.

Peter Tosh

Real Name: Winston Hubert McIntosh
Born: 9 October, 1944, Westmoreland, Jamaica
Died: 11 September, 1987
Age: 42

In the sixties a new form of black music emerged from the sunny skies, clear blue waters and abject poverty of the Caribbean. Reggae, the fusion of folk music with African rhythms and electric guitars, originated in Jamaica.

Peter McIntosh, as he was known in his early years, was born in Westmoreland, but raised in the island's capital, Kingston. His father, James McIntosh, had deserted the family, and Alvera, Peter's mother, unable to cope on her own, sent the boy to live with his aunt in Kingston.

There was little escape from the poverty and drudgery of ghetto life in Kingston, but Peter was a very musical boy and saw music as his salvation. He borrowed a guitar from the local church, fixed it up, and formed a group with two other boys from the same neighbourhood, Bob Marley and Bunny Livingstone.

For stage purposes, Peter dropped the first part of his

name, becoming simply Peter Tosh. It was as part of The Wailers that he first rose to fame. A very handsome young man, he quickly established a reputation for himself as the ladies' man of the group.

By the early 1970s The Wailers were beginning to achieve international stardom. But as their success grew Peter became dissatisfied with his role in the band. When Chris Blackwell of Island Records, who had signed them to a contract, began to promote Bob Marley over the other Wailers, Peter and Bunny Livingstone both decided to leave the group.

Peter decided to set up his own recording label. A committed Rastafarian, he named it Intel-Diplo HIM – Intelligent Diplomat for His Imperial Majesty – in honour of Emperor Haile Selassie. Rastafarians, members of a Jamaican religious cult, believe that the late Emperor Haile Selassie is God, and that Ethiopia is their true home. Famed for their dreadlocks and woollen caps, they are also well-known for their music. The hills of Jamaica, where the Rastas prefer to live, reverberate to the sound of their music.

As a Rastafarian Peter also believed that marijuana should be legalised, which made him a prime target for police harassment. His separation from The Wailers left him in an even more exposed position. On one occasion he was knocked senseless by the police and his ribs were dislocated. Admitted to hospital, he was left untreated and in great pain to serve as an example to others.

In retaliation, Peter wrote the album, 'Legalise It', an attack on the laws governing the use of marijuana. The title track was banned on the radio in Jamaica, yet despite this it became a top-selling single.

Although alienated from The Wailers as a group, Peter remained friendly with Bob Marley and Bunny Livingstone.

However, a tragic accident caused an estrangement. A car crash after a party at Marley's Kingston home left Peter's girlfriend dead and his face badly scarred. Peter retreated into himself.

It wasn't until 1977 that he was reunited with Marley. Peter appeared with him in the One Love concert, a concert given in the mistaken belief that it would make peace between rival political factions in Jamaica.

Peter still suffered constant police harassment because of his campaign to have marijuana legalised. Following 'Legalise It' he made a further apolitical statement with the release of the album, 'Equal Rights', before signing with The Rolling Stones' record label.

For a time it looked as though his career was taking a turn for the better. He recorded three albums with The Rolling Stones, and the most successful of these was not 'Bush Doctor' (1978), which included collaborations with Keith Richard and Mick Jagger, but the solo album 'Wanted: Dread Or Alive' (1981).

Peter had become very friendly with Keith Richard. However, when major success continued to elude him, Peter began to blame the Stones and Richard in particular, for his failure. There was a personal altercation regarding the tenancy of Richard's Jamaican house and Peter's contract with the Stones was terminated.

In 1983, Peter produced his best-selling album, 'Mama Africa'. But afterwards his creativity seemed to desert him and his career began to falter. His personal life was not much better. The father of eight children (by different women), he lost a bitter custody battle for the youngest. His common-law wife was not popular and his house in Jamaica was burnt down.

On the evening of 11 September, 1987, three men (one of whom was known to Peter) burst into the house where he and his wife were staying and demanded money. A fight broke out and Peter was stabbed and shot. Peter was declared dead on arrival at hospital, and two other men were also murdered.

All Peter's children gathered together as 12,000 mourners filed past his body where he lay in state. His final resting place is in Westmoreland, overlooking the Caribbean Sea.

Of the three men charged with Peter Tosh's murder, two were acquitted. The third, Dennis 'Leppo' Lobbhan, who admitted to extortion, was condemned to hang for murder.

Dennis Wilson

Full Name:	Dennis Carl Wilson
Born:	4 December, 1944, Inglewood, California, USA
Died:	28 December, 1983
Age:	39

The Beach Boys were one of the most influential and commercial pop groups of the sixties. Like the Mamas And The Papas, they were synonymous with the lush sound explosion that emanated from California.

Dennis Wilson was the middle son in a very musical family. Being a middle child was difficult for him, and Dennis never felt that he received enough love or attention. His father, Murry, ran a machine tool shop and was an aspiring songwriter in his spare time. Audree, his mother, was a pianist. All the boys were expected to sing and play instruments: Brian played the piano accordion, Carl the guitar and Dennis the piano. Murry was very strict and, perhaps because he had himself suffered abuse as a child, he was given to violence. Only a love of music united the family.

Brian, the oldest, began writing songs in high school. He was fascinated by the vocal harmonies of The Four

Freshmen and decided to form his own group. Murry insisted on joining in.

Dennis seemed to be the major target of their father's violence. He was regularly beaten, punched and kicked. Refusing to participate in the group if their father was a member, he absented himself from home as much as he could. As a teenager he was wild and rebellious. By the age of fifteen he was smoking and drinking and spending all his time at the beach on his beloved surf-board.

Carl, the youngest, was the best adjusted. He had a carefree personality and provided a sense of stability for the others.

When, in 1961, Brian decided to reform the group, excluding Murry, Dennis was persuaded to join in on drums. The other members of this group, The Pendletones, were their cousin, Mike Love, and a schoolfriend, Al Jardine.

Murry Wilson, determined to be included, arranged for the boys to play for Hite and Dorinda Morgan, who were small music publishers. Dennis, the great surfer, prompted the group to sing 'Surfin', one of the songs composed by Brian Wilson and Mike Love.

Surfing was a big craze in California. Records, films and radio all extolled the pleasures of riding the big waves. The Morgans immediately saw the potential of this rock music with its blend of sun, fun, sex and surf, and agreed to record it.

Through a very complex series of events, 'Surfin' was eventually released as a single. More by error than design, the boys had acquired a new name, The Beach Boys. It was a great formula: five clean-cut, nice-looking guys, with an up-beat, fun sound based on the latest Californian craze, surfing (even though Dennis was in fact the only surfer in the group).

The record sold well, but because of the complexities of the contract, everyone made money except the boys themselves. Murry Wilson, feeling himself better equipped to deal with business affairs than the boys, took over as manager.

Al Jardine, disappointed at the small amount of money the record had accrued for them, dropped out of the group to return to college, thus necessitating a rearrangement in the line-up. David Marks replaced Jardine, playing rhythm guitar and Brian switched to bass. Dennis was on drums and Carl on guitar, leaving Mike Love as the only member who did not play an instrument as well as sing.

Brian began to write songs with another friend, Gary Usher. He and Brian began to produce some unusual effects on the tracks, adding surf sounds on 'The Lonely Sea', and background car noises on '409', a hot-rod song. Murry, though, felt threatened by Usher's influence and forced him out.

In 1962, Murry secured a contract for The Beach Boys with Capitol Records, who were bowled over by the new sound. The first single released by them was '409', with 'Surfin' Safari' on the 'B' side. This was the kind of music that a whole generation of teenagers had been waiting for, and they greeted it with enthusiasm. 'Surfin' USA' followed and became the first Top Ten hit for The Beach Boys. They hit the road for their first tour of the United States to publicise it. Once again, the line-up had changed. Al Jardine had returned to the group and David Marks had quit, eventually going on to form his own group, David Marks and The Marksmen.

Dennis loved life on the road. It was a heady mixture of freedom and sex. Blond, tanned and muscular from his athletic life, Dennis had sparkling blue eyes and a devastating smile. He was undoubtedly the most attractive member of the group. The girls were all over him and he lapped it up. He boasted that they lined up to sleep with him, and on the tour there was certainly no shortage of groupies. A constant rivalry went on between Dennis and Mike Love as to who could pull the most girls. Their relationship was often violent and it grew increasingly acrimonious over the years when Dennis tormented Love about his thinning hair.

When Brian decided to give up touring and remain in the studio to write, he was replaced by Glen Campbell, and later by Bruce Johnstone. The Beach Boys continued to tour, taking in Europe, Australia and the Far East.

Riding on the crest of their 'surfing' wave, the group were totally wiped out when the unique sound of The Beatles exploded on the scene. The music of The Beatles had a more universal appeal than the California sound, and for two years they vied for position as the world's most popular group, The Beatles gradually edging ahead.

In 1966, the Beach Boys bounced back to the top with their biggest-selling hit ever, 'Good Vibrations', which temporarily returned them to the position of the world's best group. The boys cultivated a new image, abandoning their 'preppy' striped shirts and summer slacks for a new, more sophisticated look.

Life was treating them well, but it wasn't to last. As true sons of California, they were invited to appear at the Monterey Pop Festival alongside Janis Joplin, The Who, The Mamas And The Papas and Jimi Hendrix. Brian, however, was afraid that audiences would compare them unfavourably with the acid rock bands. They declined the invitation and Otis Redding took their spot. It was a fatal error of judgement. Fifty thousand people turned up for this, the first benefit rock concert, and Jimi Hendrix put the final nail in their coffin when at the end of his act he told the audience: 'You heard the last of surfing music'.

Dennis thought life was wonderful. He loved being a rock star. He didn't like the work involved, but he was happy with the rewards. He bought one fabulous car after another, a Ferrari, a Jaguar and a Rolls Royce. He had married and owned a large mansion in Beverly Hills. Marriage didn't cramp Dennis's style, however. He had an endless series of affairs and boasted about his sexual prowess. And he was into drugs. Finally, his wife could no longer tolerate the public humiliation and they separated.

In 1968, through his friend Terry Melcher, Dennis became involved with Charles Manson, the sinister leader of a strange cult group. Manson wanted to be a recording star. In the hope of furthering this ambition, he moved his entourage of willing and nubile girls into Dennis's mansion. Life became a long round of drugs and wild sex orgies, but ultimately Manson proved to be too weird even for Dennis's tastes. After one very expensive summer, Dennis moved out of the house leaving Manson to fend off the bailiffs.

Nevertheless, Manson continued to call on Dennis, once leaving a bullet from his gun with the message, 'This is for Dennis'. When Manson and his 'family' were arrested for the savage murder of Sharon Tate and five others, Dennis lived in a state of fear until Manson was convicted.

Brian was still writing and the boys were still touring, but their popularity had waned and it was obvious that their music was not keeping abreast of the times. The new trend in music was for bands like Led Zeppelin, The Who, The Rolling Stones and The Grateful Dead.

In 1969, Dennis embarked on his second marriage to a lovely young girl from Indiana, Barbara Charren. Unfortunately, he was soon up to his old tricks and this marriage, too, ended in divorce.

Without Brian, who was out of the line-up due to ill health, The Beach Boys continued to tour. They were enjoying a resurgence of popularity but Dennis felt frustrated. For the first time in his life he had begun to write his own songs but the other members of the group didn't take him seriously. He retaliated by behaving childishly and making life difficult for everyone. During an argument one day he smashed his fist through a window and injured his right hand. He was unable to play the drums for some time and had to drop out of The Beach Boys.

By 1974, he was back in the group. But he had gained a reputation for drunken and wild behaviour, and he was once arrested for carrying a gun without a licence. Relationships between the group members deteriorated and it seemed as though The Beach Boys had come to an end.

Dennis began to spend his time on board his boat, *The Harmony*, sailing up and down the coast and enjoying the freedom of the open sea. There was a new lady in his life, a beautiful blonde model and actress, Karen Lamm. They were the perfect couple: golden, young, rich and famous. But their two volatile personalities clashed head-on and theirs was a very explosive and passionate affair. The couple were married in 1976, divorced in 1977, and briefly remarried in 1978.

In 1977, Dennis gave the other Beach Boys a major shock when he became the first of the group to produce a solo album, 'Pacific Ocean Blue', which was released to critical acclaim.

Brian, meanwhile, had suffered a breakdown and was not producing any new material. Carl, who had taken over the leadership of the group, was finding the in-fighting difficult to handle and formed his own band. And Dennis, who had split up with his wife, was a mess. He was drinking heavily and taking heroin and cocaine. He was also broke. His drugs and drinking were expensive and he had always spent extravagantly.

For a couple of years Dennis solved his problem by moving in with Christine McVie, a singer with the British group Fleetwood Mac. But his drinking and cocaine addiction got completely out of hand and made him impossible to live with. Once again, he was left on his own. Now even more of Dennis's time was spent aboard his boat which he kept anchored at Marina Del Rey. He was his own worst enemy and seemed bent on self-destruction. He was grossly overweight and heavily dependent on cocaine, heroin and booze. His behaviour became so bad that he was asked to leave the ailing Beach Boys. The group were still not doing well: Brian was a mess, sitting in a sand box with his grand piano, Dennis had been fired and Carl was trying to build a solo career. Often the line-up on stage did not include any of the Wilson brothers.

But in 1983 Dennis was back in the group. His relationship with his cousin, Mike Love, was still extremely acrimonious. The punch-ups of the early days on tour had escalated into full-scale warfare. Dennis blamed Love for all the ills that befell him. He took the perfect opportunity for revenge by marrying Love's illegitimate teenage daughter, Shawn Love. Despite the arrival of a son, Gage Dennis Wilson, whom Dennis clearly adored, the marriage didn't stand the test of time, and Dennis filed for divorce.

One cold, grey, December day, Dennis went diving off a friend's boat. *The Harmony* had long since been repossessed and Dennis said he was looking for some of his belongings that he had once been thrown overboard. He surfaced once and went under again. At first his friend, Bill Oster, didn't worry when he didn't reappear. But as the minutes went by and Dennis still didn't come back up, Oster panicked and called the Harbour Patrol. Forty-five minutes later they discovered Dennis's body directly under the spot where *The Harmony* had been berthed. Dennis had drowned, but the coroner attributed his death to misuse of alcohol and drugs.

There was some disagreement between Dennis's ex-wives as to where he should be buried. But as his divorce from Shawn had not yet been finalised, she prevailed. There was a quiet funeral service followed by a burial at sea.

Although a federal law prohibits burial at sea, President Reagan was willing to grant the family a special dispensation. It seemed a fitting resting place for Dennis Wilson, the surfing California Beach Boy.

Brian Wilson underwent intensive therapy to cure his drug addiction and improve his health, and eventually returned to the Beach Boys. Although the rambling speech given by Mike Love when the Beach Boys were inducted into the Rock 'n' Roll Hall of Fame in 1988 showed how much relationships within the group had deteriorated, they have managed to stay together. And, as their 1989 album claims, they are 'Still Cruisin'.

Bob Marley

Full Name: Robert Nesta Marley
Born: 6 February, 1945, St Ann's, Jamaica
Died: 11 May, 1981
Age: 36

Bob Marley, the undisputed king of reggae, was responsible for introducing Jamaican music to a wider audience. Now his name and music can be appreciated worldwide and his influence can be clearly seen in the work of other musicians. But his originality still reigns supreme in the world of reggae.

Bob was the child of a mixed marriage. His father, Captain Norval Sinclair Marley, was white, and his mother, Cedella, was black. Captain Marley, having defied his family in marrying Cedella, found himself financially unable to support his wife and family and left Cedella to raise their child alone.

Cedella was the daughter of a country medicine man and herbalist. She and her father brought up young Bob in the traditions of Jamaican rural life. They were devout churchgoers and Cedella, with her fine, rich voice, sang in the church.

When Bob was five, his father re-entered his life for

a short time, putting him in school in Kingston. But within a year Bob was back home with his mother and grandfather, and his father departed from his life for good.

Cedella was ambitious and wanted more from life than a day-to-day existence in the hot, dusty atmosphere of the shanty town. By the time Bob was ten she had moved them to Kingston and placed him in a small private school.

During the forties and fifties Jamaica had gone through a significant growth period, both socially and politically. It had become a member of the West Indies Federation with full autonomy, and exports had begun to provide welcome revenue. But the social divisions were stronger than ever and life in the Trenchtown ghetto where Bob was raised was very tough. By necessity he was very fit, needing to know from an early age how to defend and protect himself.

But there were some pleasures in his life. With the influx of money from the outside world had come a greater interest in music and a new radio station, the Jamaican Broadcasting Company. JBC played the music of the United States – soul, rhythm and blues and rock 'n' roll – but it also gave local musicians an airing. The teenage Bob had his first taste of the music that was to change his life. Sam Cooke was his hero, but his great love was ska, the music of Jamaica, a fusion of folk music and American rhythm and blues.

By the time he had finished school, Bob was writing songs. To please his mother, he had agreed to take an apprenticeship as a welder, but this career came to an end when a steel splinter lodged in his eye and it was feared he might lose his sight.

Bob had already had one of his songs 'One Cup

Of Coffee', recorded, in 1962. Now with two other boys, Bunny Livingstone and Peter Tosh, he formed a vocal trio, attending a free music clinic run by Joe Higgs. Higgs, the songwriting half of a well-known ska duo, Wilson and Higgs, and a committed Rastafarian, wanted to encourage young talents and to give them an opportunity to escape their background.

Bob's group, originally The Teenagers, became The Wailin' Wailers and increased in number to include six vocalists. In 1965, The Wailers joined producer Clement Dodd's Studio One label. There they released the single, 'Simmer Down', an enormous success which went to Number One in the Jamaican music charts. The group kitted themselves out in gold lamé suits and Beverley Kelso, their new female vocalist, in a sequinned dress to provide a more professional image.

There was still a great deal of political unrest in Jamaica, and the population was clearly divided into 'haves' and 'have nots'. The Rastafarians, because of the part played in their lives by the smoking of marijuana, which was outlawed, were the most persecuted. Cedella felt that this would be a good time to move her family to Delaware, where she had relations. However, Bob was firmly entrenched in his musical career and refused to accompany her.

The Wailers became very popular very quickly, playing at concerts and turning out a string of hits. They avoided becoming involved in the political issues which had been stirred up by the civil rights movement in the United States, happy just to be playing their music.

About this time a new group, The Soulettes, began recording in the same studios. Bob became involved with their lead singer, Rita Anderson, and when he found himself without a roof over his head he moved in with her and her illegitimate daughter, Sharon. Determined to realise his dream, and to become not only his own boss but also a big star, Bob went to visit his mother in the United States to try to raise some money. But first he married Rita, so that he could confront his mother with a *fait accompli* in case she disapproved of his choice of bride.

Using another name, Bob found various employments in Delaware, but life in the United States did not really suit him. The weather was too cold and the lifestyle too frenetic. When he was called before the draft board, he gathered together his belongings and the money he had earned and headed back to Kingston.

Back home he set about establishing his own record company, Wailin' Soul. Bob had managed to write enough songs while visiting his mother to begin recording, but now he devoted himself to expanding his material.

The Wailers had by now become Rastafarians and the police seemed to have a personal vendetta against them. Bunny Livingstone was convicted of possession of marijuana and was sent to jail, Peter Tosh was arrested for participating in an anti-Rhodesian demonstration and Bob was arrested on a traffic offence. Despite this, the three continued to record together and when Bob's funds began to run out, they amalgamated with producer Lee Perry.

The first album of this collaboration was 'Soul Rebels' (1970), which had a stronger rock beat than Bob's previous work. It was first example of true reggae, and sold well in both the United States and Britain.

In 1970, Bob went to Europe to collaborate on a film soundtrack with American soul singer Johnny Nash. While he was there he was joined by the other Wailers for a tour of Britain. The large West Indian population of the United Kingdom welcomed them enthusiastically. They also won over a section of the white teenage population known as 'skinheads', who adopted reggae music as their own.

Chris Blackwell, the boss of Island Records, signed The Wailers to a contract in 1972. Their first album for Blackwell was 'Catch A Fire' (1972). With the strong promotional backing of Island Records it brought The Wailers international recognition. Blackwell insisted on an accelerated touring programme to consolidate this success and, by 1974, the reggae cult was firmly established. The influence of reggae music also began to appear in the work of other artists, as seen in The Beatles' 'Ob-La-Di, Ob-La-Da' and some of The Rolling Stones' numbers. And Bob's song 'I Shot The Sheriff', which The Wailers had sung on their album 'Burnin', was a major hit for Eric Clapton.

Bunny Livingstone didn't like touring and Peter Tosh was unhappy with Blackwell's promotion of the group as 'Bob Marley and The Wailers'. Before they had always been a brotherhood under the one umbrella of The Wailers, but now Bob received the lion's share of the publicity. The other two quit.

With the departure of Peter Tosh, the atmosphere within the band lightened and they had a very successful European tour which established Bob as an international rock star. With this fame came an altered lifestyle. Bob and Rita had a house in Newland Town, where Rita was raising the family in the traditions of the Rastafarian faith. Now Bob acquired a large house in Kingston and a silver BMW, enjoying the fact that the initials on his car stood for Bob Marley and The Wailers. He remained married, but not faithful to Rita. Temptations are many for a big star, and a steady number of women enjoyed relationships with him over the years. By the end of his life Bob had eleven acknowledged children by eight different women.

In 1976, further turmoil hit the troubled island of Jamaica. Bob was injured when he and his family were the targets of a failed assassination attempt. Believing this to be a political act, Bob left Jamaica to convalesce in Miami. His health suffered a further setback when, in 1977, one of his toes had to be operated on following the discovery of a cancerous growth.

For some time Bob remained in Europe, working on an album and discovering a new form of music that was blossoming in London, punk rock. To Bob, the punk rockers seemed closely aligned to the Rastas through their belief in their rejection by society. In 1978 he returned to Jamaica, where a major attempt was being made to reunify the various warring political factions. All the major reggae artists agreed to appear at the One Love peace concert and Bob brought together Prime Minister Michael Manley and his opponent Edward Seaga as a demonstration of unity.

This was the first public indication given by Bob that he was involved with the turmoil of the political situation and supported the complete independence of Jamaica. His major concern was that heavy drug-pushers had infiltrated the Rastas and were offering cocaine and heroin in place of marijuana. However, much of his time was spent overseas, where he was using his music to act as an ambassador for peace.

One morning in September, 1980, Bob collapsed while out on a morning run. Doctors diagnosed a brain tumour. When conventional treatment did not seem to be working he was admitted to a clinic run by Josef Issells, a German doctor who employed radical treatment in cases of terminal cancer. Sadly, it was too late for Bob. The man who had practised healthy living as advocated by the Rastafarians died in 1981, eight months after his first collapse.

Thousands of people attended a Rastafarian service in Kingston, and as a Jamaican legend he was honoured with a full state funeral. Four of his children, billed as The Melody Makers, sang at an international reggae festival held in tribute to him in August, 1981.

There has been a considerable amount of legal dispute over Bob's worldly goods, with his mother, his wife, The Wailers and and Chris Blackwell all claiming their share.

But his music lives on through his children. Ziggy Marley and The Melody Makers will carry his name forward.

Ron 'Pigpen' McKernan

Full Name:	Ronald Charles McKernan
Born:	8 September, 1945, San Bruno, California, USA
Died:	8 March, 1973
Age:	27

Raised in the San Francisco Bay area of California, the son of an R&B disc jockey, 'Pigpen' began singing at school. By the age of sixteen, he knew that this was what he wanted to do with his life and he dropped out of school to follow his star.

A versatile musician, he played blues harmonica before meeting guitarist Jerry Garcia and switching to the organ. The two formed a group with several other musicians, including Bob Weir, rhythm guitar, Bill Kreutzmann, drums, and Phil Lesh on bass. Originally The Zodiacs, they became The Warlocks, and in 1965, The Grateful Dead.

Born of the folk music trend of the sixties, The Grateful Dead began as an electric R&B band. Introduced to LSD while still The Warlocks, they adapted their music to suit the hippie acid culture that was sweeping the area, changing their name with their style. They became the house band for Ken Kesey's famous Acid Test parties, gatherings where mass experimentation with LSD was practised, accompanied by dazzling light shows and explosive music.

And the Dead dropped acid along with everyone else. But Pigpen was one member of the band who didn't need drugs. Like his friend Janis Joplin he didn't like the disorientation associated with hallucinogenic drugs. Cheap wine and hard liquor were his poisons.

Live music was essential to the psychedelic lifestyle of the Bay area, and music flowed freely along with the drugs. The Dead, in their communal house at 710 Ashbury Street, were right in the heart of it, performing in spontaneous free-flowing jam sessions and giving numerous free concerts. Pigpen's bluesy forty-minute rendition of Wilson Pickett's 'In The Midnight Hour' became a favourite on the concert circuit.

Pigpen wasn't a hippy, however. Although in 1967 he was one of eleven arrested in the Haight Ashbury house for the possession of marijuana, he didn't take LSD. He didn't dress like a hippy, either. True, he wore his black hair long, but in all other respects he resembled a biker. He had swapped the cowboy hat of his early years for a biker's cap, wore a studded black leather jacket with Hell's Angels insignia (he was an honorary member), and sported a moustache and goatee beard.

Having established their reputation by appearing at live concerts, the Dead were finally offered a recording contract with Warner Brothers in 1967. Their début album, 'Grateful Dead', was too R&B in flavour for their public and didn't capture the true essence of their performance.

It wasn't until 1970, when the Dead's music began to reflect the changing mood of the time, that they achieved a more commercial success. It was the end of the hippy era and the band had abandoned their psychedelic sensitivity to return to their country roots. Deeply in debt to their record company, they were grateful for their new marketability.

By 1971, when their live album, 'Grateful Dead', was released, Pigpen was very ill. He had suffered the adverse effect of an inadvertently-taken heavy dose of LSD from a doctored drink can. When his friend Janis Joplin died in 1970, he sank into a depression. As a tribute to Janis, he pledged that he would 'sit back and get ripped on Southern Comfort', Janis's favourite drink. But he didn't really need any excuse. His heavy drinking had caught up with him anyway, leaving him with a severely damaged liver. He was forced to drop out of a European tour, and although he rejoined the band for a brief time, he was too weak to perform. Eventually he retired to devote himself to work on a solo album.

Sadly, it was never completed. As Pigpen wrote in one of his final songs, 'Don't make me live in this pain no longer You know I'm gettin' weaker, not stronger'. In March, 1973, his anguish ended. He died at the age of twenty-seven – the same age as Janis Joplin had been at the time of her death. The causes of Pigpen's death were stomach haemorrhages and acute liver failure. Always a big man, he had weighed 200 pounds before his illness: at the time of his death he was a shadow of his former self, weighing only 100 pounds.

But The Grateful Dead, with their ever-changing list of players, have remained one of rock's most popular live bands. Never achieving great commercial success, they still endure, giving freely of their time and talent to charities: Rainforest Action, Cultural Survival, Greenpeace and AIDS.

And theirs is probably one of the most highly-organised fan clubs of all times. Ninety thousands 'Deadheads' follow their heroes around the world to watch them perform.

In 1972, **Keith Godchaux** and his wife, Donna, joined The Grateful Dead, Keith replacing Pigpen on keyboards. In 1980, Keith followed Pigpen to untimely death when his car collided with a truck. He was two days past his thirty-second birthday.

Brent Mydland, who replaced Keith Godchaux, was the third ill-fated keyboard player with The Grateful Dead. He died in California, at the age of thirty-eight, from an overdose of morphine and cocaine.

Donny Hathaway

Full Name: Donny Pitts
Born: 1 October, 1945, Chicago, Illinois, USA
Died: 13 January, 1979
Age: 33

Donny Hathaway was raised in St Louis, his childhood steeped in gospel music. His grandmother sang, his parents sang and, inevitably, he sang. He studied music at Howard University, Washington DC, before becoming a professional musician.

Although he began his career as a producer-arranger, he enjoyed an early vocal début with singer June Conquest, billed as June and Donnie.

In 1969, a close friend, saxophonist King Curtis, introduced him to Atlantic Records, where he began to record as a solo artist. However, it was his duets with Roberta Flack that brought him to prominence. Donnie and Roberta had known each other since their days at Howard University, and when Atlantic teamed them together, they enjoyed an immediate rapport.

Their single, 'Where Is The Love' (1972), won them a Grammy Award for Best Pop Vocal Performance by a duo. Both the single and their album, 'Roberta Flack and Donny Hathaway' (1972) were Gold Records, selling over a million copies.

But Donny found the performing spotlight too glaring and decided to return to production. He set up his own company, working with such stars as Aretha Franklin and soul singer Jerry Butler. His friend King Curtis had been stabbed to death in a street fight and his own mental state was very fragile.

In 1978, Roberta Flack managed to coax him back into the studio. Their single, 'The Closer I Get To You' was a major success and they began to work on a new album.

Although Donny was prone to bouts of depression, it was nonetheless an enormous shock to his family and friends when he fell to his death from the window of his fifteenth-floor hotel room. The bedroom door was locked from the inside, and the verdict was suicide.

Roberta Flack was struck by grief and retired temporarily from the recording world. The album the two had been working on at the time of Donny's death, 'Roberta Flack Featuring Donny Hathaway', was released the following year and became another Gold Record.

Donny's wife, Eulalah, was an operatic soprano, so it is little wonder that their daughter, Lalah, is carrying the family's musical tradition forward. Her debut album, 'Lalah Hathaway' (1990), produced immediately following her graduation from music school, was released to critical acclaim.

Freddie Mercury

Real Name:	Farokh Bulsara
Born:	5 September, 1946, Zanzibar, Tanzania
Died:	25 November, 1991
Age:	45

Zanzibar conjures up images of the exotic, the mysterious and the glamorous. Freddie Mercury, one of its most famous sons, was all of these. A flamboyant, often outrageous, personality, he was the ultimate showman.

Freddie's early childhood was idyllic. He was brought up on this small island in the Indian Ocean, where life was relaxed and friendly. The children were free to roam happily on the golden sands and splash in the warm waters of the ocean. Nevertheless, in later life Freddie didn't like the sea, overcoming his fear only because of his love for the island of Ibiza.

Bomi Bulsara, Freddie's father, was an accountant for the British government (Zanzibar was still a British Protectorate). Both he and his wife, Jer, were of Persian descent and Parsees of the Zoroastrian religion, and raised their son as an orthodox member of their church. Zoroastrianism was the major pre-Islamic religion of

Persia. The Parsees fled from Persia following the Arab conquest in the eighth century AD, settling in India, where they were allowed to practise their religion without persecution.

At the age of five, Freddie was sent to Bombay to begin his education. Schooling there was of a very high standard, and the school he attended would rank alongside a typical British public school. In Bombay, Freddie received a good all-round education, enjoying the freedom of the city with its colourful bazaars. He excelled at art, literature and sports, particularly table-tennis and cricket. Piano lessons were part of the curriculum and Freddie manifested an early talent for music, enjoying classical Indian music as well as the small amount of rock 'n' roll that filtered through from the United States.

When Freddie was fourteen, his world changed dramatically. His father was transferred to Britain and the family settled in a small, semi-detached house in Feltham, Middlesex. What a contrast he found between the grey skies and dreary houses of suburbia and the sunshine and hustle and bustle of India! And at school here, Freddie was a misfit. Teased because of his strange accent, foreign appearance and buck teeth, he was a bird of paradise in a garden of sparrows.

In 1966, teenagers had come into their own. Girls were wearing mini-skirts and tons of make-up, and boys were into 'mod' gear too, hipster pants, Nehru jackets, high-heeled boots and long hair. Rock 'n' roll had crossed the Atlantic in earnest and teenagers were listening to The Beatles, The Rolling Stones and Jimi Hendrix.

Although Freddie enrolled at art school to study graphic design, he was already entertaining ideas of becoming a rock star. He was fascinated by the flamboyant wizardry of Jimi Hendrix and loved to imitate his singing. Unable to play the guitar, he sang and played the piano. He joined a blues band called Wreckage, running a bygone clothes stall in Kensington Market to augment his income.

In 1970, Brian May, a guitarist with a band called Smile, persuaded Freddie to join him and drummer Roger Taylor to form a group. The line-up was completed a year later by the recruitment of John Deacon on bass. Freddie had already chosen a name, Queen. In his words, 'The concept of Queen is to be regal and majestic. Glamour is a part of us, and we want to be dandy'.

It was during this period of his life that he met Mary Austin. Mary, who was to remain a close friend to the end of Freddie's life, worked in Barbara Hulanicki's Kensington boutique, Biba. Biba was *the* boutique of the sixties. Here, in the dark, womb-like atmosphere, the 'in' crowd could buy their exotic clothes and unusually-coloured cosmetics in green, aubergine and black.

Freddie and Mary moved in together, and Mary become an important part of his life. She guided his choice of clothes and stage gear, taught him make-up tricks and introduced him to the black nail polish that later became his trademark. Eventually Mary became his personal assistant, helping Freddie to develop into a polished performer and master of the theatrical.

Queen began their professional career by cutting demos at De Lane Lea Studios in return for testing new equipment. Two engineers at the studios, Roy Thomas Baker and John Anthony, were responsible for bringing them to the attention of Trident Audio Productions, which in turn led to a contract with EMI.

The group set to work to produce their first album, 'Queen'. However, audiences were not receptive to them, unsure of whether they were part of the new breed of glam rockers or a heavy metal band.

Freddie, meanwhile, had released a single, 'I Can Hear Music', under the name Larry Lurex. This and their debut single 'Keep Yourself Alive' didn't fare much better than their album, but Queen gained a lot of exposure on their first tour as support to Mott The Hoople. Freddie's extrovert nature and flamboyant stage presence singled him out as a star, but he wasn't the group's leader. Queen were the sum of the whole, each member contributing their own particular talent, and May's guitar-playing was as essential as Freddie's vocals.

In 1974, their second album, 'Queen II' was released. Through a stroke of luck, Queen were called to replace David Bowie on *Top of the Pops*. The single they performed, 'Seven Seas Of Rhye', a perfect blend of the band's hard rock and high camp style, became their first Top Ten hit.

Through the rest of that year, and the next, Queen climbed to international stardom with 'Killer Queen', 'Now I'm Here' and the seven-minute 'Bohemian Rhapsody'. Now considered a rock classic, 'Bohemian Rhapsody' was thought at the time to be too long for release as a single. But thanks to Capitol Radio DJ Kenny Everett, who played it repeatedly on air, it rushed to Number One in the charts and stayed there for nine weeks over Christmas, 1975.

A promotional video of 'Bohemian Rhapsody', made at a cost of £5,000, was also a great success and heralded a new industry for which Queen could take the credit. It was the dawning of a new age. Thereafter, no respectable pop group would consider launching a record without a promotional video to accompany it.

Freddie was a very private person and he tried to maintain a wall of secrecy around his life. His relationship with Mary Austin, after seven years of living together, had evolved into close friendship, and his homosexuality became common knowledge. He purchased a house in Kensington to which he could retreat and enjoy seclusion between the long, exhausting tours Queen undertook.

Tales of his excesses and extravagance spread. He enjoyed casual relationships and one-night stands, preferring not to become involved with his lovers. He became renowned for his promiscuity. He once boasted that he had had more lovers than Elizabeth Taylor. He loved Russian vodka and it was said that he could drink a bottle at a sitting. His cocaine-snorting was as legendary as his fabled, if somewhat vulgar, parties.

Freddie loved to throw parties, particularly theme parties. He thought nothing of hiring a plane to fly 1,000 guests to Ibiza for an evening, or Concorde for a sky-high party. Champagne and cocaine were free-flowing and Freddie's extravagance topped even that of the other great showbusiness party-giver, Alma Cogan, each occasion costing a mere £50,000. One of Freddie's most glamorous parties took place in 1986 at London's Roof Gardens club. The guest list was impressive, and included almost every name in the rock world. Naked girls, their bodies painted as works of art, served champagne and food. Another party had a 'hat' theme, and one featured flamenco dancers and a fireworks display that set the sky alight with his name.

Freddie was an innovator, constantly seeking to break new musical barriers. He stretched his vocal chords to the limit and consequently suffered frequent bouts of laryngitis. He learned to play the guitar and performed on Queen's 1979 release of the rockabilly number 'Crazy

Little Thing Called Love'. In 1976, he branched into production with Eddie Howell's 'Man From Manhattan' album.

His stage act never became dull. At the beginning of Queen's career, Freddie sported the long hair, flares and platform shoes that were in fashion. In the early eighties he changed his camp image for a new look. He cut his hair short, a moustache appeared above the famous teeth and his costumes became less elaborate. Still the message Freddie put across was gay. In liberal-minded Europe it was of no consequence, but in America his popularity dropped. Yet he claimed that some of his happiest days were spent in New York, which he dubbed 'sin city'.

In the late seventies, Queen went from strength to strength. They were constantly in the charts or on tour, and their soundtrack for the film *Flash Gordon* was a major achievement. But by 1983 they were exhausted, not only by the extensive tours, but also by the creative energy their music demanded. There were rumours of rifts in the group, but with four such highly-talented and volatile people working together, this was only to be expected. They were all feeling the strain, and decided to take a year off. Freddie, not one to be idle for long, used 1983 to begin work on a solo album.

By 1984 Queen were back in action with the release of 'Radio Ga Ga'. The video that accompanied this single was impressive, incorporating scenes from Fritz Lang's classic film *Metropolis*. An even more remarkable video accompanied their next release only two months later. 'I Want to Break Free' featured the group dressed in drag and was consummately professional. Queen had turned pop video-making into an art form.

A great deal of controversy lay in store for Queen in 1984. Freddie's obvious homosexuality had already diminished their popularity with conventional rock audiences in the United States, and then an ill-advised series of shows at the Sun City leisure complex in South Africa alienated many liberal-minded anti-apartheid fans. And when Freddie appeared in full drag on stage in Rio to perform 'I Want To Break Free', he was booed.

The Live Aid concert at Wembley (1985) was organised by Bob Geldof for famine-struck Ethiopia. Queen's appearance there was a triumph. Coming the year after the Sun City concerts, it did much to appease their detractors, and their popularity, which had slipped since their sabbatical in 1983, was once again sky-high.

Freddie always gave everything to his performance. His costumes ranged from the sublime to the ridiculous, from fur-trimmed crown and ermine robe to mascara and leotard, but the drama of his performances mesmerised the crowds. His charisma reached out and touched them, and they didn't care whether he wore sequins or singlets.

As the saying goes 'When the going gets tough, the tough go shopping', and this adage is certainly applicable to Freddie. His spending sprees were legendary. He had acquired a houseful of valuable antiques and one of the best fine art collections in the United Kingdom. He was also unfailingly generous with his friends and lovers, giving them expensive items such as cars and jewellery. It seemed as if he had everything in life that he could want, money, looks, talent and friends.

When, in 1985, it became apparent that AIDS was gaining a stranglehold on the gay community, Freddie changed his lifestyle. He gave up partying and promiscuity, adopting a quiet life in London with a regular boyfriend.

In 1987, he rose to a new challenge, bringing opera to

pop in a duet with opera *diva* Montserrat Caballe. He had composed 'Barcelona' to launch Barcelona's bid for the 1992 Olympics. Despite experiencing throat problems and having been advised not to sing, he appeared with Montserrat at the launch concert in October, 1988, miming to his own recording. Sadly, this was to be Freddie's last live concert appearance.

In 1988, when two of his friends died of AIDS, Freddie began to practise celibacy. But it was already apparent that he was not well. He had lost weight and appeared withdrawn. Rumours circulated that he was suffering from a 'mystery illness', usually a press euphemism for AIDS.

By the time 'Innuendo' was released in January, 1991, Freddie was looking gaunt and thin. He was rarely seen outside the ten-foot wall that surrounded his house, and was living as a recluse.

In November, Freddie broke his silence to announce to the world that he had AIDS. Twenty-four hours later, on 24 November, 1991, he died of bronchial pneumonia engendered by the disease. In the month before his death Queen had released the single 'The Show Must Go On', but for Freddie Mercury, the curtain had come down for the final time.

Fans came from all around the world to pay tribute, keeping an all-day vigil outside his house. Floral tributes poured in from thousands of friends and admirers. The funeral was a quiet and dignified affair, with two Parsee priests in white cotton robes conducting chants and prayers in the ancient language of the Zoroastrian religion.

Freddie once said: 'Excess is part of my nature. Dullness is a disease'. His life was full of excesses, and it was certainly never dull. He had expressed a wish to have all his treasures buried with him like the Pharoahs on Egypt, but was there a vault large enough?

For nearly twenty years Queen dominated the rock music world, selling over eighty million records. And, in December, 1991, 'Bohemian Rhapsody' was once again top of the charts. All proceeds from record sales were contributed to AIDS charities.

In April, 1992, a tribute concert, which is said to have raised over twenty million pounds for AIDS charities, was held in Freddie's honour. A crowd of 72,000 packed Wembley Stadium and rock stars from around the world participated. Elizabeth Taylor, one of the celebrities taking part, described Freddie as 'an extraordinary rock star who rushed across our cultural landscape like a comet. The bright light of his talent still exhilarates us, even now that his life has been cruelly extinguished'.

Freddie's composition 'Barcelona' opened the 1992 Olympic Games in that city.

There have been few showmen the like of Freddie Mercury, and he will be sorely missed.

Gram Parsons

Real Name:	Cecil Ingram Connor III
Born:	5 November, 1946, Winter Haven, Florida, USA
Died:	19 September, 1973
Age:	26

Gram Parsons was born Cecil Connor, the son of 'Coon Dog' Connor, a country and western singer. His mother, Avis, came from a wealthy Florida family, whose fortune stemmed from hard work, astute real estate acquisitions and the Florida citrus industry. Each member of the family had a trust fund set up for him that more than amply provided for his needs.

Gram's early years were spent in Waycross, Georgia, where his father worked in the family's timber plant. Waycross, a small town in the deep south, close to the wildly beautiful Okefenokee Swamp, had a strong church-going community. But beneath the surface ungodliness bubbled. There were rumours of wild parties, wife-swapping and alcoholism. Whether the Connors participated or not is unknown, but what is known is that Gram's mother had a drinking problem, even in those days.

The Connors lived in a comfortable house in the wealthy neighbourhood of the town, and Gram and his sister, young Avis, had all the material benefits that life could offer, including musical tuition. Like most wealthy families, the Connors boasted a piano, but Gram could also play the trumpet and drums. An instinctive musician, he improvised music in the style of Hank Williams, Elvis Presley, Buddy Holly, Jerry Lee Lewis and anyone else who was played on the radio.

The first major change in Gram's life came at the age of ten when he was sent as a boarder to a military school in Jacksonville, Florida. Then, when he was thirteen, his father committed suicide and the family moved back to Winter Haven, Florida.

Avis lost no time in remarrying. Her second husband, Robert Parsons, was a salesman, very slick and very handsome. He assumed responsibility for Gram and his sister, legally adopting them and latching firmly on to his wife's wealth.

A handsome and sensitive boy, Gram expressed the unhappiness he felt about these changes in his life through his music. He was popular at school and did well in his studies, but it was his music that brought him the most pleasure. A fellow student had taught him to play the guitar and he was adept at his Elvis Presley impersonation. Where Gram went, his guitar went, and the girls were never far behind. He had a good voice and he joined a country group, The Pacers, as a singer, developing his own singing style. A year later he became lead singer and rhythm guitarist with another group, The Legends.

Life at home was difficult. His stepfather was unfaithful and his mother was very unhappy. She was drinking heavily and had a permanent supply of prescription drugs on hand. Gram's first experimentation with drugs began in his mother's medicine cabinet.

In 1963, he joined a South Carolina folk group called The Shilos. They played the popular music of the day – Peter, Paul and Mary, the Kingston Trio and Woody Guthrie – interspersed with some of Gram's own compositions. Their opportunites were limited, however, by their age. Gram was still at school, they were under the legal age for signing a contract, and they missed an opportunity to appear on that great showcase for young talent, the *Ed Sullivan Show*. It fell to Gram's stepfather, Bob Parsons, to provide them with a venue. He opened a teen nightspot in Winter Haven expressly for Gram to display his talents.

Life had more shocks in store for Gram. On the day of his high school graduation, his mother died of alcohol poisoning. His stepfather was even suspected of smuggling bottles of whisky into her as she lay in her hospital bed because he was in a hurry to remarry! Then Gram was called before the draft board. The United States was in the thick of the Vietnam War and was calling up the cream of its young manhood to go and die for their country. Through the intervention of his stepfather Gram was declared 4F (unfit for service) and instead he enrolled at Harvard University to study theology.

However, Gram was a true child of the sixties. He found the university atmosphere too inhibiting and traditional and he dropped out, although not before he had established a new band, called The Like. Gram's first love had always been country music. He had abandoned it for folk music with The Shilos, but now he returned to it, although the influence of The Beatles' music could also be heard – and the influence of LSD, which Gram had first sampled at Harvard.

The band moved to New York, changing their name to The International Submarine Band. While they struggled to find their own sound, Gram's trust fund kept them afloat. They toured and played the clubs, even made one record, but they had no audience appeal. Easterners wanted to hear rock music, or even Indian music – Ravi Shankar was enjoying popularity – but not country.

In California, The Mamas And The Papas were big. So, too, were The Byrds, The Grateful Dead, Jefferson Airplane and Big Brother and The Holding Company with Janis Joplin. Gram decided that the International Submarine Band would find more success in this atmosphere and moved them out to the west coast. His decision may have been influenced by the fact that he had fallen in love with a Californian girl, Nancy Ross. Nancy had been introduced to him by his friend and sometime singing partner, actor Brandon deWilde.

Work was very sporadic, but Gram, decked out in full 'Hank Williams' cowboy regalia, was happy to play the country and western clubs. He still wanted to be a star in the traditional country and western style. The band's album, 'Safe At Home' (1967) was the first country album to include rock songs, but it wasn't a success. Gram decided it was time for him to move on again – courtesy of his trust fund, he had the freedom to walk away.

In 1968, he joined The Byrds, a folk-rock band whose hits included 'Mr Tambourine Man' (1965) and 'So You Want To Be A Rock 'n' Roll Star' (1967). Chris Hillman, singer and bassist with The Byrds, was to enjoy a long association with Gram.

Gram had a vision. He wanted to blend traditional country with rock music. Now, with the Byrds, he was given the opportunity. His first and only album with them, 'Sweetheart Of The Rodeo' (1968) was recognised as the first rock-based country album. It featured much of Gram's own work, including the haunting 'Hickory Wind'. Most of his vocals, however, had to be overdubbed because of a legal problem with his previous recording company.

Recognition of Gram's contribution to 'Sweetheart Of The Rodeo' was not forthcoming, and on the pretext of social conscience, he was once again ready to move on. As he had never before shown any political affiliations, it amazed everyone when Gram refused to accompany The Byrds on a tour of South Africa, claiming that he had always hated racial segregation. It was the end of his relationship with The Byrds.

Gram had also left his girlfriend and their daughter, Polly. Although he had arranged to marry Nancy, he wasn't ready to be tied down and pulled out at the last minute. Like his hero, Elvis Presley, he couldn't relate to the mother of his child as a love object.

Back in Los Angeles, Gram and Chris Hillman formed a new group with a wacky name, The Flying Burrito Brothers. Herb Alpert's label, A&M, who were looking for a more modern approach in their artists, signed them to a contract. Finally, Gram thought he had found the right creative atmosphere for his talents.

Still in pursuit of his dream of stardom, Gram insisted that the band dressed in eye-catching and colourful outfits. Not for them mundane jeans and cowboy boots: red roses, peacocks and submarines adorned their flamboyant outfits. Gram, who was heavily into drugs, even had the audacity to decorate his jacket with rhinestones in the form of the flowers and leaves of the cannabis plant.

Collaborating with Hillman, Gram wrote the début album for the Burrito Brothers, 'Gilded Palace Of Sin'

(1969). It was a triumphant blend of country and rock, and included the memorable song 'Sin City'. 'Gilded Palace Of Sin', despite the critical acclaim it received, didn't sell, but that was the least of A&M's problems.

The Flying Burrito Brothers didn't believe in rehearsals, and it showed. Gram's drug habit was completely out of hand. He was snorting cocaine openly, ingesting marijuana in cookies and popping downers, and his performance suffered accordingly. A tour of the United States was a disaster, and the band's first single, 'The Train Song', was unreleasable.

Gram, still cushioned by his trust fund, moved into a bungalow in the grounds of the exclusive Beverly Hills hotel, Château Marmont. The Château had seen many famous stars come and go, among them three who died drug-related deaths, Janis Joplin, Jim Morrison and John Belushi.

A&M finally managed to get the band back together and into the studio. Another album was produced, 'Burrito Deluxe' (1970) which included the successful track written by Mick Jagger and Keith Richard, 'Wild Horses'. But Gram wanted out. Although it was a buffer against reality, his wealth had robbed him of self-discipline and provided him with the means to buy a constant supply of drugs.

The year 1972 saw Gram with a wife, and back in the studio putting together a solo album. He had married a beautiful young blonde actress, Gretchen Burrell. Gretchen did her best to keep Gram off drugs, even following him into the studio to see that he remained clean. But he substituted alcohol for the drugs, and physically he was still a mess.

Then he discovered Emmylou Harris. Emmylou was a southern girl, struggling to make a living singing folk and country music in Washington DC. Gram was looking for a girl to sing duets with and Emmylou fitted the bill perfectly. The first album they made together, 'GP' (1973), with Emmylou's true, sweet tones providing the perfect foil for Gram's cracked vocal style, featured sentimental country music. It was well received by the critics but went virtually unnoticed by the public.

The tour that followed it was, in true Gram style, a disaster. He was falling apart. Drugs and alcohol had taken their toll and he was very overweight. He had to stuff his body into his clothes as Elvis did in his later years. His marriage was coming apart, too. He and Gretchen fought in public and private. And Gram was still taking drugs secretly. He pulled himself together for the recording of 'Grievous Angel'. This also featured Emmylou Harris, fuelling the rumours that the two were having an affair, although they both denied it.

When completed, this album was everything that Gram had been working towards. But his marriage was over and he filed for divorce from Gretchen. While waiting for the release of the album he decided to take a much-needed break from the world in the desert sanctuary of Joshua Tree, California.

Joshua Tree National Park stands in the high desert land where the Mojave Desert meets the Colorado Desert. This hot, arid region is the home of the Joshua tree, a weird and wonderful plant that provides nourishment and shelter for desert life. To this place Gram came when he was in need of peace and solitude.

On the night of 19 September, 1973, after consuming a lethal mixture of morphine, cocaine, amphetamines and tequila, Gram found eternal peace. The press release claimed that he died of heart failure, but in truth it was yet another life wasted by an overdose of drugs.

The circumstances surrounding Gram's final resting place are bizarre. Bob Parsons, his stepfather, claimed Gram's body and arranged for it to be shipped to New Orleans. Under Louisiana law, if Gram were proven to be a resident of the state Parsons could inherit his estate, and he was determined to do so.

But Phil Kaufman, Gram's friend and manager, had made a pact with Gram before his death. The first one to die was to bury the other at Joshua Tree. Phil rented a hearse, and with another friend, both posing as freelance undertakers, stole the body from Los Angeles International Airport and transported it back to Joshua Tree. Here, in the high, desert land, they set it alight and made a quick getaway.

Phil Kaufman was arrested and eventually fined several hundred dollars. In order to raise the money he gave a Gram Parsons funeral party, charging an admission fee of five dollars.

Bob Parsons reclaimed the remains of the body. A small gravestone marks the spot where they lie, in a quiet cemetery in New Orleans, a place with which Gram shares no history.

Gram once said that he liked to sit in the high land at Joshua Tree and imagine that he was a bird drifting above. A dedication has been inscribed on a rock by a faithful fan at this, Gram Parsons' unofficial resting place: 'A Bird Flying High Over The San Andreas Fault'.

With his death, Gram achieved the fame and recognition he sought for his work. His final album was released posthumously and was well received. Emmylou Harris has kept his music alive and become known as the 'keeper of the flame'. Her career has gone from strength to strength and she is still touring.

Gram's influence has been seen in the work of The Rolling Stones and Elvis Costello. Many songs have been written about him, and 'Sin City' is in the Smithsonian Collection of Classic Country Music. Gram Parsons has joined his heroes Hank Williams and Elvis Presley as a cult figure.

Duane Allman

Full Name:	Howard Duane Allman
Born:	20 November, 1946, Nashville, Tennessee, USA
Died:	29 October, 1971
Age:	24

Duane Allman was another son of the south. Although he was born in Tennessee, Duane and his younger brother, Gregg, were raised in Florida. Duane was only three when their father, an army officer home on Christmas leave from the Korean War, was murdered. Their mother moved the family to Daytona Beach, where she could more easily find work.

Both boys attended a military academy but Duane, always a loner and a rebel, hated it. The great love of his life was a motorcycle that he had acquired when he was only fourteen. Music first came into his life when Gregg taught him to play the guitar. They formed a duo playing rhythm and blues around the clubs. This first band was The Y-Teens, and it evolved through The Shufflers, The Escorts and The Houserockers before it finally metarmorphosed into The Allman Joys in 1966.

After touring for much of the year, the Allmans

found themselves in Los Angeles, where The Allman Joys became Hour Glass. Signed to the Liberty label, the band recorded two albums. But Duane was restless; he thought the two albums were inferior and best forgotten. And he felt that his creativity was being stifled.

Hour Glass broke up and the brothers returned to Florida. Duane became a session musician, working with many of the foremost artists of the day, such as King Curtis, Aretha Franklin and Wilson Pickett. It was Duane who suggested that Pickett record the Beatles song, 'Hey Jude', on which recording he played lead guitar.

Although he was still very young, Duane's reputation as a guitarist grew. Gregg, meanwhile, had returned to Los Angeles to record a solo album. The brothers had been committed to Liberty for one more album and Liberty were happy to have Gregg as a soloist. The arrangement suited Duane, too.

In 1969, Duane formed his own band with guitarist Dickey Betts, bassist Berry Oakley and drummers Jaimo Johanson and Butch Trucks. They lacked a lead singer, but Duane already had someone in mind. Gregg was called back from Los Angeles and The Allman Brothers Band came into being.

The appearance of the group was typical for a rock band in the late sixties. The groomed look of The Beatles and The Beach Boys was out of fashion, and in came unkempt shoulder-length hair, walrus moustaches, flared jeans, fringed jackets and, because they were southerners, cowboy boots. In their first year, they toured extensively, establishing themselves as the foremost southern rock band. They had novelty value too, because theirs was the first band to feature two lead guitars. And the dual guitars of Duane and Dickey Betts produced an exciting new sound.

Duane also continued to record as a session musician. Other considerations aside, the money was useful while the band was still establishing itself. King Curtis's single, 'Games People Play' (1970), on which Duane played guitar, won a Grammy for Best R&B Instrumental Performance, and Duane's slide guitar duet with Eric Clapton on the Derek and the Dominoes' album 'Layla' (1970), became one of Clapton's greatest hits. Duane's guitar-playing was at its peak and the Allman/Clapton duet was electrifying. Yet although it is now considered one of the greatest rock and blues albums ever recorded, at the time of its release, 'Layla' received little acclaim.

Meanwhile, The Allman Brothers Band had released their own debut album, 'Allman Brothers Band' (1969). But it was their second album, 'Idlewild South', (1970) that finally began to bring them recognition.

Duane was a true son of the rock 'n' roll era. He lived for speed, of any description. He had a heavy drug habit and he rode his beloved motorbike much too fast. It seemed certain that if one vice didn't kill him, the other would. In 1971, all the members of the band were arrested for possession of heroin and marijuana, and in later years it would be drugs that would cause the final split in The Allman Brothers Band.

The band's third album, 'Live at The Fillmore East' recorded live in New York, was an enormous success. But, sadly, it was Duane's last recording and he didn't live to see its triumph.

On 29 October, 1971, returning from Berry Oakley's house in Macon, Georgia, Duane swerved to avoid a truck and crashed his motorbike. He died of massive injuries three hours later in hospital. He was only twenty-four years old but already Duane Allman was celebrated as one of the great guitar heroes.

Duane was buried in Macon's Rose Hill Cemetery, the location of many of the band's nocturnal rehearsals.

On 11 November, 1972, on the same stretch of road, Duane's close friend, **Berry Oakley**, also twenty-four, met his fate. He crashed his motorbike into a bus and followed Duane to the Rose Hill Cemetery, where they lie side by side.

The band, united in their grief, carried on until 1975, when Gregg Allman testified at a drugs trial against their former manager. The rest of the band, seeing this as a betrayal, refused to work with him. However, they have since reformed and, in 1991, they were given a Comeback of the Year award.

Gregg Allman, briefly married to Cher, overcame his drug addiction to cocaine and heroin to follow a solo career, forming his own band, The Gregg Allman Band. In 1992, he made his film debut in 'Rush', for which the music provided by Eric Clapton.

Steve Marriott

Born: 30 January, 1947, London, England
Died: 20 April, 1991
Age: 44

Steve Marriott was always destined for a career in showbusiness. He attended the Italia Conti theatrical school and made his debut on the London stage as the Artful Dodger in Lionel Bart's hit musical *Oliver*.

When he was eighteen, he teamed up with fellow R&B enthusiasts Ronnie Lane (bass), Jimmy Winston (organ), and Kenny Jones (drums) to form a group. The mod youth culture was just getting into its stride in the mid-sixties. Modernists wore stylish clothes, preferably Italian, rode Lambretta motor scooters, worshipped speed (amphetamines), and loved black American rhythm and blues music. The group chose their name accordingly: The Small Faces were small in stature and they wanted to be 'faces', a mod idiom.

Formed in June, 1965, the group secured a contract with Decca only a couple of months later. Their first hit, 'Watcha Gonna Do About It', appeared in October. By the time their second record, 'Sha La La La Lee' (1966) appeared, the line-up had already changed, Winston having been replaced by Ian McLagan.

Steve loved to wear trendy gear and the group were soon hailed by teenagers as *the* mod group. The Small Faces went from strength to strength with their live performances. Steve and Ronnie Lane had also begun a songwriting partnership that later produced their hits 'Hey Girl' (1966), 'All Or Nothing' (their only Number One) and 'My Mind's Eye'. But the group were having problems with Decca, who wanted to remodel their image. The Small Faces had always been most happy performing live, enjoying a close rapport with their audiences. Now Decca wanted to polish and refine their sound. In 1967, they parted company with Decca and joined Andrew Loog Oldham's independent label, Immediate.

Drugs were very much a part of the youth culture of the sixties, despite the police force's crackdown on celebrity users. The group caused controversy with their single 'Here Comes The Nice' (1967), co-written by Steve, which alluded to amphetamines. It was one of the few drug-orientated rock numbers to get past the censors to be aired on the radio.

Their next single, 'Itchycoo Park', was a more complex and humorous affair altogether. It was a direct parody of Scott McKenzie's 'San Francisco (Be Sure To Wear Some Flowers In Your Hair)' and brought the group international recognition. 'Lazy Sunday' (1968), their next offering, with its strong rock beat, gave an indication that Steve wanted to break away from his teenage mod image and gain acceptance as a serious rock musician.

In 1968, he linked up with singer/guitarist Peter Frampton to form Humble Pie, a blues and rock band. The band had an immediate success with 'Natural Boogie', but it was their only hit. Frampton left to embark on a solo career and Steve went on to form Steve Marriott's All Stars.

A second release of 'Itchycoo Park', in 1976, relaunched The Small Faces and Steve reformed the group. But fame is very fickle and 'Lazy Sunday' didn't enjoy the same resurgence of interest as 'Itchycoo Park' had. The Small Faces went their separate ways once more, Steve to pursue a solo career.

For some years he kept the enthusiasm for R&B alive on London's pub and club circuit, returning to the studios for the rather disappointing album '30 Seconds to Midnight' (1989).

In 1991, Steve flew to the United States for a recording session with his ex-Humble Pie partner, Peter Frampton. He was on the brink of a new career. Returning to Britain, he spent an evening with friends before retiring to his sixteenth-century Essex cottage to sleep off his jet-lag. It is thought that he fell asleep with a cigarette in his hand and set the cottage on fire.

Death from carbon monoxide poisoning, due to smoke inhalation, was the post-mortem finding. There was no evidence of suicide and the coroner's verdict read accidental death, although traces of valium, alcohol and cocaine were discovered in the autopsy.

Rod Stewart, who joined the Faces when Steve quit in 1968, said, 'He was a great musician and a great bloke. Life deals some cruel blows'.

Marc Bolan

Real Name: Mark Feld
Born: 30 July, 1947, London, England
Died: 16 September, 1977
Age: 29

Marc Bolan was undoubtedly an original. Blessed with the elusive aura of star quality, he invented himself as a pop star, developing his singing voice, writing his own songs of magic and fantasy and giving his audiences what they wanted to hear. Although wordly-wise, he still maintained a fey and mystical quality.

Marc was born the son of a truck driver in London's east end. His mother ran a stall in a London street market and was Marc's firmest supporter in his quest for fame. Both his parents fostered his belief in himself, his father providing him with a drum set and his mother supplying a guitar.

He had a happy childhood but, being physically small, he had to learn to defend himself from an early age. Academically, he was very bright, but his active mind fluttered so quickly from subject to subject that he never attained very high grades at school.

It was of little consequence to young Marc. His true

love was rock 'n' roll and his ambition was to be a pop star. In secondary school he joined his first group, Susie And The Hoola Hoops. The singer was a young girl called Helen Shapiro, who became one of the first child rock stars, and a symbol to Marc of the success that he could attain.

He dropped out of school, and with the benefit of his pretty face and mod style of dress he quickly found work as a model. In his spare time he hung around the record shops and coffee bars and anywhere else that music was playing.

In these early days of his career, Marc's charm and overwhelming ambition served him well. He was generous with his sexual favours, sharing them equally between men and women, and soon he had a very wide acquaintance among showbusiness personalities, all of whom he hoped would assist his efforts.

Bob Dylan was his hero. With a cap perched on his mad mass of corkscrew hair, Marc determined to emulate Dylan's success. He toured the coffee bars, singing and playing the guitar and mouth organ. He cut one record under the name of Toby Tyler, but in 1965, when he moved to Decca, he became Marc Bowland (eventually contracted to Bolan).

Marc's first record, 'The Wizard', was not a success. Committed to his vision of fame, however, Marc engineered an audition for himself with producer Simon Napier Bell. Bell loved Marc's voice and elfin personality, although he felt that his guitar-playing needed some improvement. Nevertheless, he placed Marc as a guitarist with another group he managed, John's Children.

Much of Marc's time with this group was spent on the road and it gave him the opportunity to write his songs. But John's Children lacked the professionalism to perform the songs to his satisfaction. Marc realised that if he wanted to be a star it would not be as part of this group, and he quit.

With drummer Steve Peregrine Took, he formed his own group. Convinced that they would be a mega-success, he christened them Tyrannosaurus Rex.

The hippy era was in its prime. Marc, with his love for all things magical and mystical, became an exponent of flower power music. His initial concept of a powerful electric band had to be set aside because of a lack of equipment. Instead, taking up his acoustic guitar, with Took on the bongo drums, they began to play all the outdoor rock festivals. Marc became a familiar sight. Seated cross-legged on his Indian blanket, singing his tales of magic and enchantment, he looked rather like a pixie himself.

The producer Tony Visconti discovered him in 1968 and, entranced with the whimsical quality of the two, signed Tyrannosaurus Rex to a contract. Their first album, 'My People Were Fair And Had Sky In Their Hair, But Now They're Content To Wear Stars On Their Brows', put Marc on the path to stardom. The follow-up, 'Prophets, Seers And Sages, The Angels Of The Ages', was full of enchanted imagery. And the single 'One Inch Rock' showed that Marc was capable of producing a harder rock sound.

He had, in the meantime, met and moved in with June Child. The couple were deliriously happy in their one-room flat, existing on very little money, and June was a great help to Marc in his career. But he could be difficult to live with when his life wasn't going according to plan.

And it wasn't going according to plan in 1969. He had embarked on a tour of the United States, determined to be an international star. But he was disappointed. The hippy era was over in the States and the Americans did not understand the pixie-faced singer with the voluminous mass of hair.

Back home, Steve Peregrine Took, who was spaced out on drugs, was replaced by Mickey Finn. Marc bought an electric guitar and turned to the great guitar hero Eric Clapton for help with his technique.

The year of 1970 was a turning-point for Marc. He married June Child; he added a bassist, Steve Currie, and a drummer, Bill Legend, to the group; and he abbreviated their name to T. Rex, accepting that it would be easier for fans and disc jockeys alike to pronounce. Finally, he found the fame he sought in the singles charts with 'Ride A White Swan'.

Marc was in his element. He loved everything about success, the money, the adulation of his audiences and the acceptance by the entertainment world. But it had its downside, too. The money enabled him to indulge in more expensive pleasures – brandy and cocaine. His friends, alienated by his conceit, dropped away. Carried away by his own self-image and superstardom, Marc found himself surrounded by sycophants.

The 'T. Rex' album, released in 1971, was also a smash hit. Marc became a cult figure. Wherever he performed masses of screaming teenyboppers would appear. The glam and glitter rockers, David Bowie, Gary Glitter and Alvin Stardust, were just arriving on the scene, but Marc was the trail-blazer.

He was the first of his generation to go overboard with the make-up and put glitter on his face. As he strutted around the stage, 'Elvis Presley' fashion, in his satin jacket, his magnetic sex appeal brought hysterically screaming fans to their feet. Marc was riding high. Hit followed hit: 'Hot Love', 'Get It On', 'Electric Warrior', 'Metal Guru' and 'Born To Boogie'. His narcissism was at its peak. He preened and posed, loving to be looked at, photographed and adored.

He had been bitterly disappointed when major success on the other side of the Atlantic had eluded him, however. 'Get It On', retitled 'Bang A Gong' for the American market, did quite well, but Marc was still too effete for American tastes. Even his bold new 'electric' image didn't stand up well beside heavy rockers like The Grateful Dead. He was simply too *avant garde* for the United States.

By 1973, Marc's popularity was fading in Britain, too. Critics claimed that his work was repetitious and audience numbers dropped. In an effort to attract new audiences, Marc toned down his style of dressing and make-up, improved his material and added backing singers.

One of these vocalists was American singer/songwriter Gloria Jones. Marc had separated from his wife, June, although they remained friendly,. He and Gloria fell in love and moved in together. But as far as Marc's career was concerned, his magic seemed to have deserted him. He began to drink heavily and retreated to Monte Carlo for several months to hide out.

Not one to be out of the spotlight for long, Marc bounced back in 1975 with 'New York City', and turned his attention to television and videos. But the joy of his life at this time was his son by Gloria Jones, Roland.

By now punk rock was in its infancy and Marc was one of the first to realise its potential. He dyed a golden streak in his Medusa-style hair, assembled a new band of first-rate session musicians, recorded an album, 'Dandy

In The Underworld', and went on tour with a punk band, The Damned.

And a new career was waiting in the wings for him. He devised a television interview programme to introduce the new wave of punk rockers. His guests included David Bowie, The Boomtown Rats, Billy Idol's Generation X and The Jam.

Marc had always had a premonition that he wouldn't live to celebrate thirty and he was to be proved right. On 16 September, 1977, at five o'clock in the morning, he was returning home after an evening out. The car, driven by his girlfriend, Gloria Jones, swerved off the road and crashed into a tree, killing Marc instantly. He was just two weeks away from his thirtieth birthday. It was a strange twist of fate that Marc, who hated cars and never learned to drive, should die in a car crash.

Many famous stars and friends attended the funeral. David Bowie was there, and Rod Stewart, Alvin Stardust, The Damned and The Brotherhood of Man. Floral tributes poured in from those who could not be present. A giant swan, constructed entirely of white flowers, commemorated Marc's first hit, 'Ride A White Swan'.

The tree on Barnes Common where Marc lost his life serves as a shrine to those fans who gather there on the the anniversary of his death.

Steve Peregrine Took did not fare much better – he died of asphyxiation, in 1980, at the age of thirty-one.

Sandy Denny

Full Name:	Alexandra Elene Maclean Denny
Born:	6 January, 1947, Wimbledon, Surrey, England
Died:	21 April, 1978
Age:	31

Fairport Convention were an important British folk band. They were the first to set folk songs to rock music, and Sandy Denny contributed a great deal to this success.

She began her singing career on the traditional folk club circuit that had sprung up in the wake of Tom Paxton and Bob Dylan. A very pretty blonde girl from a comfortable middle-class background, she little resembled the rather unkempt, lank-haired young men with whom she sang. But she had an expressive voice with a wide musical range and was an asset to the folk scene.

After a short spell with The Strawbs, she replaced Judy Dyble in 1968 in the ever-changing line-up of Fairport Convention. Joining them when they were at their peak of productivity, Sandy had a profound influence on the group's music. Fairport Convention described themselves as having a country-American folkrock repertoire. Sandy, through her experience as a folk singer, was able to introduce more traditional English folk songs to the group.

Fairport Convention then released a trio of albums with Sandy as vocalist including 'Liege and Lief' (1969). It brought them enormous popularity and is regarded as *the* definitive British folk-rock album. It included a French version of a Bob Dylan song, '*Si Tu Dois Partir*', and the hauntingly beautiful 'Who Knows Where The Time Goes'. This was Sandy's own composition, and it was later a hit for Judy Collins.

In 1969, Sandy left Fairport Convention to form her own band with her boyfriend, Australian singer-guitarist Trevor Lucas. Sandy took the group, named Fotheringay for one of her best songs, on tour. But she had other interests, too. She produced a solo album, sang the Buddy Holly classic, 'Learning The Game', on a compilation folk-rock album, and duetted with Robert Plant on 'Led Zeppelin IV'.

When Lucas, by now Sandy's husband, joined Fairport Convention in 1972, there were inevitable separations. Unhappy with this arrangement, Sandy rejoined Fairport Convention on their world tour. But when financial difficulties tested personal relations within the band to the limit, Fairport Convention finally split up. Sandy, who wanted more control over the musical direction of her career, decided to go solo.

She retired temporarily for the birth of her daughter, returning to record her album 'Rendezvous' (1977). Only a few short months later, Sandy was dead, at the age of thirty-one. She had fallen down a flight of stairs and suffered a brain haemorrhage. At her funeral the plaintive notes of a lone piper mourned her passing with 'Flowers Of The Forest'.

Another great loss to Fairport Convention was **Martin Lamble**, their drummer. Returning from a gig one night in the band's van, Martin was killed in a motorway accident. He was only nineteen years old. The group threw themselves into their work to assuage their grief, producing that classic album, 'Liege and Lief'.

Keith Moon

Born:	23 August, 1947, London, England
Died:	7 September, 1978
Age:	31

Keith Moon was 'drummer extraordinaire' for the innovative sixties band The Who. Originally, a mod R&B band, The Who moved with the times, combining hard rock with anti-establishment lyrics to produce a solid string of hits.

Keith left school at the age of sixteen to follow a career in rock 'n' roll. He was a great fan of The Beach Boys and joined a surfin' band called The Beachcombers. In 1964, he became the drummer for a mod band, The High Numbers. Legend has it that Keith turned up drunk at a High Numbers gig and asked to sit in on their session. They were so impressed with his abandoned style of drumming that they asked him to join them.

The group consisted of guitarist Pete Townshend, vocalist Roger Daltrey and bassist John Entwistle. Their first record, for Fontana, 'I'm The Face!' was not a success. Undiscouraged, they took on new management, a new image and a new name, The Who.

The Who's new image involved a smash-up stage act.

They smashed up their guitars, their amplifiers and Keith's drum kit. It was an expensive exercise, but a worthwhile one: audiences were fascinated, and by the time The Who released their first record, 'I Can't Explain' (1965), they already had a large following among young people.

Two more hits in the first year, 'Anyway, Anyhow, Anywhere' and 'My Generation', consolidated their success. And they performed live extensively, expanding their fame.

There were frequent power struggles and squabbles in the group. Townshend was anti everything that wasn't young or radical. Daltrey threatened to quit because he didn't like the onstage violence. On one occasion, Keith was late for a gig. When he walked on stage, Townshend attacked him with his guitar, giving him a black eye. And Keith considered life one long party, of which drink, drugs and groupies were essential ingredients.

Dubbed 'Moon the Loon' because of his crazy behaviour, Keith's antics were not confined to his stage act. The tales of his escapades were legion. The Who were founder members of the 'hotel wreckers' brigade and Keith was the instigator. It all began on their exhausting tour of the United States in 1967. Like most other British groups, they wanted to break into the lucrative American market and were willing to give their all. The hours were long and arduous and the group spent all their time either in hotel rooms or performing. Keith developed a reputation for being a destructive force. Under the influence of drugs and alcohol he found it entertaining, to destroy hotel rooms. He threw television sets out of windows, exploded fireworks in bathrooms and took furniture apart, stick by stick. When Jimi Hendrix set his guitar alight at the Monterey Pop Festival, Keith vied with him by smashing into his drum kit and kicking the whole lot over.

He also had a propensity for practical jokes which involved itching powder, stink bombs and other childish gags. Even his beautiful Rolls Royce once ended up parked in his swimming pool. Keith loved dressing up and could be very offensive, such as when he paraded in the strongly Jewish Golders Green district of London in a Nazi uniform. While on their tour of the United States, The Who were invited to perform on The Smothers Brothers' television show. Keith exploded flash powder in his drum kit, leaving Townshend with singed hair and the other guests on the show in shock. Nevertheless, they were a huge success in America – although they were not welcome in many hotels.

In 1969, The Who revolutionized rock 'n' roll with the release of Townshend's pop opera, *Tommy*. Coming as it did so long before Freddie Mercury's venture into the operatic world, it opened new vistas for music-lovers. *Tommy* told the story of a deaf, dumb and blind boy who was a pinball wizard. It was critically acclaimed and The Who took it on another highly-successful tour of the United States.

Keith had secretly married in 1966, but he saw this as no obstacle to his wild lifestyle. However, in 1970, he was involved in a tragic accident that altered his outlook on life. He and his wife were leaving a disco in Keith's purple Rolls Royce when they were accosted by a gang of youths. Keith's chauffeur left the car to reason with them. Keith, who didn't drive, moved into the driving seat. He started the car up, inadvertently running over and killing his chauffeur in the process. He was charged with drunk driving but was given an absolute discharge although the incident was always to play on his conscience.

In need of a new career direction, Keith branched out into films, appearing in *That'll Be The Day* (1972), *Stardust* (1974) and *Tommy* (1975). But these were troubled years. He and his wife had separated; his solo album, 'Two Sides Of The Moon' (1975) was a disaster and he was drinking heavily. He still performed live with The Who but he was showing the effects of alcohol. He was tired, ageing and overweight, and had attempted suicide on at least four occasions.

On 8 September, 1978, after an evening spent with some friends to celebrate Buddy Holly week, Keith died of an overdose of heminevrin, a prescription drug that is often used to overcome alcoholism. By a macabre coincidence, he died in the flat in which Cass Elliott had lost her life four years earlier.

The Who have continued to play on. They have replaced their drummer several times, but there was only one Keith Moon, the ultimate rock 'n' roll drummer.

Kit Lambert was The Who's manager in the early days. The son of an alcoholic composer, Kit seemed bent on following in his father's footsteps, and cocaine, heroin and alcohol were all part of his lifestyle. When his services as manager to The Who were no longer required, he became a complete eccentric. He moved to Venice, bought himself a *palazzo* and called himself Baron Lambert.

In 1981, when he was forty-five years old, Kit fell downstairs at his mother's London home. He died three days later with significant levels of drugs and alcohol still in his body.

John Bonham

Full Name:	John Henry Bonham
Born:	31 May, 1948, Redditch, Worcestershire, England
Died:	25 September, 1980
Age:	36

If Keith Moon was the ultimate rock 'n' roll drummer, then John Bonham filled the same bill for heavy metal. A larger-than-life character, he was a heavy hitter in every sense of the word. He hit his drums with massive strength and stamina, playing solos with his fists. And he hit the bottle with all the enthusiasm of hedonist.

Born and raised in Worcestershire, John looked destined to follow in his father's footsteps as a builder and carpenter. But fate stepped in. John discovered drumming. At the age of five he had begun hammering on his mother's kitchen utensils. At fifteen he was the proud possessor of his first drum kit. There was never any doubt in his mind that drumming was what he was meant to do. And he reasoned that if it didn't work out, he could always fall back on the building trade.

John began his professional career with the Birmingham-based R&B group Band Of Joy. But he was too loud and overwhelming for Birmingham audiences and he moved south. Life on the club circuit in the south was more lucrative anyway.

In 1968, John was invited by another Brummie, ex-Band Of Joy vocalist Robert Plant, to join him in The New Yardbirds. Their line-up consisted of John on drums, Robert Plant as vocalist, Jimmy Page on guitar and John Paul Jones on bass. Between the four of them they could produce a lot of volume!

After their first tour, of Scandinavia, The New Yardbirds adopted a more arresting name. They became Led Zeppelin, a name, legend has it, supplied by loony Who drummer Keith Moon, who described disastrous gigs as having gone down 'like a lead Zeppelin'. This was one Zeppelin that wasn't going down – on the contrary, it was well on its way up.

Although the quality of their recorded performances was never quite to match that of their live appearances, their debut album, 'Led Zeppelin' (1969), was an enormous success. They toured extensively on both sides of the Atlantic to promote both this and their second album, 'Led Zeppelin II' (also 1969), which hit Number One in Britain and the United States.

Suddenly, Led Zeppelin were creating a stir wherever they went. Their performances were wildly explosive and, because they whipped their fans into a frenzy, concerts usually ended in riots. They left a trail of destruction behind them in hotels, too, equalling that left by another British band, The Who. They threw television sets out of top-floor rooms into the sea, and on one occasion, John sliced a Tokyo hotel room to pieces with a Samurai sword.

In fact, John had a great deal in common with his friend Keith Moon. They both loved practical jokes and John's exploits became so legendary that he was eventually banned from all the top London hotels. He drank heavily, too. It soothed his stage fright and helped to while away the long monotonous hours on the road. Once he staggered drunk on to the stage at a Deep Purple concert and insulted their guitarist. He put so much energy into his performances that his health began to suffer. It became necessary for him to travel with a doctor present.

And it began to seem as if the band was jinxed. Rumours abounded that Page's fascination for the Occult was responsible for many of the untoward incidents that befell Led Zeppelin.

In 1970, Robert Plant was involved in a car accident and suffered facial injuries. Later that year, on a European tour, a member of the aristocratic von Zeppelin family threatened legal action if the band used their name in Denmark. They were forced to play a Danish concert under another name, The Nobs.

In 1975, Robert Plant and his wife were involved in another near-fatal car crash. And not long after that, their five-year-old son died suddenly of a viral infection. Then two other people, Keith Harwood and Keith Relf, who were tenuously linked with the group, died in mysterious circumstances. John broke three ribs in a car crash, and he and the group's manager, Peter Grant, were arrested in the United States and charged with assaulting a security guard.

Robert Plant and his wife were suffering from shock over their son's death, and the extensive worldwide tours, as well as his drinking, had taken a toll on John's health. John and Jimmy Page, as well as most of the road crew, were reported to be heroin addicts. John wanted to spend more time at home with his wife and family. In 1977, therefore, Led Zeppelin decided to take a break. John made the most of these months, working on his farm and indulging his love of fast and powerful cars.

Led Zeppelin were still proving a commercial success despite the band's personal troubles. If Page jinxed the band, he also influenced the music. His mysticism was especially evident in Led Zepplin IV, which included the classic single 'Stairway to Heaven'. The single became a popular finale at The Doors' concerts.

In September, 1980, it was back to work. The band gathered at Page's Windsor mansion to rehearse for their forthcoming tour of the United States. John, in his customary manner, had been drinking vodka all day, and he carried on well into the evening, when he had to be helped to bed. It was not until the following day that his body was discovered. Like Jimi Hendrix, he had choked on his own vomit.

The coroner's report stated that John had the equivalent of seven measures of vodka in his system. He died as he had lived, over-indulging himself. Without his pounding rhythms and larger-than-life presence, Led Zeppelin disbanded, and the other members of the band pursued solo careers.

In 1990 they were reunited for a five-hour session. The occasion was the wedding of John's son, Jason. Jason, also a drummer, sat in for his father with those pioneers of progressive rock, Led Zeppelin.

Ronnie Van Zant

Born: 15 January, 1949, Jacksonville, Florida, USA
Died: 20 October, 1977
Age: 28

Ronnie Van Zant was the eldest of three bothers, Ronnie, Donnie and Johnny. Their father was a great music-lover and the boys were raised in Florida to the beat of folk and blues music.

In high school, Ronnie and two of his friends, Gary Rossington and Allen Collins, formed their first group, My Backyard. Ronnie, a self-confident young man, took on lead vocals and songwriting, with Rossington and Collins on guitar.

In appearance they were much like other bands of the day. The Beatles influence had arrived in Florida and long hair was in. All the members of My Backyard had exceptionally long hair, a feature that one of their teachers, Leonard Skinner, did not appreciate – gym teachers in the sixties were notorious for objecting to this new trend. And Leonard Skinner made life difficult for the band, penalising them when he could. Little did he know that one day a corruption of his name would be used to identify one of the south's best rock bands.

My Backyard started out touring the clubs and bars of the southern states. In 1972, they were discovered in an Atlanta bar by Al Kooper, an ex-Blood, Sweat And Tears member, who was trying to get his own label, Sounds of the South, off the ground.

Changing their name to Lynyrd Skynyrd (after the hapless Leonard Skinner), they produced their first album, entitled 'Pronounced Leh-nerd Skin-nerd' (1973). It was a runaway success. By far the best, and most popular, track on the album was 'Freebird', a tribute to Duane Allman. The Allman Brothers Band had been the foremost southern rock group until the death of Duane, and Ronnie wanted his group to surpass them.

Determined that they would succeed, the band went on the road, initially supporting The Who. In their years together Lynyrd Skynyrd were to notch up the enviable record of over 2,000 live performances. Ronnie, who had fallen easily into his role as leader of the band, often liked to escape to the peace of the Florida wilds to write his songs.

Although these songs attacked bigotry and drugs, make no mistake, these were not nice guys! They were 'good ole boys' from the south, and they liked rough living, fist-fighting and drinking. Ronnie was arrested on numerous occasions for brawling, and they wrecked hotel rooms and cars. There were frequent tales of infighting in the band and members came and went.

Because of their high profile on the concert circuit, Lynyrd Skynyrd were now one of the most popular live bands, and their albums, eulogising the macho lifestyle of the southern male, sold well. After the release of their second album, however, they changed labels. Producer

Tom Dowd took over. But the two albums he produced lacked the hard rock sound that the previous ones had. Taking a revolutionary step, they added a third guitarist, Steve Gaines.

Exhaustion, always a major problem for a rock 'n' roll band, overtook them and, in 1976, they took some time off. But they continued to work on their new album. 'Street Survivors' was the studio debut of their third guitarist, Steve Gaines, and it looked like being their best album ever.

But before it could be released, tragedy struck. In October, 1977, the band, refreshed from their break, embarked on yet another round of live performances. Experts by now at getting from gig to gig, they chartered their own plane. En route to Baton Rouge, Louisiana, the plane crashed in swampland, killing Ronnie Van Zant instantly. Also to die were Steve Gaines, his sister Cassie, a backing singer with the group, Dean Kilpatrick, their manager, and two members of the crew. Allegations that as the plane had not caught fire it had run out of fuel, or that it was not airworthy, were never authenticated.

Ronnie Van Zant was buried in Jacksonville, Florida. 'Freebird', the number he wrote as a tribute to Duane Allman, was played in dedication to him. Strangely, in 1982, the marble headstone, weighing over three hundred pounds, was stolen from Ronnie's grave, although it was later found nearby.

'Street Survivors', their final album, had to be recalled because the sleeve, rather tastelessly, in view of the turn of events, depicted the band surrounded by a sheet of flame.

Collins, who had survived the crash, lost his wife in 1980 and his girlfriend in 1986, and, in 1990, he himself died of pneumonia. Both Donnie and Johnny Van Zant are musicians, keeping the family name alive. Johnny has recently appeared with a reformed Lynyrd Skynyrd and Donnie performs with a heavy metal band.

Karen Carpenter

Born: 2 March, 1950, New Haven, Connecticut, USA
Died: 4 February, 1983
Age: 32

Karen Carpenter was the product of a happy and close-knit middle-class family. Although she was born in the eastern United States, her father's job took them to the west coast in 1963. They settled in the pleasant California suburb of Downey, but Karen always dreamed that one day she would return to live in Connecticut.

Richard, Karen's brother, showed considerable musical talent and he began studying classical piano as a child. Karen herself also possessed natural musical ability, and wanted to take up an instrument. Refusing to conform to a feminine stereotype, she chose the drums.

When Richard formed an instrumental jazz trio, Karen joined him on drums, and a friend, Wes Jacobs, on bass. In 1966, they won first prize at the Hollywood Bowl Battle of Bands. They also won a recording contract with RCA, although little came of it.

Jacobs left the trio to study music and Richard, aiming

to use original compositions and complex arrangements, formed a folk-rock band called Spectrum. Spectrum was very short-lived, however. It was 1968 and musical trends had changed. Groups like The Doors were playing the same clubs as Spectrum, and offering rock 'n' roll.

Never one to be discouraged, Richard developed a more mainstream sound, persuading Karen to do vocals. Karen's voice was wonderful, velvet-smooth, perfectly pitched and expressive. The harmonies Richard achieved with his arrangements were quite outstanding.

In 1969 they met the forward-thinking record producer Herb Alpert. Realising the potential of The Carpenters' music, he signed them to a contract, and allowed them the freedom to develop the unique sound that was to bring them international fame.

Their début album for A&M was not a great success. Critics lambasted them as middle-of-the-road, out-of-date and out of touch. But Herb Alpert persisted. Their second album, 'Close To You' (1970), rewarded his patience with two hit songs, the title track and 'We've Only Just Begun'.

Richard's friend John Bettis, who had also been a member of Spectrum, was now writing lyrics to accompany Richard's music and skilful arrangements. The result was dynamite. A string of hits followed: 'For All We Know', 'Rainy Days And Mondays', 'Superstar', 'Hurting Each Other', 'Sing', 'Yesterday Once More', 'Top Of The World' and 'Please Mr Postman'. They won three Grammies, Best Contemporary Performance by a Group, Best New Artist and Best Pop Vocal Performance by a Group.

But it was apparent that Karen's health was suffering. Since the early days of their career she had been obsessed with her weight. She believed that it wasn't possible to be too thin. Despite her lovely face and slim figure she was convinced that she was fat. She embarked on one diet after another, and as the weight dropped away from her, her family became very concerned.

It was a vicious circle. The more concerned her family became, the more Karen found their attention stifling. She felt that she could never live up to her mother's expectations and that she had no control over her own life. The only facet of her life over which she did have control was her ability to lose weight. In 1974, she took her first independent step and moved out of the family home.

Richard, too, felt the demands of their fame, resorting to prescription drugs, quaaludes to relieve the pressure. In 1975, severely underweight and exhausted by their hectic schedule, Karen collapsed. Her family rallied round, and after two months' recuperation she had regained some weight. The Carpenters returned to work, although they slowed down their frenetic work pace.

However, their popularity seemed to be on the decline. They were aggravated when the critics labelled them as bland, wholesome, squeaky-clean and whiter than white. All of this made them seem boring, which was quite patently not true. Their sound had mellowed and they were consummately professional. Their 1977 release, 'Calling Occupants Of Interplanetary Craft', a triumphant blend of Karen's melodious vocals and Richard's piano arrangements, illustrated their all-round appeal.

In 1978, Richard collapsed and was hospitalised for several months. His dependence on prescription drugs, which enabled him to survive the killing pace of their lives and his own relentless quest for perfection, had caught up with him. Karen took this opportunity to produce a solo album. But when Richard was discharged from hospital she rejoined him in the studio and her album was never released.

Karen had never had much time in her life for romance, and most of the men she did meet were overawed by her image. Finally, in 1980, she thought she had found the man of her dreams, a real estate developer named Tom Burris. But the marriage was brief and a complete disaster. It was impossible for them to conduct a normal marriage in the constant glare of the public eye, and Karen continued to work exhaustingly long hours. Their divorce was inevitable.

Once again Karen's weight was causing her family concern. Finally, she voluntarily entered therapy. Her condition, anorexia nervosa, was relatively unknown at the time, but Karen was fortunate in her choice of medical advisors. She began to gain weight and seemed to have her anorexia under control.

But the long battle had weakened her heart. In February, 1983, Karen suffered a cardiac arrest and died at her parent's home in Downey, California. All attempts to revive her were in vain. She was only thirty-two years old.

Karen's story is one of the most tragic in popular music. She was not bent on self-destruction, as so many rock stars seemed to be, she was merely a lost soul crying out for love and understanding. And she was the victim of modern society's obsession with slimming.

Two films have been produced about Karen's life, one The Karen Carpenter Story, by CBS, under the guidance of her brother, Richard. The other, which shall remain nameless, is a totally tasteless affair, depicting Karen and her brother as Barbie and Ken dolls.

Richard Carpenter produced a solo album, 'Time', in

1987, with guest vocalists Dusty Springfield and Dionne Warwick, and in 1989 an album, 'Lovelines', featuring previously unreleased Carpenters recordings, appeared.

The music of The Carpenters has proved timeless. Theirs was a triumph over the generation gap, uniting young and old, rock and pop fan. Karen Carpenter put her heart into her singing. The loss of her sweet, true voice leaves a void that has yet to be filled.

Paul Kossoff

Born: 14 September, 1950, London, England
Died: 19 March, 1976
Age: 25

Paul Kossoff should have been quite at ease with showbusiness. His father, David Kossoff, was a well-known film actor and Paul was raised in a theatrical atmosphere. However, he himself was an introverted character. He decided to train in classical music – until he saw Eric Clapton perform, that is. Then he knew that the guitar, and the blues music of black America, were for him.

His first band, Black Cat Bones, played in clubs up and down the United Kingdom. But Paul sought new horizons, and in 1968, he and Simon Kirke, the drummer, broke away to form a band in the style of Cream, Eric Clapton's blues-based rock band. With the aid of their mentor, Alexis Korner, the R&B band leader, Paul organised a new line-up. It comprised himself, Kirke, Andy Fraser on bass and Paul Rodgers on vocals. Korner gave them their name, Free, after his own sixties trio, Free At Last.

Free's first album, 'Tons Of Sobs' was released

and virtually ignored. But the band soon gained an international reputation through their extensive touring, sometimes playing as many as seven nights a week.

Success arrived with the release of the single 'All Right Now' (1970). But with success came trouble. There were new pressures for Paul. Being the son of a famous father was stressful enough, but coping with his own fame was worse. Coupled with a punishing touring schedule and the need to produce another hit, it was all too much for Paul. He turned to drugs, seeking relief from the tension.

Rifts began to appear among the band members. The more disagreements there were, the more Paul used drugs to escape the acrimony. When Free's single 'Stealer' failed to reach the heights of its predecessor, the band split up.

Paul was much in demand as a session musician, and he linked up with John 'Rabbit' Bundrick, a Texan keyboard player, Tetsu Yamauchi, a Japanese bassist, and his old friend Simon Kirke to produce the album 'Kossoff, Kirke, Tetsu and Rabbit' (1971).

In 1972, in a show of unity, Free reformed. Paul was obviously addicted to heroin by now, and the band hoped that with their support he could kick the habit. Paul played on the reunion album 'Free At Last'. But his behaviour was very erratic and he was forced to withdraw from a Japanese tour because of ill health caused by his drug abuse.

When he was back on his feet again, he officially left Free and began a solo career, recording the album, 'Back Street Crawler'. He made a determined effort to kick his heroin addiction. In 1974, he formed his own band, named Back Street Crawler after his solo album, and triumphantly announced that he had 'killed the drug habit'.

A tour of the United Kingdom was announced, but before it could begin Paul suffered a massive heart attack.

Unwilling to disappoint his fans, he forced himself to carry out his commitments. But he looked very ill and his speech was slurred. At one concert he stumbled around, seemingly unaware of his surroundings, and played out of tune.

Nevertheless, he kept going. Then, in March, 1976, he took a plane to New York for discussions with a record company. He never reached his destination, suffering a coronary on board the plane.

As a result of his drug abuse, Paul Kossoff died at the age of twenty-five, another victim of the self-destructive rock lifestyle. David Kossoff, his father, has continued the fight against drug abuse.

An album, 'Koss', released in 1977, contains the best of Paul's work.

Tommy Bolin

Born: 1 August, 1951, Sioux City, Iowa, USA
Died: 4 December, 1976
Age: 25

Tommy Bolin was another sad victim of the 'too much, too soon and too fast' lifestyle. A guitar hero and prolific composer, he seemed destined for a brilliant future.

Born and raised in middle America, Tommy resembled those handsome Sioux braves after which his home town was named. Like many other teenage boys of his time, he grew his hair long. Then he was expelled from school for refusing to cut it.

Blessed with innate musical ability, Tommy could play drums, keyboard and guitar. Fame came easily to him: he began playing the guitar with a succession of bands and had cut his first album, 'Zephyr', when he was only eighteen. After that he was never short of work. He was highly regarded by his fellow musicians as a jazz-rock guitarist and, in 1973, he joined The James Gang. A greater honour awaited him in 1975, when he was asked to replace the legendary Ritchie Blackmore in Deep Purple.

Tommy was ecstatic. But Deep Purple were already in trouble. There were personality clashes among their superstar egos, and Tommy's heavy drinking and drug-taking didn't help. After the disappointing release of 'Come Taste The Band', the album on which he made his début, Deep Purple disbanded.

On his own again, Tommy formed another band and returned to his native land to tour. But on 4 December, 1976, he died in a Miami hotel room from an overdose of heroin, alcohol, cocaine and barbiturates. He was only twenty-five.

Phil Lynott

Full Name:	Philip Lynott
Born:	20 August, 1951, Dublin, Eire
Died:	4 January, 1986
Age:	34

Phil Lynott was born of a black Brazilian father and an Irish mother: an irresistible combination of music and charm. His father deserted them when Phil was just a baby. Bringing up a child as a single-parent was tough enough in those days, even tougher when the baby was black. So Philomena, Phil's mother, turned the care of the young boy over to her own mother, Sarah, and moved to Manchester in search of work.

Full of personality, Phil was a handful for his grandmother. And, living in a tough area, he had to learn to defend himself at an early age. Like Bob Marley, he saw music as a means of escape. As soon as he was old enough, he joined The Black Eagles, a local R&B band, as a vocalist.

The Black Eagles proved to be Phil's stepping-stone to a better life. When the band broke up, he wasn't disheartened but moved on to join another group, Skid Row. Here he learned to play bass guitar and discovered that he had the ability to write songs. Leaving Skid Row, Phil formed his own group, Orphanage, with drummer Brian Downey and guitarist Eric Bell.

The three worked well together, building themselves a reputation as one of the top live Irish bands. After their first hit, 'Morning Dew', they decided on a change of name. With a great deal of difficulty, they finally selected the name of a comic-book hero, Tin Lizzy, adding an 'h' as a touch of humour.

In 1970, Thin Lizzy were signed up by Decca and moved to London. Their success in Ireland was not instantly repeated in Britain, however. Their first album was a dismal flop. So, too, were their first tour of the United Kingdom and their second album. But Phil wanted to be a star, and he drove the others on. In 1973, his persistence paid off when 'Whiskey In The Jar', a rock version of a folk song, hit the charts.

Phil had gained some valuable lessons in showmanship. He had learned how to dress up the band's image in general and his own image in particular, emphasising his similarity to Jimi Hendrix. He had also learned that drugs helped survival on the road. He also knew how to manage members of the band. Even so, Eric Bell left the group and was replaced by Gary Moore.

Hard rock, LSD, cannabis, booze and girls were the order of the day on tour. The members of Thin Lizzy steadfastly enjoyed them all, except for Moore, who wanted to work, not party. He quit after only four months; then Brian Downey left and Phil realised the major problems that faced him in his search for stardom.

It was Phil, with his determination to succeed, and as the songwriter of the group, who held Thin Lizzy together. The responsibility for the band's presentation also rested with him. Now he recruited two guitarists, Scott Gorham and Brian Robertson, to cover himself should one drop out. But still the full measure of fame eluded them.

In 1976, Thin Lizzy's single 'The Boys Are Back In Town' finally signalled their arrival as international superstars. But their troubles were not over. One of the guitarists cut his hand in a brawl and had to be replaced. Then Phil contracted hepatitis and a tour of the United States had to be cancelled, damaging their credibility as a band.

Advised by doctors to give up drugs, sex and alcohol, Phil slowed down for a while. He had his hands full enough dealing with the various temperaments within the band, not to mention the musical chairs. Gary Moore had replaced Brian Robertson, then he dropped out, and was replaced by Midge Ure, then Dave Flett, and later Snowy White. Brian Downey left briefly and was replaced by Mark Nauseef. When Scott Gorham also announced his intention of leaving, Phil knew that the band's days were numbered.

In 1980, Phil married Caroline Crowther, the daughter of British comedian Leslie Crowther, and began a solo career. His first album, 'Solo In Soho' was a moderate success. But his life did not have the stability he needed and once again he became dependent on drugs and alcohol.

With the release of his second album, it was obvious that his career was in decline. His marital, drink and drug problems were attracting more media attention than his music. On Christmas Day, 1985, Phil fell into a coma induced by a drug overdose. Ten days later, on 4 January, he died of liver, kidney and heart failure and pneumonia.

Phil Lynott was a charismatic and talented musician. In the years that have followed his death, Thin Lizzy's work has stood the test of time and is now more appreciated than it was during his lifetime.

Stevie Ray Vaughan

Born: 3 October, 1954, Dallas, Texas, USA
Died: 27 August, 1990
Age: 35

Stevie Ray Vaughan was born in Texas, the son of Big Jim and Martha Vaughan. Stevie Ray's elder brother, Jimmie, a great guitar enthusiast, owned an extensive record collection which included all the great guitar heros of the time, B.B. King, Albert King and Django Reinhardt, and Stevie Ray loved to listen to them.

Stevie Ray wanted to be a drummer or saxophonist, but as neither instrument was available to him he had to be satisfied with his brother's guitars. However, as soon as he picked one up he knew that the guitar was his instrument. The brothers were close, and it was Jimmie who gave Stevie Ray his first electric guitar.

When he was eight, Stevie Ray taught himself to play the guitar and quickly became hooked on the blues, listening to records to improve his technique. By the age of fourteen he had joined his first band, an R&B group called Blackbird. In high school he played with the Chantones, then A Cast of Thousands, and occasionally he joined brother Jimmie's Texas Storm.

In the spring of 1972, Stevie Ray dropped out of high school and followed his brother to Austin, Texas. Austin was where the blues were to be found, and that is where Stevie Ray wanted to be. He joined a blues-rock group, Crackerjack, playing the bars and clip joints. Stevie Ray was a great guitarist, but now he also developed his singing voice until he could use it as sensitively as an instrument.

Within a year Stevie Ray had acquired the 1959 Fender Stratocaster guitar, nicknamed Lenny, that was his constant companion for the rest of his career. He served his apprenticeship as a blues musician with The Nightcrawlers, The Cobras and Triple Threat Revue, covering all the popular songs of Jimi Hendrix and Janis Joplin.

In May, 1979, Stevie Ray formed his own band, called Double Trouble after one of Otis Rush's blues numbers. The band, with Tommy Shannon on bass and Chris Layton on drums, was strongly influenced by both Albert King's blues and Jimi Hendrix's technique. Stevie Ray had a great empathy with Hendrix and the Hendrix style even pervaded his stage act. He played the guitar behind his neck and with his teeth! His inspired rendition of the Hendrix classic 'Voodoo Chile' was as close to the original as is possible and gained Stevie Ray a Grammy nomination.

The 1982 Montreux Jazz Festival saw the beginning of Stevie Ray's international career. David Bowie heard him play and asked him to perform on his next album, 'Let's Dance', and John Hammond, the well-known CBS talent scout who had played an important part in the careers of Benny Goodman, Billie Holiday and Bob Dylan, signed him to a recording contract.

'Texas Flood' was the debut album for Stevie Ray Vaughan and Double Trouble. Stevie Ray, pictured on the cover, was the quintessential Texas gunslinger in his black Mexican hat, poncho and cowboy boots. The album consolidated Stevie Ray's position as a guitar giant and earned him a new nickname, 'Texas Flood', for the flowing style of his playing. It won two Grammy nominations and sold over 500,000 copies.

Stevie Ray was constantly on the go. He was committed to extensive touring and he pushed his creative talents to the limits in the recording studio. Alcohol and cocaine enabled him to work twenty-four hours a day until sometimes he didn't know whether he was coming or going. Finally, in 1986, it all caught up with him. He collapsed on stage in London and had to return to the United States.

Stevie Ray and Tommy Shannon both entered a detoxification rehabilitation programme. Openly admitting his alcoholism and drug abuse proved cathartic for Stevie Ray, and within a few short months he was back in the recording studios. Life was looking good again.

He had received many awards and nominations over the years: Best Electric Blues Player, Instrumentalist of the Year, Entertainer of the Year, among them. In 1990, Stevie Ray won a coveted Grammy, Best Contemporary Blues Recording, for his album 'In Step' (1990).

Next, Stevie Ray fulfilled another lifetime ambition. He was reunited with his brother, Jimmie, to make an album. Jimmie, a mean guitarist himself, had until recently been the lead guitarist with the Fabulous Thunderbirds. 'Family Style', a brilliant collection of numbers from blues to rockabilly, showed the versatility of Stevie Ray's own style.

But, sadly, it was his swansong. In July, 1990, Stevie Ray's beloved 1959 Fender Stratocaster was snapped in half and some of his other guitars damaged by falling scenery. It was an omen.

One month later, Stevie Ray was on an Eric Clapton Blues tour. Flying to Chicago, in heavy fog, the helicopter in which he was travelling crashed into the side of a man-made ski hill, killing him and four other passengers.

At his funeral, held in his home town of Dallas, Texas, Jackson Browne, Stevie Wonder and Bonnie Raitt led the mourners in a touching rendition of Amazing Grace.

In 1991, 'Family Style' won two Grammies, one track for Best Instrumental Performance and the album itself for Best Contemporary Blues Recording.

Stevie Ray Vaughan's contribution to contemporary blues was great. His personal courage in defeating his alcoholism and drugs problem serves as an example to all. But how tragic it is that having won such a victory he should lose his life as the result of an accident.

Ian Curtis

Born:	15 July, 1956, Macclesfield, Cheshire, England
Died:	18 May, 1980
Age:	23

As punk music was evolving, so, too, was another musical direction: new wave. It shared the same aggressive spirit as punk but was more sophisticated, both lyrically and musically. In the vanguard of this movement was one band, Joy Division.

Joy Division was made up of four young Manchester lads. Ian Curtis was the vocalist and lyricist. Breaking new ground is never easy, and the band struggled through a long apprenticeship before gaining recognition. Their first album, 'Unknown Pleasures' (1979), which was funded privately by their record company's boss, brought them comparisons to The Doors.

Ian, sensitive, and an epileptic, poured his feelings of despair and loneliness into his songs. He laid his soul bare to his listeners, often bewildering them with his physical parodies of his epilepsy. But his stage presence was charismatic, and by the end of 1979, Joy Division, championed by John Peel had attracted a large cult following.

While the band were on the brink of commercial success in Britain, an American tour was planned. But the pressures were too much for Ian's sensitive soul. On Sunday 18 May, shortly before the band were scheduled to fly to the United States, Ian hanged himself leaving behind a wife and child.

Joy Division disbanded. They were innovators and their greatest success arrived only after they ceased to exist. Their single 'Love Will Tear Us Apart' entered the charts and was later covered by Paul Young and P.J. Proby. Their albums, 'Unknown Pleasures', 'Closer' and 'Still' continue to sell.

The remaining members of the line-up reformed to become the enormously successful cult band New Order.

Sid Vicious

Real Name:	John Simon Ritchie
Born:	10 May, 1957, London, England
Died:	2 February, 1979
Age:	21

Sid Vicious was a member of The Sex Pistols, a group that had a massive impact on the British music scene, perhaps the greatest of their decade. Punk music had been quickly adopted by the rebellious younger generation of the mid-seventies as an alternative to progressive (soft) rock. It was aggressive, violent music, designed to shock and intimidate. And its disciples followed the theme in their attire. Leather gear and bicycle chains (which could also be used as weapons) were the order of the day. Chains of safety pins adorned their noses, ears and clothes, and spiky Mohican haircuts in rainbow colours completed the look.

Sid was raised in a single-parent family in the grime and poverty of London's east end. It was a tough part of the world and Sid grew up well able to take care of himself, but hating authority and the establishment.

He was dubbed Sid by his friend, John Lydon (Vicious was added later as an indication of Sid's character).

Lydon (later to become known as Johnny Rotten), was the vocalist for a group called The Sex Pistols. Managed by Malcolm McLaren, they were breaking new ground and were to emerge as leaders of the punk music movement.

In 1976, one of the major record companies, EMI, realised that this new youth movement, however unsavoury it might be, spelled money, and The Sex Pistols were signed to a recording contract. They burst on to an unsuspecting world in a volley of profanities. The media loved them because they were good copy, and their record company loved them because the more controversy they caused, the more money rolled in.

In 1977, the bassist, Glen Matlock, left The Sex Pistols. Sid, until then just a high-profile fan of the group, was asked to step in as bassist. Bearing in mind Sid's complete lack of musical background, this may seem unusual. But it posed no dilemma to the group; they were not renowned for their musical ability, anyway. Sid was willing to learn to play bass guitar. He had a violent, punk image that suited them. And it increased their publicity to add such an outrageous character to their line-up.

EMI, meanwhile, had dropped their contract, hoping to distance themselves from the adverse publicity The Sex Pistols were generating. A&M rushed in to take their place, but a week later, after a particularly disgusting drunken exhibition by the group, they, too, backed out. Virgin Records, less squeamish about their artists' reputations, entered the picture.

The Sex Pistols' first single for Virgin was 'God Save The Queen', an anarchic attack on the establishment. Coming as it did in Jubilee year, it caused a great deal of antipathy towards the group and violent personal attacks were made on them. Although television and radio refused to play the single, it moved up the charts to the Number Two position.

Drugs were also very much a part of the punk scene. Depending on financial circumstances, the choice ranged from glue-sniffing to amphetamine sulphate. Sid could afford the latter. Perhaps it explained why he seemed impervious to physical pain, routinely gouging himself with razor blades, broken glass, flick knives, or anything sharp and close to hand.

Sid was arrested in 1977 and 1978 for possession of illegal substances and he was fast becoming addicted to heroin. Quoted on numerous occasions as 'hating sex', and being 'the most sexless person on earth', Sid had nevertheless become involved with a young American groupie, Nancy Spungen. Whether united by sex or by their mutual dependence on heroin, the two were inseparable.

When Nancy was facing deportation from the United Kingdom, it was provident that a tour of the United States was scheduled for The Sex Pistols. However, the tour was doomed. First, Sid stabbed himself with a knife at a Memphis concert. This was not well received by the southern audience. Then Johnny Rotten quit and headed back to New York. Sid stepped in on vocals. But he took an overdose and had to be admitted to hospital. The other two members of the group, bored with the whole proceedings, took off to Rio de Janeiro to record a single with the great train robber Ronnie Biggs.

Back in London, without The Sex Pistols, Sid was directionless. He gave a farewell concert, appropriately called Sid Sods Off, and moved to New York with Nancy Spungen. Sid started life in the United States very much as he meant to continue. He was so spaced out on arrival that he had to be carried off the plane. He and Nancy settled into the Chelsea Hotel.

On 11 October, Sid called the police to say that Nancy was seriously injured. In fact, she was dead, stabbed several times in the stomach. Sid seemed the obvious suspect. Despite his protestations that he had no memory of the event, and that he couldn't be arrested because he was a rock 'n' roll star, he was arrested and charged with murder. Rumours flew around. It was suggested that Nancy had been attacked by a mugger. Or that she was the victim of a drug hit.

Virgin, who, like previous record companies had tried to distance themselves from The Sex Pistols, put up $50,000 bail. Five days later Sid was released and, with his mother's help, he made an unsuccessful suicide bid. A couple of months later he was back in jail for attacking a man in a nightclub.

Two months later, Sid was free again. His two months' incarceration had cleaned him up. Foolishly, he reverted to type and asked his mother to obtain some heroin for him. It was too much for his detoxified body. Sid Vicious, at the age of twenty-one, died of a heroin overdose.

Andy Gibb

Born: 5 March, 1958, Manchester, England
Died: 10 March, 1988
Age: 30

The youngest of the four Gibb brothers by many years, Andy Gibb was only four years old when his brothers, Barry, Robin and Maurice achieved fame as The Bee Gees.

Their father, Hugh, was a band leader, and their mother, Barbara, a singer. Little wonder that all the members of the family were musically-minded.

In 1958, the family had emigrated to Australia, where The Bee Gees rose to fame, but by the time Andy was ready for school, they had returned to England. Life in the shadow of his brothers' fame was not easy for young Andy. He began playing the guitar and singing when he was in his teens, drawing the inevitable comparisons. However, his brothers were very encouraging, and in 1976, he was given his own recording contract.

The disco boom was at its height in the mid-seventies and The Bee Gees were at their peak. It is to Andy's credit that his debut single, 'I Just Want To Be Your

Everything' (1977), penned by Barry, was not overshadowed by his brothers' success. It went to the Number One position in the US charts, as did his next singles, '(Love Is) Thicker Than Water' and 'Shadow Dancing' (both 1978).

But Andy found the pressures of fame difficult to cope with and he became a cocaine addict. Two more hit singles followed as he strugged to overcome his drug problem. His girlfriend, beautiful *Dallas* actress Victoria Principal, endeavoured to pull him out of it, but the strain on their relationship was too great and they split up.

Andy hit rock bottom. His brothers rallied around: they had seen the problems caused by the pressures of the rock world often enough themselves. Andy was persuaded to enter the famous Betty Ford Clinic for treatment, and it seemed as though he was ready to pick up the pieces of his life again. He joined his brothers in Florida looking for a new start.

In 1988, Andy was in Britain when he was struck down by a viral infection of the heart. His heart, damaged by the years of drug abuse, was unable to fight the virus and he died of heart failure just five days past his thirtieth birthday.

The Bee Gees' album 'Ordinary Lives' (1989) was dedicated to their young brother, Andy, who now lies buried beside their beloved father, Hugh, at Forest Lawn Cemetery.

Steve Clark

Born: 23 April, 1960, Hillsborough, South Yorkshire
Died: 8 January, 1991
Age: 30

Steve Clark was born and brought up in Hillsborough, where his father was a taxi driver. His father was also a rock 'n' roll fan, and when his son showed an interest in music, he was delighted. However, he insisted that Steve have proper tuition, guiding him into learning the classical guitar.

But Led Zeppelin, the heavy metal group, were young Steve's heroes. In 1978, he joined a burgeoning band, Def Leppard, as joint lead guitarist. The other members were Pete Willis (guitar), Joe Elliott (vocals) and Rick Savage (bass). Steve had met Pete Willis at Stannington College, and saw the offer to join the band as an excellent opportunity to play the kind of music that he preferred.

The band was packed with talent and it showed in their original material. Joe Elliott wrote the lyrics and Steve the music. They added a drummer to the line-up, fifteen-year-old Rick Allen. Their first years were tough. They all had to hold down regular jobs at the same time as rehearsing and performing in pubs – their first gig paid them the princely sum of five pounds.

To cut their first EP, 'Getcha Rocks Off', they formed their own label, Bludgeon Riffola, with the aid of funds from Joe Elliott's father. Phonograph Records picked up their EP and signed Def Leppard to a contract. Their debut album for Phonograph, 'On Through The Night', was released shortly afterwards and a tour was arranged to promote it.

Fame followed the album release quite quickly and the band set their sights on the highly-lucrative American market. Success in the United States brought antipathy from British fans, however, and it was some time before Def Leppard regained their previous popularity on home ground.

An extensive touring schedule brought with it the problems that faced most rock groups on the road. Drugs and alcohol helped to overcome tedium and exhaustion. Pete Willis was drinking heavily and so was Steve. Eventually Willis was replaced by Phil Collen and Steve was persuaded to seek psychiatric help.

Phil Collen and Steve made a good team. The first album produced with the new line-up, 'Pyromania', was released at the beginning of 1983 and sold over twelve million copies, remaining in the US charts for ninety-two weeks. Def Leppard had achieved their aim of superstar status in the United States.

Steve found his stardom hard to handle. He was the most glamorous of the group, he was rich and he was famous, but he was very insecure. Drugs were always available and he was drinking heavily. He entered rehabilitation on a regular basis.

In 1984, a tragedy awaited Def Leppard. Rick Allen, their young drummer, injured his right arm and lost his left one in a car accident. In an act of supreme courage, using a custom-built drum kit designed specially for him, he overcame his disability and was back with the band within six months. This drew them all closer together and now there was no stopping them.

Hailed as the major heavy metal band of the decade, Def Leppard once again grew popular in the United Kingdom. Their album 'Hysteria', which was three years in the making, was released in 1987. It topped the album charts on both sides of the Atlantic and outsold 'Pyromania'.

This overwhelming success should have brought happiness. But Steve was still grappling with his own private demons. His basic insecurities drove him to drink, and although he attended Alcoholics Anonymous he just couldn't cope with the pressures of his fame.

On the night of 8 January, 1991, following a massive drinking session, Steve died at his Chelsea home. The cause of his death was excessive drinking. He was thirty years old and a multi-millionaire, but now just yet another victim of the rock 'n' roll lifestyle.

His friends paid tribute to him, praising his personal attributes, his gentleness, shyness, quietness and modesty, and his vital and consummately professional stage persona. Without his creative force, the future of Def Leppard lies in the balance.

More Untimely Deaths

SECTION ONE

Any final list of untimely deaths in the music world will undoubtedly have omissions. Notable among those whose lives I have been unable to chronicle within the confines of this book are:

GEORGE GERSHWIN, who was born in New York the son of Russian immigrants. He learned to play classical piano at an early age, but it was the music of Tin Pan Alley that held the greatest attraction for him. With his brother Ira writing the lyrics, George went on to become one of America's most popular song writers.

This wasn't enough for the musically ambitious George and he began to experiment with more complex pieces. *Rhapsody In Blue* (1924) and the folk opera *Porgy And Bess* (1935) were two examples of his versatility.

A very popular figure in society, George, at the age of 38, lapsed into a coma and died of a brain tumour.

Born in the American state of Iowa, **BIX BEIDER-BECKE** was a virtuoso of the cornet and trumpet. The first white musician to become a leading jazz soloist, Bix made a number of recordings in the few short years of his career, and these have recently enjoyed a resurgence of popularity. He was at the peak of his powers when he died from pneumonia at the age of 28.

Also an Iowan, **GLENN MILLER** was the leader of one of the most popular swing bands of the 1930s. Although best remembered for 'In The Mood' and 'Moonlight Serenade', he produced a wide variety of music.

Drafted into the Air Force during World War II, Glenn was travelling to entertain troops when his plane disappeared over the English Channel. He was 40 years old.

Another talented performer of the same era, colourful pianist-singer-composer **THOMAS 'FATS' WALLER**, was also a child of the American midwest. Whether exuberantly performing his own composition 'Ain't Misbehavin'', or calling for another of his endless bottles of whiskey, he was an inveterate showman and equally popular on both sides of the Atlantic. At the age of 39, he died from pneumonia.

The big band sound flourished in the 1930's and piano-playing **EDDY DUCHIN** led one of the most popular of these bands. But after World War II the new swing movement swept America and Eddy's popularity faded. Leukaemia claimed his life at the age of 41.

Gypsy guitarist **DJANGO REINHARDT** was an early influence on European jazz. Born in Belgium, he travelled extensively in Europe before settling in France. Despite losing the use of two fingers from his left hand which was badly damaged in a caravan fire, Django was a founder member of France's foremost jazz group, the Quintette de Hot Club de France.

His unique jazz style and technique was a major influence on later jazz guitarists. He died at the age of 43.

SECTION TWO

There are many other untimely deaths I would have dearly liked to enlarge upon, stars bent on self-destruction, lives thrown away in search of the ultimate experience, others lost in senseless tragedies, but unfortunately time and space precluded. However, it would be amiss to omit the following:

Robert Johnson, a blues singer who was an inspiration to the likes of Jimi Hendrix and Eric Clapton. He was said to have sold his soul to the devil in return for fame and fortune. He was on the brink of achieving both of these when he was murdered by a jealous husband at the age of twenty-six.

Graham Bond was a musician who had escaped from the grey world of insurance to play the R&B circuit. But he dabbled in black magic and drugs and ended his days, at the age of thirty-seven, under the wheels of an underground train.

Frankie Lymon enjoyed early success with the vocal group Frankie Lymon and The Teenagers. The number for which he will be best remembered is 'Why Do Fools Fall In Love?', released when Frankie was just thirteen. It was later a big hit for Diana Ross. But by then Frankie had already lost his battle with heroin addiction. He overdosed at the age of twenty-five. Two other members of The Teenagers also followed Frankie to early graves.

Sherman Garnes was thirty-eight, and **Joe Negroni** was thirty-seven.

John Rostill joined The Shadows to replace Brian Locking. After the group split up, John joined Tom Jones' backing group and took to writing songs. His death was a most unfortunate accident. His body was discovered in his home studio – he had been electrocuted by his bass guitar while working at night. He was only thirty. **Claude François**, the French pop star, was also electrocuted, in his bath while changing a light bulb, and **Les Harvey**, guitarist with Stone The Crows, suffered an even more horrifying end. He was electrocuted on stage by his equipment.

Canned Heat, an electric blues band, lost two of its number. **Al 'Blind Owl' Wilson** and **Bob 'The Bear' Hite** were founder members of the band. In 1970, Al Wilson, aged twenty-seven, died of a drugs overdose, and in 1981, Bob Hite died of a heart attack at the age of thirty-six.

Lowell George was the songwriter, guitarist and inspiration behind Little Feat. Very much a cult band, they combined traditional American music, blues, country and jazz into a whole. George quit the band to pursue a solo career, but died of heart failure, caused by drug abuse, at the age of thirty-three.

Bon Scott of AC/DC, according to the coroner, drank himself to death. He was thirty-three.

Gary Thain was the bassist with Uriah Heep. He had a most disappointing career. After he was electrocuted onstage at a Dallas concert, his erratic behaviour and drug habit forced the band to sack him. He died of a drugs overdose. **David Byron** was another casualty of Uriah Heep. He, too, was sacked from the band. His attempts to pursue a solo career failed and he died at the age of thirty-eight.

Robbie McIntosh was the drummer with The Average White Band, a soul band from Scotland. At a party in Los Angeles he took a good snort of what he thought was cocaine. Unfortunately, it was heroin, and to the shock of all the guests present, Robbie McIntosh died. He was twenty-four. The Average White Band's 1975 Gold Album 'Cut The Cake' was dedicated to their drummer.

Two more drug related deaths were those of **Pete Farndon** and **James Honeyman-Scott** of The Pretenders. Pete Farndon was thirty when he died of a drugs overdose in his bath. James Honeyman-Scott was twenty-five when his cocaine and heroin addiction caught up with him. Honeyman-Scott's widow is still chasing royalties from his work through the courts.

Jimmy McCulloch, who had been the guitarist for Thunderclap Newman, replaced Les Harvey in Stone The Crows and played in Wings and The Small Faces, also died of an overdose. He was twenty-six.

Charlie Christian, the jazz guitarist responsible for bringing the electric guitar to the forefront of jazz, died of tuberculosis at the age of thirty-five.

Mildred Bailey, the smoky voiced blues and ballad singer, died of ill health at the age of forty-three. And blues guitarist, **Freddie King**, whose technical brilliance was a major influence on Eric Clapton and John Mayall, succumbed to an heart attack when he was forty-two.

Michael Holliday's hit, 'The Story of my Life' (1957), brought him instant fame. But the changing beat of music in the early sixties caused a drop in his popularity. He tried his hand at acting, but, this too proved unsuccessful. In 1963, depressed by his failure, he committed suicide at the age of thirty-seven.

Another big hit in 1957, was 'At The Hop' by Danny and the Juniors. A couple more hits followed but, by 1963, their success, too, had evaporated and they split up. The lead singer, **Danny Rapp**, was found dead in 1983, having apparently shot himself. Danny and the Juniors have now reformed (retaining the name) and are very popular on the rock 'n' roll revival circuit.

Johnny Kidd and The Pirates enjoyed success for several years following their hit 'Shakin' All Over' (1960). But, in 1966, Johnny split from The Pirates and reformed another group as The New Pirates. On tour with this new group, Johnny, aged twenty-six, perished in a car accident.

Of the same era as Johnny Kidd came **Joe Meek**. Joe was more a producer than a musician, and he will be best remembered for his production of 'Johnny Remember Me' (1961), with its unusual echoing sounds – which, it is said, he created by recording in the toilet! Also, the highly constructed sound of 'Telstar' (1962), which he made with the Tornados. A great Buddy Holly fan, Joe committed suicide on the anniversary of Holly's death in 1967. He was thirty-five.

Twin brothers, Barry and **Paul Ryan**, were also pop stars of the sixties. Although their hits included 'Don't Bring Me Your Heartaches' (1965), 'I Love Her' (1966), and 'Have Pity On The Boy' (1966). They were never major stars. However, 'Eloise' (1968), written by Paul, and sung by Barry, reached No 1 on the charts in Britain, and eighteen other countries. In 1992, Paul died of cancer at the age of forty-four.

Jeff Porcaro, the son of percussionist Joe Porcaro, was, with his brother Steve, a founder member of the rock band Toto. Their most successful album 'Toto IV' (1982), won them seven Grammy Awards, and three hits resulted from this album alone; 'Rosanna', 'Africa' and 'I Won't Hold You Back'.

In 1992, at the age of thirty-eight, Jeff died suddenly of heart failure. The coroner's report, however, refuted this. The pathologists stated the cause of death was linked to the use of cocaine.

The New York Dolls was an innovative group with a glamrock look and a punk-glitter sound, reflecting the youth mood of the early seventies. But the youth culture embraced drugs and the group seemed fated. By 1972, when the Dolls visited Britain as a support act to Rod Stewart, guitarist **Rick Rivets** had died of a lethal combination of alcohol and chemicals. Followed by **Billy Murcia**, the Dolls' drummer, who died of a drink and drugs overdose at the age of twenty-one. Guitarist, **Johnny Thunders**, the enigmatic personality who went on to join cult punk group 'The Heartbreakers', died in mysterious circumstances in 1991. And, in 1992, Murcia's replacement on the drums, **Jerry Nolan** died of a stroke.

Musical Youth shot to fame with the reggae number 'Pass The Dutchie' (1982), but they were unable to sustain their success and became 'one hit wonders'. Disbanded after eighteen months, the group all went their separate ways. **Patrick Waite**, the bass player, never came to terms with life after success. He turned to a life of crime, amassing a string of arrests for robbery, theft, reckless driving and assault on the police. Then, in 1993, at the tender age of twenty-four, Patrick fell over at a friend's house and couldn't be revived. The cause of his death remains a mystery.

In their memory, let it read:
Their time on earth was far too short,
They lived too fast and died too young.

Index